THE BIRTH OF MELBOURNE

Tim Flannery is a naturalist, explorer and writer. He is also director of the South Australian Museum and chair of the South Australian Science Council. His books include the bestsellers *The Future Eaters*, *Throwim Way Leg* and *Country*, and he has made contributions of international significance to the fields of palaeontology, mammalogy and conservation.

THE BIRTH OF
MELBOURNE

EDITED AND INTRODUCED BY
TIM FLANNERY

TEXT PUBLISHING
MELBOURNE AUSTRALIA

The Text Publishing Company
Swann House
22 William St
Melbourne Victoria 3000
Australia
www.textpublishing.com.au

First published 2002
This edition published 2004

Printed and bound by Griffin Press
Designed by Chong Wengho
Typeset in Stempel Garamond by Midland Typesetters

National Library of Australia
Cataloguing-in-Publication data:

The Birth of Melbourne.

Bibliography.

ISBN 1 877008 89 3.

1. Melbourne (Vic.) – History – 1788–1900. I. Flannery,
Timothy Fridtjof, 1956–.

994.4102

Cover painting by Henry Burn, *Swanston Street from the Bridge*, 1861, oil on canvas, 71.8 x 92.2cm, gift of Mr John H. Connell, 1914, National Gallery of Victoria, Melbourne.

Contents

Tim Flannery

The Passing of Birrarang

All cities spring from twin fountainheads—the nature in which they are grounded and the human enterprise that builds them. Nature works slowly and at times can be set on her beam-ends by ecological disruptions, yet ultimately she determines the fate of every living thing. Melbourne's history has been one of prodigious human activity and unimaginable ecological catastrophe. Just 170 years ago the city did not exist. In its place was *Birrarang*, a bountiful land beside a bay, through which ran the sparkling river *Barrern*. This was a place of astonishing beauty and abundance, with roots deep in Gondwana.

A remarkable insight into Birrarang's origins came in early 1980 when a builder on Melbourne's underground rail loop noticed a strange shape in a rock fragment that had broken off the tunnel wall. At first glance it looked like a Wild West sheriff's badge—a suitable emblem of Melbourne's frontier phase—but when held to the light it proved to be the immaculately preserved impression of a starfish. Although the creature lived 400 million years ago, even its smallest details remained discernible.

That lonely, pioneering starfish was probably entombed by a mudslide as it wended its way across the sea floor. Could we have taken a bird's-eye view of Melbourne back then we would have seen nothing but water. Below that horizon-spanning expanse of salt water lay a vast gash in the ocean bottom called the Melbourne Trough—a sort of prototypical Marianas Trench. It occupied much of what is now central Victoria, and the muds and silts that filled it were destined to form the rolling hills of Melbourne, as well as much of the rock underlying the city itself.

A place near the outer suburb of Lilydale tells us how this ancient mud was transformed into solid rock. The Europeans called it Cave Hill and dug a quarry there. The Aborigines, however, knew it as *Bukker Tillible*, and believed that a falling star had created a bottomless pit on the site. The cave the legend refers to had been carved from a mass of limestone, rich in shells and other ancient marine life. How this great slab of limestone, kilometres in extent, ended up on the floor of a deep ocean trench was a mystery until geologists discovered evidence nearby of volcanoes. This primitive coral reef must have grown on the summit of such a peak, near the sunlit surface of the ocean, until a tremendous paroxysm of the earth's crust some 380 million years ago detached the limey mass from its pinnacle, sending it hurtling into the abyss.

This was only one of countless geological movements that over tens of millions of years would bury errant starfish and close the Melbourne Trough—eventually folding and heating the sediment, then thrusting the mass of new-formed rock skyward. Tectonic forces also squeezed great bodies of magma into the rock, which slowly cooled and solidified to form the granite that now outcrops around Melbourne. In time these processes would transform the entire region from sea to land, creating the continental crust that would come to be known as Victoria.

These continent-creating processes also emplaced a thin trace of metal in the sediment, which was concentrated in north–south running 'belts'—two to the east of Melbourne and one to its west. After lying dormant for over 350 million years the immense motivating power of this golden trace was released like a genie from a bottle. Although only 2500 tonnes of gold have been mined in Victoria, this was enough to create marvellous Melbourne in the geological blink of an eye.

From the age of fishes some 350 million years ago, through the age of dinosaurs and into our own age of mammals, we know little of what passed in Melbourne-to-be, for few rocks are preserved to inform us. But by around 40 million years ago a vital geological event took place that enables us to pick up the story once more. Volcanoes began erupting around Victoria, particularly in the west, and the rocks their lava produced—including Melbourne's famous 'bluestone'—can be dated by geologists. In time the basalt would break down to form the largest area of rich soils in Australia. This, combined with the region's reliable winter rainfall, would make it one of the continent's most productive regions, and it was this that drew Melbourne's first settlers.

Lava flows occurred only to the west of the Yarra in the Melbourne area, so the city sits astride two very different natural realms—rich volcanic plains, and infertile sand-sheets and swamps to the east. The place is like a two-faced god, offering either fortune or heartbreak. The first Europeans to settle the area turned right when they passed through the Heads into Port Phillip Bay. This fateful choice meant that they encountered Melbourne's poorer if more picturesque side, and were defeated by the sterility of the land. In 1835, thirty-three years later, Batman turned left on entering the bay and the natural riches he unlocked astonished the world.

When the volcanoes were first roused to life millions of years ago, the continental crust began to sag, allowing the sea to approach once again and sediment to accumulate. These deposits are preserved in many places around the bay, but nowhere are they as brimful of early life as at Beaumaris, some eighteen kilometres south-east of the city. There, in rocks that are exposed only at the lowest of tides, the remains of many unexpected creatures are found.

Huge bones attest to the fact that prehistoric sperm and baleen whales spouted in that long-vanished sea, while around them sported penguins, seals and diverse kinds of sharks, some of which made meals of the whales. One such species had teeth almost fifteen centimetres long, and one fossilised whale jawbone has the tooth of a shark embedded in it, testimony of an ancient attack.

Rivers or creeks—perhaps ancestors of the Barrern itself— debouched in the area, carrying the bloated carcasses of giant marsupials into the sea. As they decomposed, bones and teeth dropped to the sea floor, providing some idea of what life was like on land. They indicate that the region was inhabited by pigsized relatives of wombats, and wallabies the size of the larger living species. We can infer that the shores of the bay supported a rainforest vegetation, for the teeth of these animals seem capable of chewing little else.

At this time the human settlement of Melbourne was still six million years in the future, and earth was yet to enter the ice age. On seventeen separate occasions during this period the planet's glaciers would advance, its oceans synchronously dropping as water froze at the poles. The ancestors of much of the modern Australian flora and fauna would take form during this period, and so would the topography of Birrarang.

We do not know exactly when human eyes first lit upon Birrarang's seven hills. My guess is that it was around 47,000 years ago, perhaps just a few centuries after the first humans made landfall in northern Australia. Then, giant marsupials roamed the region. One such creature, the size of a rhinoceros, left its bones below what is now Arden Street in North Melbourne, while herds of others comprised a veritable graveyard of marsupial giants in the outer suburb of Keilor. By around 46,000 years ago such creatures had vanished across the continent. The cause of their demise is still debated, but it is likely that hunting by the first Australians was a significant factor.

Those same first settlers would begin burning the landscape, restricting fire-sensitive plant species like tree ferns and Antarctic beech to the wetter gullies and mountains, and allowing grasses and eucalypts to inherit the rolling hills and broad valleys of the city-to-be. We have no clear evidence of what those first, fire-wielding inhabitants were like, but later peoples did leave traces, including an ancient skull found during the excavation of a soil pit near Keilor in 1940. The bone, later to be known as the 'Keilor cranium', came to the attention of the Reverend Edmund Gill, one of the last parson-naturalists and the curator of fossils at the marvellously named National Museum of Victoria. Years later, using early Carbon-14 technology, Gill determined the skull was between 8000 and 15,000 years old.

In 1965, at a place called Green Gully, three short kilometres from the Keilor soil pit, a second spectacular discovery was made. It was a human grave so strange that it has baffled archaeologists ever since. The excavators at first assumed that the skeleton interred in the floodplain sediments was of a single individual. When they examined it more closely, though, they discovered that some bones were from a man while others, including the skull, were from a woman. The pair appear to have been exposed above the ground after death, allowing relatives to retrieve the bones. In a feat worthy of an expert anatomist, enough bones to make up a skeleton were subsequently placed in the grave, without a single bone being duplicated.

It is difficult to comprehend the significance of this extraordinary burial. Did the remains belong to a man and wife who loved each other so dearly that they wished to be joined in eternity? Or does the assemblage denote some other, long-lost meaning? Sadly, excavation of the Green Gully site has now ceased, a casualty of the great breach between Aboriginal communities and archaeologists in Victoria. Perhaps the site will yield its secrets to some future Australia, in which black and white can work together in exploring the continent's past.

At the time Australia's first human inhabitants were familiarising themselves with their new estate, the planet was about to experience a rapid cooling. As ice accumulated at the poles, the sea level dropped. By 20,000 years ago the waters had deserted the bay—indeed, all of Bass Strait was dry. Then the Barrern flowed through a vast, swampy bottomland as it meandered towards a distant ocean. Because the sea level was so low, it cut a deep valley. At Port Melbourne water flowed more than thirty metres below its present bed, and at the Spencer Street Bridge it was twenty metres below. The deep valley thus created has proved an expensive handicap for development as it greatly increased the building costs of structures such as Port Melbourne's Breakwater Pier and the Westgate Bridge. The cost comes in the foundations, which must be sufficiently deep to reach the bedrock many metres below. In the case of Breakwater Pier, muck had to be first excavated to a depth of twenty metres, and sand from Hobsons Bay used to create a stable base.

During this period of low sea level, known as the last glacial maximum, Melbourne was a much colder, windier place than today. Huge dust storms borne on winds generated over a Sahara-like central Australia would have been a dramatic annual occurrence. The cold and aridity allowed a bizarre mix of species to proliferate. Red kangaroos (whose bones have been found at

Sunshine) and desert wallabies grazed among the alpine tussocks and sphagnum-moss swamps, while stands of snow gums struggled to survive in sheltered places on what is now the eastern side of the bay. While this Melbourne seems very alien to us, it is not entirely unfamiliar, for El Niño brings similar, though milder conditions to the city. The last such ice-age reminder I recall was in 1983, when great dust clouds blew over the city and water was in short supply.

About 15,000 years ago, for reasons that no one fully understands, the last glacial maximum abruptly terminated. The sea rose, first flooding into Bass Strait and then into the Heads, so that by 6000 years ago the shoreline stood where it does today. When workers were excavating for the south pylon of the Spencer Street Bridge they were surprised to come upon the stump of a mighty red gum at a depth of twenty metres. It last saw daylight 8200 years ago. The sea continued to rise and by around 5000 years ago the waters of the bay lapped as far inland as Essendon. In the slightly warmer conditions that then prevailed, Sydney cockles thrived in the lower reaches of the Barrern. By 4000 years ago the sea had begun a gradual retreat and the river carried sediment towards the bay, smothering the ancient shell-beds. At the time the Egyptians were building their pyramids, the Melbourne that John Batman knew was finally taking shape.

By the time John Murray of the *Lady Nelson* sailed past the Heads in 1802 and named the waterway beyond, this dynamic history had given rise to a most beautiful and bountiful region. A limpid river flowed over a rocky waterfall known as the *Yarra Yarra*, at what is now the foot of Market Street, before debouching into a large, deep pool at the head of a paperbark-lined estuary. Billabongs and swamps were sprinkled right around the bay, and they teemed with brolgas, magpie-geese, Cape Barren geese, swans, ducks, eels and frogs. So abundant was the wildlife that we can imagine the Melbourne area in 1830 as a sort of temperate Kakadu and, as in Arnhem Land, it was the wetlands that were the focus of life.

Few pioneers saw the beauty of the so-called swamps, but George Gordon McCrae has left us a precious vision of the Blue Lake, which in his childhood occupied low ground near the Flagstaff Gardens. It was:

> intensely blue, nearly oval and full of the clearest salt water; but this by no means deep. Fringed gaily all round by mesembryanthemum ('pigs-face') in full bloom, it seemed in the broad sunshine as though girdled about with a belt of magenta fire. The ground gradually sloping down towards the lake was also empurpled, but patchily, in the same manner, though perhaps not quite so brilliantly, while the whole air was heavy with the mingled odours of the golden myrnong flowers and purple-fringed lilies, or ratafias. Curlews, ibises and 'blue cranes' were there in numbers…black swans occasionally visited it, as also flocks of wild ducks.

When the wattles bloomed in the chilly air of August, the entire Yarra Valley was lit up with gold, and each spring the sand-sheets of what are now the city's bayside suburbs would glow with orchids, banksias and other heathland flowers. This plant community was known as the 'Sandringham flora', and was remarkable for its orchids—in fact most of the state's species were said to be found there.

For all its beauty and deep Gondwanan roots, much of this magical landscape was not entirely 'natural', for Aboriginal hunting and fire played a central role before, during and after the ice age in shaping and maintaining it.

The Aboriginal tribes of the Melbourne area—the Jajowrong, Wudthaurung, Taungerong, Woiwurrung and Bunurong—were impressive, for the land was bountiful and they were well-fed. The Jagajaga brothers with whom John Batman negotiated in

1835 were around six feet tall (183 centimetres). The tribes lived healthy, settled lives, and at densities far greater than was possible for the rest of Aboriginal Australia.

Some sense of the resources available to them can be gained from mid-1840s accounts of the superabundance of Melbourne's fish. In four hours' angling at the Yarra falls it was commonplace to catch over 150 bream, each weighing up to a kilogram. Great knob-headed snapper weighing over fifteen kilograms were so plentiful in the bay as to sell for a mere ninepence each, while crayfish and large flathead were to be had for the spearing in the shallows.

The *Ocean* and *Calcutta*, which comprised Victoria's own 'first fleet', entered this beautiful bay in 1803. They were packed with convicts and stores, and were led by David Collins who had first arrived in Australia in 1788. They settled at Sullivans Cove near Sorrento, where the soils and water were so appalling that within a few months they gave up and fled, leaving the escaped convict William Buckley as the sole human legacy of this failed venture.

The next wave of settlers, led by John Batman and soon followed by John Fawkner, were very different. They had come in search of cheap land, and at least at the beginning were beyond the law. One of Batman's earliest acts was to 'purchase' a vast tract of country—the first of many land acquisitions that would dispossess one people and enrich another. Batman himself had an enlightened view towards the Aboriginal people, and his treatment of them was the closest thing to a fair deal they would see from colonial Victoria. But Batman's sympathy was rare and—once the veneer of legality had been obtained by the settlers—guns, sheep (which obliterated the yam daisy) and the black police would do the real work. The first 'criminals' to hang in the Old Melbourne Gaol were Aborigines, but for all the massacres, rapes and poisonings that so terribly marred Victoria's first few decades, not a single European would be brought to justice. It is a shameful history, concealed by the perpetrators and largely ignored by today's

Victorians. Yet despite efforts to hide such racism, it is clear that from 1835 to around 1850 Victoria was one of the very worst places to be an Aborigine.

The ruthless treatment of Aboriginal society left the tribes in despair. In June 1837, as Melbourne's first land sale was held with Robert Hoddle holding the gavel, they watched with increasing bitterness. Their disillusionment was given voice by Derrimut, who had saved the infant settlement from massacre in October 1835. 'You see, Mr Hull,' he told a magistrate he met on the street some years later, 'Bank of Victoria, all this mine, all along here Derrimut's once; no matter now, me tumble down soon.' Hull asked if Derrimut had any children, at which the enraged Aborigine replied, 'Why me have lubra? Why me have piccaninny? You have all this place, no good have children, no good have lubra, me tumble down and die very soon now.' A fragment of Derrimut's vast tribal estate was at last regained by him when, in 1864, he was buried in the Melbourne general cemetery. The generosity of the settlers even extended to a headstone.

Melbourne's first Aboriginal mission was established in 1837, near what is now the Royal Botanic Gardens. It lasted just three years before the land became too valuable and the blacks were removed to a site near Narre Warren, far to the east. William Thomas, a protector of Aborigines, wrote in his diary the day the Aborigines were relocated:

> From sun rise to sun set spent in arguing, reasoning, and
> persuading the natives—They declare that they will not remove.
> They had camped on private property …I tell them again that
> they make *willums* on White Man's ground, and cut down trees
> and cut off bark, make White Man sulky—they say no White
> Man's ground Black Man's.

The Narre Warren reserve was a catastrophe for the blacks, for despite the determined resistance of the elders it was used as a recruiting depot for the black police. The young men were taken away, armed and used to kill, dispossess and arrest other Aborigines. In an effort to avoid the loss of their finest youth the tribes finally deserted the site, leaving it as a base solely for use by the black police, most of whom suffered gross alcohol abuse and appallingly early deaths. Soon thereafter they were gathered up again and dumped on reserves at Mordialloc and Warrandyte, but these too failed. Then 23,000 acres was allocated on the Goulburn River, and at first the Aborigines prospered because of new agricultural and employment opportunities. Again, though, the land was considered too valuable to remain in black hands, and after allegations were made by settlers about its operation, it was de-gazetted and sold to the whites.

In 1859 the remaining Woiwurrung took matters into their own hands, requesting land on the Acheron River in central Victoria where eighty-odd people had begun establishing farms. White hostility, primarily from local squatters, soon crushed this attempt at independence, and the bureaucrats ordered the Aborigines further down river. 'No worse site could have been chosen,' noted one observer, but the Melbourne blacks were to be moved a second time before the Acheron was permanently abandoned.

A brief halt to this hideous tale of greed, dispossession and official incompetence occurred in 1863 when the Coranderrk reserve near Healesville was gazetted for Aboriginal use. At 2300 hectares it was a flyspeck compared with the tribes' holdings of twenty-five years earlier, but the Aborigines had also diminished terribly; only 200 remained from all five of the once populous Melbourne tribes.

There they developed several viable businesses, but their greatest success lay in the growing of hops. Coranderrk hops gave the Aborigines a sense of achievement and control worth even more than the cash, for the product was highly esteemed, winning

prizes at the Melbourne Agricultural Show and being in demand
by brewers. The Aborigines even employed white labourers to
help harvest the crop. But, once more, the land that supported this
remarkable experiment would not be left in black hands. In 1886,
the land-boomers triumphed when a law was passed ordering the
removal from reserves of all people of mixed blood. This effec-
tively destroyed many Aboriginal families and removed most of
the Coranderrk workforce, allowing the government to reclaim
and sell the half of the reserve not subject to flooding.

William Barak was a boy when Batman landed and was the
last traditional leader of the Woiwurrung. By the time he died on
the remaining fragment of the Coranderrk reserve in 1903 there
was just a handful of Victorian Aborigines surviving. Forty-five
thousand years of Aboriginal occupation in the Melbourne area
had come to an end.

From Batman's time onwards the settlement experienced rapid
growth as the pioneers, led by pastoralists, land speculators and
traders, made the place their own. Just what they did with it
hardly bears thinking about.

It started with the laying out of the town. Assistant surveyor-
general Robert Russell recalled that it was done from 'a plan in the
Sydney office'. The 'plan' was nothing but a grid, which Russell
plonked down in an afternoon on the undulating landscape adjacent to the Yarra falls. This meant that the city would start life at
odds with its topography as well as with its traditional owners.

Much of the road grid running up hill and down gully was
soon transformed into quagmires. The worst was Elizabeth Street,
which during the 1840s was known as the 'River Townend', after
the grocers' store that stood near the head of the gully. There,
entire bullock drays along with their bullocks were reputed to
have been swallowed up. To highlight the appalling conditions

of the street one wit placed an advertisement in a Melbourne newspaper:

> Wanted immediately one thousand pairs of stilts for the purpose of enabling the inhabitants of Melbourne to carry on their usual avocations—the mud in most of the principal thoroughfares now being waist-deep.

Even worse, the plan and the populace abused their best asset—the Yarra River. Not a word of protest appears to have been raised when the pretty waterfall was blasted out of existence. In fact the settlers were busy turning the stream into a chamber of horrors. Here is how the wife of an Italian businessman recalled it in the 1850s:

> these banks are merely a long series of slaughterhouses where sheep are killed; tanneries where their hides are prepared; and factories where their fat is prepared for the market. Here and there appear white mountains twenty-five, thirty and forty feet high; these are the bones. These slaughterhouses…give forth a pestilential odour that made me regard Port Phillip with horror even before arriving.

In the 1860s an event occurred that exceeded even these barbarities. A terminus was needed for the new country train lines, and to accommodate them Melbourne's most picturesque elevation and favourite pleasure ground—Batman's Hill—was gouged flat and the refuse used to fill the Blue Lake. With trains and pollution replacing eucalypts and herons, the Yarra had finally been made fit only for a fast getaway—and the network of railyards, roads and docks that now crowded its banks facilitated the exit.

While Melbourne's environment and its Aboriginal inhabitants were on a slippery slope to oblivion, the city's entrepreneurs were riding a crazy roller-coaster of boom and bust. Land purchased for as little as £54 in 1837 sold for £10,250 two years later. Champagne lunches were the inevitable prelude to frenzied auctions, and for years after visitors commented on the number of discarded champagne bottles that littered the region. Yet by 1842 this first bubble had burst, and the infant settlement fell into the grip of recession.

The discovery of gold a decade later revivified the city, paying for the erection of instant testimonials to European culture such as the town hall and treasury building. In 1856 alone around 95 tonnes of the yellow stuff was scratched from the ground, enough to intoxicate the whole world with gold fever and to bring whatever was wanted to Melbourne. Yet that golden fortune only added to the misfortune of the natives, for Melburnians now possessed the wealth to realise their European dreams, and what they wished to do was to re-create their homeland in the Antipodes. They yearned for English-style gardens full of English birds and animals and, once this flora and fauna was imported, Melbourne's rich soils and defined seasons allowed them to flourish. Among the newcomers were foxes and rabbits, both released near Geelong. Within fifty years these creatures had turned the dream to a nightmare, for they both spread like wildfire, devastating native Australia and pastoralist alike.

Gold also created a frontier society on a scale never experienced in Australia before or since. Melbourne lay at the epicentre of this new world where the pursuit of wealth was the great *raison d'être* and where, in true frontier fashion, life was cheap. The British writer William Howitt described the place as being in the grips of a 'hairystocracy'—men in bowyangs with flowing locks and beards who galloped their horses through the streets—and who brawled and drank equally freely whether at the opera or the pub. To the British upper class they represented a perversion of the social order, a complete breakdown of class and authority.

The social changes engendered during this period, however,

were to endure. December 1854 saw government troops attack digger rebels near Ballarat, an incident which came to be known as the Eureka Stockade. Following the capture of many of the diggers, Melbourne juries refused to convict the rebels. These events were to precipitate radical administrative reforms. City workers were also gaining power, as was demonstrated in April 1856 when stonemasons working on the University of Melbourne quadrangle held a protest which won them an eight-hour working day. It was perhaps this freedom of the working man, along with other frontier aspects of Melbourne society, that led nineteenth-century visitors to describe the place as decidedly American in character, and unlike any other Australian city. Even Karl Marx commented upon the American flavour of the resolution passed during the Eureka protests.

By the 1850s Melbourne was already a multicultural city. It had large Jewish and Chinese communities, diggers from many nations and a floating population of sailors drawn from around the world. Then, as now, Little Bourke Street was Chinatown, but nineteenth-century Chinatown was a very different place from today. For a start it was profoundly masculine—almost no Chinese women came to Australia and few European women married Chinese—and perhaps as a result, gambling and opium smoking were rife. The opium dens also acted as hideouts for prostitutes and petty criminals, so although the quarter had an orderly veneer it hid many a dark secret.

By the 1870s and 1880s some of the frontier aspects of Melbourne had begun to fade. Grand buildings were giving the city gravitas, while new arcades and an elegant area known as 'the Block'—Collins Street—were stages for the city's elite to promenade and display their sophistication and wealth. The pursuit of riches and a determination 'to get ahead', however, still stamped the character of its inhabitants, and you did not have to go far to find reminders of a more raucous Melbourne.

Larrikins—idle young men with no good on their minds—
gathered in the lanes and on street corners, and after dark wild
brawls would spill out of the more notorious pubs.

The city also had a decidedly quirky side. On Saturday
evenings the Eastern Market—on the corner of Exhibition and
Bourke streets—was taken over by large numbers of pigeon
fanciers, and tumblers and other strange breeds were set loose to
strut their stuff. Even the main streets displayed more than their
fair share of the bizarre. Had you walked down Swanston Street
in the late 1880s you might have seen, in a sombrely wreathed
shop window opposite the town hall, an emaciated figure standing
inside a coffin. He was the 'living skeleton', a man so wasted by
tuberculosis that doctors gave him just two weeks to live. A freak-
show operator had seen a way to make a buck out of this grim
situation, and while the poor fellow's strength endured he
displayed his pathetic body in public. An easiness with death has
always been part of the frontier make-up, and it is perhaps one of
the city's great incongruities that such displays could exist alongside a Collins Street that was described as having all the
sophistication of a Parisian boulevard.

Living skeletons aside, the city's entertainments were by this
time almost modern. Australian Rules football, a thoroughly local
invention, was well and truly established, cricket was being played
at the MCG and the Melbourne Cup was run each November,
drawing the most beautiful women and dashing men in the
province to the course.

By the time the cupola of the Exhibition Building rose to domi-
nate the city's skyline in 1880 it stood above a rich and grand
metropolis. This was the era of 'Marvellous Melbourne', a place
that the world looked on in amazement and envy—the commercial
powerhouse of a continent. International exhibitions were held
by the ebullient inhabitants, more ornate buildings constructed,
and wealth pursued with a singular enthusiasm. 'If you wish to

transact business well and quickly, to organise a new enterprise—in short, to estimate and understand the trade of Australia, you must go to Melbourne,' wrote English visitor Richard Twopeny in the early 1880s. Yet so dramatically had the natural environment of the city declined that he could also say, 'The situation of Melbourne is commonplace if not actually ugly.'

Marvellous Melbourne could not last, for it was based upon a kind of boosterism that brooked no limits. By 1890 corrupt business practices, over-capitalisation in railways and irresponsible land speculation threw the city into a depression unprecedented in its length and severity. It marked a turning point in the outlook of Melburnians, for the mad speculations of the get-rich-quick brigade were succeeded almost overnight by a business community with a deeply conservative turn of mind, and so it would remain for much of the twentieth century.

Even during this economic slump, however, the metropolis still teemed with ideas. Melbourne has always been at the centre of Australia's labour movement, and it has long acted as a great cauldron of politically liberal as well as conservative ideologies—home to both Trades Hall and the Melbourne Club. In the media and the arts, too, Melbourne proved to be no slouch. In the 1860s journalist and novelist Marcus Clarke was a columnist for the *Argus*, and in the 1870s John Stanley James aka The Vagabond was the same. The peripatetic political radical, poet and social commentator Francis Adams spent time in the city and found much to criticise. The 1880s also saw Melbourne as the setting for an international bestseller, *The Mystery of a Hansom Cab*, which would go on to sell more than a million copies and would help inspire a young English writer by the name of Arthur Conan Doyle. From the late 1880s painters Tom Roberts, Frederick McCubbin and Arthur Streeton—collectively known as the Heidelberg School—produced startling works of the town and bush that are now widely regarded as the true beginnings of Australian art.

Melbourne's day of triumph came in May 1901, when the city was host to the first sitting of Federal Parliament in the new Australian nation. It was unofficially proclaimed the first city of the country, and it remained as interim capital until Parliament moved to Canberra in 1927.

The twentieth century brought an unending stream of visitors to Melbourne—from sex-starved Yank soldiers bearing silk stockings during World War II to the entire world at the Olympic Games in 1956. Yet some of its most interesting visitors went unheralded. One of the most extraordinary, to my mind at least, arrived in 1959. The first person to notice her was a Mr McInnes, who was busy collecting sea-water from the beach opposite North Road at Brighton to replenish his aquarium. While knee-deep in the shallows he was startled by a disturbance caused by a live paper nautilus. She was freshly arrived from the Great Southern Ocean and, in her shell, nurtured hundreds of eggs. Soon other reports made it clear that she was but one of a great maternal fleet that had been driven into the bay by wind and water.

I was three years old when that special fleet visited. My Melbourne had been in existence for just over a century then, yet it wore the aspect of a timeless and majestic city, surrounded by formal parks and gardens. Somehow, a few natural inhabitants had survived the transformation, for I remember as a child searching for banjo frogs amid the rockeries of the Fitzroy Gardens, and fishing yabbies out of its ornamental ponds. But it was the bluestone that provided the strongest link with Birrarang. Even now when I walk through the city on a hot summer afternoon I stop and sniff the stone, for its distinctive odour somehow tells me that I've come home.

My childhood city was also the city of politicians Bob Santamaria and Henry Bolte—men whose focus was on re-igniting old

European quarrels and oiling the engines of commerce. This city's Yarra River was polluted and lifeless, its bay a receptacle of foul drains and rubbish dumps, and its suburbs vast tracts of sterile lawns and roses. I still remember as a teenager seeing a flock of birds feeding in a magnificent flowering gum in full bloom. My heart leapt at the thought that they might be lorikeets. But when I got close I saw that they were starlings, which in this mangled environment had somehow discovered that the sweet drink offered by the scarlet blossoms was going begging.

And yet my very earliest memories are of the semi-wild suburb of Sandringham, with its tracts of tea-tree, swamps and remnant heathland—the last of the magnificent Sandringham flora. By the time I was in high school that wild place had been replaced by a grid of development which like the city itself ignored the landscape and sought only to maximise financial returns.

The great fluted cliffs of Red Bluff were the wonderland of my early childhood. Erosion gullies ran right through them—a labyrinth of tunnels revealing glimpses of the blue bay far below. To the city council, however, that striking landmark represented nothing more than an opportunity to dump rubbish. Tonnes of old cars, whitegoods, even old road surface were thrown down the cliff-face—destroying and covering the spectacular red, yellow and white sandstone columns—to lie in great rusting heaps by the shoreline, near where a metre-wide pipe seeped a foul-smelling run-off into the bay.

While still very young I used to go fishing on an old trawler called the *Taivy*. It set out every Saturday morning from Middle Brighton pier with twenty or so keen fishermen, mostly men who could not afford their own boat, or kids like me. Tas the skipper was an ex-boxer turned fisherman, and he and his wife Ivy lived aboard, running the ship as a retirement project. Tas always seemed to know where the fish were, and along with the scads of flathead we were all sure to catch there was always some lucky bugger who'd hook a red emperor, a barracouta or, best of all, a huge, hump-headed snapper. Then a shout would go up, and we'd all stop to watch the battle—one man with his short rod struggling against the mighty red-and-blue-spotted fish that seemed to glow in the clear water; and Tas with his blue eyes gleaming in his weatherbeaten face beneath a black beanie, net in hand, waiting for the exhausted creature to come alongside.

The *Taivy* would set off at 8 a.m. sharp, regardless of weather, and Ivy would keep us all warm with black tea and homemade cake. On a rough day seasickness would afflict quite a few of us. Tas would then work what he called his wonder cure. He'd wait until you were looking really green, then sidle up and say, 'Want to feel better?' When he got the inevitable nod he'd continue. 'Just imagine a big lump of rancid fat—with great, black horsehairs running through it.' After you'd fed the fish he'd say, 'Feeling better now?' Of course you always were.

Those childhood experiences left me with a love for the bay that has only intensified over the years. At sixteen I learned to scuba dive with a mate, Brian. We'd take an inflatable Zodiac owned by Brian's family far out into the bay and slip over the side. It always seemed like magic to see the flathead move over the sandy bottom towards the bait, and to see the tiny crabs that the fish fed on dash down their burrows. Visibility was rarely more than a couple of metres, so you had to get really close to see the drama.

Other times we'd visit the rocky reef off Ricketts Point to search for snagged anchors, or dive around the sunken *Cerberus*— a nineteenth-century battleship that was once the pride of the navy. Sometimes we'd dare each other to enter the hold through a great rust-forged hole in the hull where a giant octopus supposedly lived.

But the place I returned to again and again with my aqualung was the magic world of the Beaumaris fossil beds. The best fossils were found off the beach in water two or three metres deep, and the time to search for them was in winter, when pollution-fed algal growth was at its lowest and the frigid waters were clear. Then you could see for metres, and the fossil whale vertebra, shark's teeth and the like could be made out on the seabed.

Sometimes the pain in my teeth and face was almost unbearable as the water found gaps between face-mask and wetsuit hood. But as the triangular shape of a fossilised shark's tooth became visible on the sea floor I would forget the pain in an instant. The dives were like a wonderful treasure hunt. You might come to the surface holding a shark's tooth stained blue with age, part of a crab preserved in stone, a delicate bone from the wing of a penguin, or struggle airwards grappling with a hunk of long-defunct whale's skull. When my air ran out, I would often snorkel until the failing light drove me to shore. Most of my findings are now lodged in the Museum of Victoria, which arguably has the most significant collection of its type in the country. A good thing too, because tonnes of landfill have been dumped atop the Beaumaris site to build a yacht club and car park.

Sometimes the living bay would distract me from my obsession with its ancient precursor. One still day as I swam offshore, I bumped into an almost surreal sight. Predators had forced a huge school of whitebait into the shallows beneath the cliffs. The tiny fish were heading determinedly north—a never-ending, shimmering curtain of silver passing by at high speed. As I swam into the mass they enveloped me, leaving a ghostly outline of my body as a safety margin between their flesh and mine. Below the school I could see the silver flash of barracouta, and the distinctive shape of small sharks. It took fifteen minutes for the fish to pass.

In Batman's time the most special part of the bay was its northern end—the shallow, nutrient-rich and relatively warm waters known as Hobsons Bay. Judging from the piles of aged and bleached seashells tossed up on Middle Park beach, the place once hosted a fauna that would have made the Great Barrier Reef flush with envy. As as kid I sorted through the whitened fragments, finding pieces of the lustrous, orange-striped zebra volute and delicate, pink-frilled venus clam, two of Australia's most striking marine molluscs. I only dived in Hobsons Bay once. The stinking, oily water and the foul, black sludge coating the bottom were enough to make you gag.

In my twenties I became so saddened by the increasingly sterile environment and mindless destruction around the city that I left for Sydney. I still remember my first morning there, and the exhilaration of counting five species of parrots in the very centre of the metropolis.

Even so, I frequently returned to Melbourne and, over the years, discovered that braver souls than I had stayed and effected a transformation. I didn't appreciate the magnitude of the change until I found myself walking the shores of Hobsons Bay one hot summer evening in 2001, hand-in-hand with my young nephews. What I saw in the sand astonished me, for among the shards of long-dead shells we found first one, then another and another, recently living zebra volute. Their shells were still stained black by the enduring pollution, robbing them of much of their beauty, but these marvellous creatures had returned, reminding me of what Melbourne once was, and what it again could be.

Premier Jeff Kennett will probably be remembered for turning Melbourne into the Los Angeles of the south, with its crowning glories a racetrack on top of the Yarra's old billabong at Albert Park, tolled freeways and the Bolte Bridge. But Kennett also completed other changes initiated by his predecessor John Cain. For over a century the city had squatted beside the lower Yarra like a person on a toilet seat, presenting its backside to the water. Cain and Kennett saw that there was money to be made from water views, and of course one could not sell real estate fronting a sewer.

So youthful is this city that in my forty-odd years I have personally witnessed a quarter of its history, my parents almost half. Melbourne now seems to be finding its place in the world. It is recovering from the booms and busts that were driven by men drunk with dreams of instant wealth and power. Those generations built a wondrous city and destroyed a paradise, and in the extracts presented here you can read eyewitness accounts of just how they did it. The present generation, however, is building roots deep into the environment. For my money, the Melbourne of the twenty-first century is the truly 'Marvellous Melbourne'.

*

Where necessary I have modernised punctuation and spelling, silently corrected a handful of obvious errors, inserted the occasional explanatory date and sometimes added a word or two of clarification in a footnote, indicated by an asterisk (*). Otherwise, the writings are presented as they were first printed, with any omissions of text indicated by an ellipsis (…).

John Murray
Port King

John Murray was the first European to lay eyes upon the waters of Port Phillip Bay. A stiff wind made approach to the unknown lee shore too risky, so he was afforded only the briefest of glimpses as he sailed past the Heads in the *Lady Nelson* in January 1802. He returned to the bay on 14 February, entering and conducting a partial survey, which resulted in a tragic first contact. Murray named the place Port King, but Governor King used his prerogative to change the name to honour the 'old Governor' Arthur Phillip.

Tuesday 5 January—Winds from SE to East with clear weather, at a quarter past 1 p.m. Cape Shanks* bore NEbN nine miles. Kept running down along the land steering west and WbN in order to train the whole of this land along, found it impossible to survey any part of the coast as yet from the numerous natives fires which covered this low shore in one volume of

* Cape Schanck.

smoke. At 3 p.m. we saw a head land bearing WNW distant about twelve miles and an opening in the land that had the appearance of an harbour NW ten or twelve miles, bore away for this at last, it having the appearance of fine steady weather, altho' the wind now blowing was dead on the whole of this shore, yet I knew she would work off in case we were deceived. Accordingly kept standing down for this entrance, which every minute from its appearance made us shure it was a good harbour. At 5 p.m. saw a small island in the entrance, and observed that between it and the main lay a reef in appearance.

On my seeing this we bore away to leeward of this rock and I had the first mate and bosun at the masthead looking out. At this time I suppose we were within $1^1/_2$ mile of the entrance as we thought, and I perceived that the sea broke short, and was withal heavy, hove the lead and found only 10 fathoms water.[*] Astonished at this I hauled our wind and call'd out to them at the masthead to know if they saw any danger, but none was at the time seen.

I bore away again and deep'd into 11 fathoms, when Mr Bowen called out rocks ahead. Immediately hauled our wind and stood off, on closer observation of my own and going often to the masthead, I saw that the reef did not nearly stretch itself across the whole way but inside saw a fine sheet of smooth water, of great extent, from the wind blowing dead on this shore and fresh. I was obliged to haul off under a press of sail to clear the land, but with a determination to overhaul it by and by, as no doubt it has a channel into it, and is apparently a fine harbour of large extent, kept pressing sail and by 8 p.m. the extremes of land bore from NW to west, distance twenty miles I fancy...

The apparent soil of all the land from Elizabeth's Cove[**] to Cape Shanks is excellent, after you round Cape Shanks and stand

---

[*] A fathom is a depth of 1.83 metres.
[**] Elizabeth Cove is on the north coast of Phillip Island.

down to the westward, the land is invariably low and sandy with little hummocks here and there of grass and small bushes till you get down as far as this supposed harbour. On the opposite side of it the land gently rises a little for about ten or twelve miles; seemingly good ground, it then sweeps away in a long bite of low land which we just could perceive at sundown. Had the wind moderated or the sea gone down I would certainly have run down to that low land and train'd it along as well as every other part of this bay; in the present state of wind and sea it would not have been prudent or safe…

14 February—…At half-past 10 south Head of the new harbour or port N by E eight miles distant; by noon the island at the entrance of the harbour bore N half a mile distant. At this time we had a view of this part of the spacious harbour, its entrance is wide enough to work any vessel in, but in 10 fathoms. Bar stretches itself a good way across, and, with a strong tide out and wind in, the ripple is such as to cause a stranger to suspect rock or shoals ahead.

15 February—Working up, the port with a very strong ebb against us, we however gained ground. The southern shore of this noble harbour is bold high land in general and not clothed as all the land at western point is with thick brush but with stout trees of various kinds and in some places falls nothing short, in beauty and appearance, of Greenwich Park. Away to the eastward at the distance of twenty miles the land is mountainous, in particular there is one very high mountain which in the meantime I named Arthur's Seat from its resemblance to a mountain of that name a few miles from Edinburgh…to the NE by N, about five miles from the south shore lies a cluster of small rocky islands and all round them a shoal of sand; plenty of swans and pelicans were found on them when the boat was down, from which I named them Swan Isles*. To the NE by E there is an opening, and

* Now known as Mud Islands.

from our masthead no land could be seen in it. The northern shores are low with a sandy beach all along. At half-past 3 p.m. we got to anchor in a sandy cove in 7 fathoms water...I went on shore and walked through the woods a couple of miles. The ground was hard and pleasant to walk on. The trees are at a good distance from each other and no brush intercepts you. The soil is good as far as we may be judges. I saw several native huts and very likely they have burnt off several hundred acres of ground. Young grass we found springing up over all the ground we walked; the only birds we saw were a few parrots. We found some shells on the beach and returned on board. I have named this harbour Port King in honour of Governor P. G. King under whose orders I act.

16 February—After dinner I took a walk through the woods of this part of the country, attended by one soldier and our carpenter to examine the wood. To describe this part I walked through is simply to say that it nearly resembles a walk on Blackheath and the Park if we set out of question the houses and gardens of the latter. The hills and valleys rise and fall with inexpressible elegance. We discovered no water nor any new wood of consequence, but it is impossible that a great want of water can be here from the number of native huts and fires we fell in with in our march...

At sundown a native fire was seen about a mile inland; in the morning early I sent Mr Bowen and Bond armed to speak with them, neither fell in with them. At 9 a.m. hove up our bower with a light air at NE and dropped a few miles further up the port. We now saw the same fire just lighted by the natives and presently perceived several of them come out of the bush, but the moment they saw the vessel they sprang into the wood out of sight. At 11 a.m. we came to an anchor in 5 fathoms of water, handed sails, etc., as there was a native fire burning a little way inland.

I sent the launch with Mr Bowen and four hands armed to see if any natives were here, and before the boat was halfway on shore we had the satisfaction of seeing eighteen or twenty men and boys come out of the wood and seat themselves down on a green bank waiting the approach of our boat with which I had sent some shirts and other trifles to give them; the boat accordingly landed in the midst of them and a friendly intercourse took place with dancing on both sides—in an hour the boat returned.

Mr Bowen had dressed them in our white shirts and invited them on board; this however they declined, but exchanged for all this. Got a basket of straw neatly enough made. They were all clothed in the skins of opossums and each had a bundle of spears, a stone mogo* and one basket. They wished much to know what our arms were and their use and did not seem entirely to believe Mr Bowen that they were only walking sticks—no women were amongst them. I sent the boat again with some bread, looking-glasses, tomahawk and a picture as presents to induce them to part with their weapons and dresses as also to inform us where there was water. This day all hands put upon two-thirds allowance of bread.

17 February—The boat proceeded to the shore and was as before received in a friendly manner by the natives, all of whom were seated in a circle on a beautiful spot of grass near a high point of land. Mr Bowen and all the crew consisting of five men and the boy, Mr Brabyn, went up with their dinners in their hands and sat down in the midst of them (eighteen in number) and began to eat showing the natives how to eat bread, etc., and gave them anything they chose to ask for. Mr Bowen gave them all the things I had sent as well as several of his own things— stripping himself almost naked to comply with their wishes, and his example was followed by the whole of the boat's crew.

* Stone axe.

As there was two fine-looking boys amongst them I sent Mr Brabyn on shore purposely to see and gain their confidence by his attention to their youngsters, both of whom he dressed in his shirts, handkerchiefs, trowsers, etc.

All matters continued in this state while our people had anything to give and all we got was two spears, a basket and a mogo and even these they again took from the seamen that had them in keeping. This, however, the officer took no offence at being determined if at all possible to keep on friendly terms with them. It was in vain that the officer and crew tried by signs too significant not to be understood to gain intelligence where water was to be found or on what beaches shells were most plentiful; to all such inquiries they turned a deaf ear and only seemed intent on getting what our people had even to the last shirt. By this time our people had nearly finished their dinners and Isaac Moss having the boat in charge got up and was walking slowly down to her.

At this time the boy Brabyn happened to turn his head towards the wood and saw a man in the very act of throwing a spear at Moss as well as a large body (not before seen) behind a large fallen tree with their spears all in readiness for throwing. The boy immediately cried out to Mr Bowen who was at that very time in the act of serving out bread to all the party he was sitting among that he would be speared. But before the words were out of his mouth, a spear of the most dangerous kind was thrown at and did not escape Moss by a yard, and in an instant the whole of the treacherous body that Mr Bowen and four of our people were sitting in the midst of opened out to the right and left, and at once left them all open to the party in ambush who immediately were on their feet and began to throw spears. Still, such was the forbearance of the officer that only one piece was fired over their heads but this was found only to create a small panic, and our party was obliged to teach them by fatal experience the effect of our walking sticks.

The first fire made them run and one received two balls between his shoulders, still some of them made a stop to heave. The second fire they all set off with astonishing speed and most likely one received a mortal wound. Before another piece was fired Mr Bowen laid hold of one of their number and held on till three of our people came up and also grappled him; strange to tell he made such violent struggles as to get away from them all, now did the contents of the officer's piece bring him up although one ball passed through his arm and the other in his side—he was traced a good distance by his blood—the remaining pieces were by this time fired and our party gave chase to them all.

On board I kept a strict lookout with the glass and we lay only a little more than a quarter of a mile off the point where they were seated on. I plainly saw the natives running through the wood which was by no means thick—one fellow in particular had been dressed in one of my white shirts and the officer had tied the wrists of it with string, which hindered his getting it off—him we plainly saw from the vessel pass the roots of black trees with such speed as more to resemble a large white bird flying than a man. To increase their panic as they passed along I gave them a discharge of our guns loaded with round and grape but am almost certain that they did them no damage; by this time our people returned from the chase, having found on the way back a number of spears, dresses and baskets, etc. Made the boat signal and they came off.

Thus did this treachery and unprovoked attack meet with its just punishment and at the same time taught us a useful lesson to be more cautious in future. With respect to the size of these natives they are much the same as at Sydney, their understanding better though, for they easily made out our signs when it answered their purposes or inclination. When it did not they could be dull enough. They were all clothed in opossum skins and in each basket a certain quantity of gum was found. Not the least sign of a canoe has been seen. I conclude they live entirely inland, and if we may judge from the number of their fires and other marks this part of the country is not thin of inhabitants. Their spears are of various kinds and all of them more dangerous than any I have yet seen. The workmanship of their dresses, their lines and baskets are far from despicable, their mogo or stone axes are such as common at Sydney.

20 February—...Sent an armed party and our carpenter a long range through the woods to try out the different kinds of wood, none however was found of use, the trees being almost invariably oak and other wood quite common at Sydney. A red waistcoat of Mr Brabyn's was found with some bread in each pocket; in this he had dressed one of the native boys, who in his fear left it I fancy, as soon as he had found how to get it off, for it was buttoned on him.

22 February—At noon the launch returned, having found an entrance into the sheet of water they were sent to overhaul, but only at high water, seven or eight feet of it, consequently no harbour for shipping. The boat proceeded a mile and a half, and, in running that, caught twenty swans of a large size without wasting one charge of shot...

5 March—I went in the launch in search of a channel by which vessels of a larger draught than ours might be got up abreast of the watering place and was fortunate enough to find one a mile at least in breadth lying off the southern shores of this port about three miles and having from 16 to 6 fathoms water in at low water and neap tides; and in this water a vessel of any draught may be secure from all winds at about a mile and a half from the spring at which today I loaded the boat with water and examined it. As far as we are judges it is most excellent water as clear as crystal— lies from the beach about ten or a dozen yards and plenty of it to water the Great Fleet of England; it is nearer the entrance than the foot of Arthur's Seat by about two miles, and can easily be found

out by the land which for a few miles before you come to it is low whereas all the other land on both sides is high with bold points; if a boat then east or E by S from Point Paterson* nine miles puts into the shore they will not be far off it, there is plenty of duck about it, but so shy that only two have been shot, a circumstance we did not a little regret as they exceed in flavour any I ever eat. We are not complete in water and will soon be wooded.

7 March—...The soil of the land all round the extensive place is good and its appearance exceeds in beauty even the southern shores. The number of large swans seen almost exceeds belief, but by this time most of them could fly, we caught eleven—ten of which were large. All of us slept this night in a pleasant little island with a few handsome trees on it, soil good and so clear as to be fit for the hoe at once. I named it *Maria Isle*** after a sister I lost some years past.

8 March—As we now intended sailing in a few days I judged it consistent with His Majesty's instructions (a copy of which I was furnished with from the Governor and Commander-in-Chief of New South Wales) to take possession of this port in the form and manner laid down by the said instructions, and accordingly at 8 o'clock in the morning the united colours of the kingdoms of Great Britain and Ireland were hoisted on board and on Point Paterson, and at one o'clock under a discharge of three volleys of small arms and artillery the port was taken possession of in the name of his Sacred Majesty George the Third of Great Britain and Ireland, King, etc., etc. Served double allowance of grog.

* Now known as Point King.
** Either Duck Island or Swan Island.

A New Discovery?

Just ten weeks after Murray's brief exploration, Flinders entered the bay during his circumnavigation of the continent. He presumed that he had made a new discovery and, not surprisingly, given the fracas with the crew of the *Lady Nelson*, Flinders saw nothing of the Aborigines.

26 April—In the morning we kept close to an east-south-east wind, steering for the land to the north-eastward; and at nine o'clock Captain Grant's Cape Schanck, the extreme of the preceding evening, was five leagues distant to the N88°E, and a rocky point towards the head of the bight, bore N12°E. On coming within five miles of the shore at eleven o'clock, we found it to be low, and mostly sandy; and that the bluff head which had been taken for the north-end of an island, was part of a ridge of hills rising at Cape Schanck…

On the west side of the rocky point there was a small opening, with breaking water across it; however, on advancing a little more westward the opening assumed a more interesting aspect, and I bore away to have a nearer view. A large extent of water presently became visible within side; and although the entrance seemed to be very narrow, and there were in it strong ripplings like breakers, I was induced to steer in at half past one; the ship being close upon a wind and every man ready for tacking at a moment's warning…

The extensive harbour we had thus unexpectedly found I supposed must be Western Port, although the narrowness of the entrance did by no means correspond with the width given to it by Mr Bass. It was the information of Captain Baudin, who had coasted along from thence with fine weather, and had found no inlet of any kind, which induced this supposition; and the very great extent of the place, agreeing with that of Western Port, was in confirmation of it. This, however, was not Western Port, as we found next morning; and I congratulated myself on having made a new and useful discovery; but here again I was in error. This place, as I afterwards learned at Port Jackson, had been discovered ten weeks before by Lieutenant John Murray, who had succeeded Captain Grant in the command of the *Lady Nelson*. He had given it the name of Port Phillip, and to the rocky point on the east side of the entrance, that of Point Nepean.

27 April—Our situation was found in the morning to be near two miles from the south shore, and the extreme towards Point Nepean bore N83°W, two leagues. About three miles to the north-by-west were some dry rocks, with bushes on them, surrounded with mud flats; and they appeared to form a part of the same shoal from which we had three times tacked in $2^{1}/_{2}$ and 3 fathoms. The mud bank where the ship had grounded is distinct from the middle shoal; but I am not certain that it is so from the south shore, from which it is one mile distant. The bluff mount (named Arthur's Seat by Mr Murray, from a supposed resemblance to the hill of that name near Edinburgh), bore S76°E; but from thence the shore trended northward so far that the land at the head of the port could not be seen, even from aloft. Before proceeding any higher with the ship, I wished to gain some knowledge of the form and extent of this great piece of water; and Arthur's Seat being more than a thousand feet high and near the water side, presented a favourable station for that purpose.

After breakfast I went away in a boat, accompanied by Mr Brown and some other gentlemen, for the Seat. It was seven or eight miles from the ship; and in steering nearly a straight course for it, we passed over the northern skirt of the shoal where the ship had touched; but afterwards had from 7 to 5 fathoms nearly to the shore. Having observed the latitude there from an artificial horizon, I ascended the hill; and to my surprise found the port so extensive that even at this elevation its boundary to the north-ward could not be distinguished. The western shore extended from the entrance ten or eleven miles in a northern direction to the extremity of what, from its appearance, I called Indented Head; beyond it was a wide branch of the port leading to the westward, and I suspected might have a communication with the sea; for it was almost incredible that such a vast piece of water should not have a larger outlet than that through which we had come.

I took an extensive set of bearings from the clearest place to be found on the north-western bluff part of the hill; and we after-wards walked a little way back upon the ridge. From thence another considerable piece of water was seen, at the distance of three or four leagues; it seemed to be mostly shallow; but as it appeared to have a communication with the sea to the south, I had no doubt of its being Mr Bass' Western Port.

Arthur's Seat and the hills and valleys in its neighbourhood, were generally well covered with wood; and the soil was superior to any upon the borders of the salt water, which I have had an opportunity of examining in *Terra Australis*. There were many marks of natives, such as deserted fire places and heaps of oyster shells; and upon the peninsula which forms the south side of the port, a smoke was rising, but we did not see any of the people. Quantities of fine oysters were lying upon the beaches, between high and low water marks, and appeared to have been washed up by the surf; a circumstance which I do not recollect to have observed in any other part of this country.

JAMES FLEMMING
The Yarra Discovered

Charles Grimes is celebrated as the European discoverer of the Yarra River. Ironically, Port Stephens, in New South Wales, and the Yarra were both distinguished by the acting surveyor-general as places unfit for settlement. The journal entries of Grimes' explorations were kept by botanist and assistant James Flemming.

2 February 1803 — ...At the usual time the same party as yesterday, with the addition of the doctor, went on shore: for about a mile the land dry, a light sandy soil; afterwards a large swamp, with three lagoons in it, all dry. The land appears to be covered with water in wet seasons. Came to a salt lagoon about a mile long and a quarter of a mile wide; had not entrance to the sea. Soon afterwards came to a large river; went up it about a mile when we turned back and waited for the boat to take us on board. The ground is a swamp on one side and high on the other. Saw many swans, pelicans and ducks.

3 February — At six o'clock the captain, Mr Grimes, self and five seamen went in the boat up the Great River; at between two and three miles it divided into two; we took the left-hand stream[*] at half past eight o'clock. The land became high, where we landed and went on a hill. The soil a reddish loam from ten to fifteen inches deep. Saw a large lagoon at a distance. Went over the hill to a large swamp. Soil black, eighteen inches with blue clay at bottom. No trees for many miles. Came to the boat and proceeded on; passed two dingles; no water; came to a third where

[*] Also known as Saltwater River until renamed the Maribyrnong River.

we found some water, where we dined and proceeded on.

Opposite this the land is stony soil, stiff blue clay, and no trees, only some straggling oaks by the side of the river. We went up the river till we came to rocks; could not get the boat over; crossed it at a place the natives had made for catching fish. It was still salt though a great fall. Went about two miles on the hills which are level at top and full of stones, the land very bad, and very few trees, and appeared so to the mountains, which appeared clothed with timber.

On our return back came to the river a little higher up and found it excellent fresh water, where it divided and appeared deep enough for a boat. Just as we got to the boat it began to thunder and rain. Stopped a little time and came back till we could procure wood to make a fire and it being sunset stopped the night.

4 February—Started at six and came to the branch we passed before, at the entrance the land swampy. A few miles up found it excellent water where we saw a little hill, and landed. The time dinner was getting ready Messrs Robbins, Grimes and self went on the hill, where we saw the lagoon seen from the hill where we first landed. It is in a large swamp between the two rivers; fine grass, fit to mow; not a bush in it. The soil is black rich earth about six to ten inches deep, when it is very hard and stiff. It is better further back. About two miles farther went on shore again; the land much better and timber larger. Soil black, ten to fifteen inches deep; bottom sand or gravel. I went to the other side where the ground was the same; went in about two miles; it began to rain. I returned to the boat and after dinner we all got on board and arrived on board the vessel at dusk. Saw a canoe and two native huts.

7 February—Early in the morning the party that went up the river before with the doctor went up to the little hill we had been at on the 4th, when we stopped to breakfast; proceeded on to a creek, where we dined. Saw some natives. The land in general is a fine black soil, ten to eighteen inches deep. Timber; gum,

Banksia, oak and mimosa of sorts, but not large except the gum. The river appears to rise to the height of eight or ten feet at times by wreck on the trees. Went alternately into the land on both sides of the river; it continued nearly of the same quality. The greatest part of the land is above the floods. Proceeded on till sunset; stopped the night.

8 February—Sowed some seeds by the natives' hut, where we slept. Continued our course up the river; the land high; rocks by side of the river; it is a freestone, the strata on edge. Came to a fall, where we could not get the boat over. We went inland a little way…Mr Robbins got up a tree; saw it to be gently rising hills, clothed with trees, for ten or fifteen miles., A little above the fall there is a small island, and the river divides in two…Returned back and crossed a neck of land 330 paces over whilst the boat went round. Came to our old station at the large lagoon. I went about two miles inland and fell in with seven natives. I saw Messrs Robbins, Grimes and McCallum at the lagoon. From the hill saw the vessel; returned to the river, and after dinner set out for the vessel, where we arrived about seven o'clock; the land at two miles inland is of a better quality than the specimen.

James Hingston Tuckey
Port Phillip's First Fleet

The HMS *Calcutta*, with her cargo of 308 convicts, and *Ocean*, carrying supplies and a handful of free settlers, were dispatched to form a settlement at Port Phillip in 1803. A year earlier the British bureaucrats responsible

for colonies and war were brought together, allowing
new thinking. The French reconnaissance of Australia's
coast had caused suspicion of a French land-grab, and it
was felt that the best response was to pre-empt them,
while on the way emptying a few more hulks and
prisons. Timber, too, was a preoccupation of the navy,
and southern Australia was widely believed to be a veritable storehouse of potential masts and beams. James
Tuckey's *On a Voyage to Establish a Colony at Port
Phillip* is by far the most readable account of the expedition. As the *Calcutta*'s first lieutenant, Tuckey was in
a good position to record events, and there are remarkable parallels between his and Watkin Tench's narratives.
Tuckey died in 1816, at the age of forty, while leading an
expedition to explore the Congo River in Africa.

10 October — ...we at last made King Island, in the entrance of
Bass's Straits, which we had anxiously looked out for the two
preceding days; the wind being from the NE obliged us to stand
within three miles of the island, which through the haze we
observed to be moderately high and level, with three sandy hills
nearly in the centre. The increasing breeze and lowering sky,
which portended a coming gale, prevented our examining the
island more minutely. Fortunately we stood off in time to gain a
sufficient offing before the gale commenced, which during the
night blew a perfect hurricane between the NW and SW.

This night of danger and anxiety, was succeeded by a morning
beautifully serene, which showed us the southern coast of New
South Wales. From the total want of information respecting the
appearance of the land on this coast, we were doubtful as to our
situation, and approached the shore with cautious diffidence; at
length the break in the land, which forms the entrance of Port
Phillip, was observed, but a surf, apparently breaking across it,
created, at first, some mistrust of its identity, until the man at the

masthead observing a ship at anchor within, which was soon recognised for the *Ocean*, removed all doubt, and without further hesitation we pushed in for the entrance.

A fair wind and tide soon carried us through; and in a few minutes we were presented with a picture highly contrasted with the scene we had lately contemplated: an expanse of water bounded in many places only by the horizon, and unruffled as the bosom of unpolluted innocence, presented itself to the charmed eye, which roamed over it in silent admiration. The nearer shores, along which the ship glided at the distance of a mile, afforded the most exquisite scenery, and recalled the idea of 'Nature in the world's first spring'. In short, every circumstance combined to impress our minds with the highest satisfaction...

The week following our arrival at Port Phillip was occupied in searching for an eligible place to fix the settlement. As it was of the first consequence that this should be of easy access to shipping, the shores near the mouth of the port were first examined. Here, to our great mortification, we observed a total want of fresh water, and found the soil so extremely light and sandy as to deny all hopes of successful cultivation. As it was, however, determined to land the people, a small bay, eight miles from the harbour's mouth, was pitched upon for that purpose, where, by sinking casks, water of a tolerable quantity was procured, and here the camp was pitched; and on 16 October, the marines and convicts were landed, while the ships immediately began to discharge their cargoes...

The face of the country bordering on the port is beautifully picturesque, swelling into gentle elevations of the brightest verdure, and dotted with trees, as if planted by the hand of taste, while the ground is covered with a profusion of flowers of every colour; in short, the external appearance of the country flattered us into the most delusive dreams of fruitfulness and plenty...

The kangaroo is the largest animal yet discovered in New Holland; it inhabits the neighbourhood of Port Phillip in considerable numbers, weighing from fifty to 150 pounds; the native dog, the opossum, flying squirrel and field-rat make up the catalogue of animals we observed.

Aquatic birds are found in abundance on the lagoons, and are black swans, ducks, teal, black and pied shags, pelicans, gulls, redbills (a beach bird), herons, curlows and sand-larks; the land birds are eagles, crows, ravens, quail, bronze-winged pigeons, and many beautiful varieties of the parrot tribe, particularly the black cockatoo; the emu is also a native of this part of the country, its eggs having been found here. Three varieties of snakes were observed, all of which appeared to be venomous. The species of insects are almost innumerable: among them are upwards of one hundred and fifty different kinds of beautiful moths; several kinds of beetles, the animated straw,* &c. The swamps are inhabited by myriads of mosquitoes of an extraordinary size; but the common fly, which swarms almost beyond belief, possesses all the offensive powers of the mosquitoe, its sting creating an equal degree of pain and inflammation. Wasps are also common, but no bees were seen.

Fish, it may safely be asserted, is so scarce that it could never be depended on as a source of effectual relief in the event of scarcity. Several varieties of the ray were almost the only ones caught, with sometimes a few mullet, and other small fish; in general, a day's work with the seine produced scarcely a good dish of fish. The number of sharks which infest the harbour may occasion this scarcity of small fish**. The rocks outside the harbour's mouth are frequented by seals and sea-elephants. The shellfish are oysters, limpits, mussels, escalops, cockles, sea-ears; and very large crayfish are found among the rocks…

* Stick insect.
** Fish were later found to abound in the bay.

The NW side of the port, where a level plain extends to the northward as far as the horizon, appears to be by far the most populous; at this place, upwards of two hundred natives assembled round the surveying boats, and their obviously hostile intentions made the application of firearms absolutely necessary to repel them, by which one native was killed, and two or three wounded.

Previous to this time, several interviews had been held with separate parties, at different places, during which the most friendly intercourse was maintained, and endeavoured to be strengthened on our part, by presents of blankets, beads, &c. At these interviews they appeared to have a perfect knowledge of the use of firearms; and as they seemed terrified even at the sight of them, they were kept entirely out of view.

The last interview which terminated so unexpectedly hostile, had at its commencement the same friendly appearance. Three natives, unarmed, came to the boats, and received fish, bread and blankets. Feeling no apprehension from three naked and unarmed savages, the first lieutenant proceeded with one boat to continue the survey, while the other boat's crew remained on shore to dress dinner and procure water. The moment the first boat disappeared the three natives took leave, and in less than an hour returned with forty more, headed by a chief who seemed to possess much authority.

This party immediately divided, some taking off the attention of the people who had charge of the tent (in which was Mr Harris, the surveyor of the colony), while the rest surrounded the boats, the oars, masts and sails of which were used in erecting the tent. Their intention to plunder was immediately visible, and all the exertions of the boat's crew were insufficient to prevent their possessing themselves of a tomahawk, an axe and a saw.

In this situation, as it was impossible to get the boat away, everything belonging to her being on shore, it was thought advisable to temporise, and wait the return of the other boat, without having recourse to firearms, if it could possibly be avoided; and for this purpose, bread, meat and blankets were given them. These condescensions, however, seemed only to increase their boldness, and their numbers having been augmented by the junction of two other parties, amounted to more than two hundred.

At this critical time the other boat came in sight, and observing the crowd and tumult at the tent, pushed towards them with all possible dispatch. Upon approaching the shore, the unusual warlike appearance of the natives was immediately observed, and as they seemed to have entire possession of the tent, serious apprehensions were entertained for Mr Harris and two of the boat's crew, who it was noticed were not at the boat.

At the moment that the grapnel was hove out of the lieutenant's boat, to prevent her taking the ground, one of the natives seized the master's mate, who had charge of the other boat, and held him fast in his arms. A general cry of 'Fire, Sir; for God's sake, fire!' was now addressed from those on shore to the first lieutenant. Hoping the report only would sufficiently intimidate them, two muskets were fired over their heads; for a moment they seemed to pause, and a few retreated behind the trees, but immediately returned, clapping their hands, and shouting vehemently. Four muskets with buckshot, and the fowling-pieces of the gentlemen with small shot, were now fired among them, and from a general howl, very different from their former shouts, many were supposed to be struck. This discharge created a general panic, and leaving their cloaks behind, they ran in every direction among the trees. It was hoped the business would have terminated here, and orders were, therefore, given to strike the tent, and prepare to quit the territory of such disagreeable neighbours.

While thus employed, a large party were seen again assembling behind a hill, at the foot of which was our tent: they advanced in a compact body to the brow of the hill, every individual armed with a spear, and some, who appeared to be attendants of others, carrying bundles of them; when within a hundred yards of us they halted, and the chief, with one attendant, came down to the tent, and spoke with great vehemence, holding a very large war spear in a position for throwing.

The first lieutenant, wishing to restore peace if possible, laid down his gun, and advancing to the chief, presented him with several cloaks, necklaces and spears, which had been left behind on their retreat; the chief took his own cloak and necklace, and gave the others to his attendant. His countenance and gestures all this time betrayed more of anger than fear, and his spear appeared every moment upon the point of quitting his hand. When the cloaks were all given up, the body on the hill began to descend, shouting and flourishing their spears. Our people were immediately drawn up, and ordered to present their muskets loaded with ball, while last attempts were made to convince the chief that if his people continued to approach they would be immediately fired upon. These threats were either not properly understood, or were despised, and it was deemed absolutely necessary for our own safety, to prove the power of our firearms, before they came near enough to injure us with their spears; selecting one of the foremost, who appeared to be most violent, as a proper example, three muskets were fired at him at fifty yards distance, two of which took effect, and he fell dead on the spot; the chief turning round at the report saw him fall, and immediately fled among the trees; a general dispersion succeeded, and the dead body was left behind.

Among these savages, gradations of rank could be distinctly traced, founded most probably upon personal qualities and external appearance. In these respects the chief far excelled the rest; his figure was masculine and well-proportioned, and his air bold and commanding. When first he was seen approaching the boat, he was raised upon the shoulders of two men, and surrounded by the whole party, shouting and clapping their hands. Besides his cloak, which was only distinguished by its superior size, he wore a necklace of reeds, and several strings of human hair over his breast. His head was adorned with a coronet of the wing-feathers of the swan, very neatly arranged, and which had a pleasing effect. The faces of several were painted with red, white and yellow clays, and others had a reed or bone ran through the septum of the nose, perhaps increasing in length according to rank, for the chief's was by far the longest, and must have measured at least two feet. Ornamental scars on the shoulders were general and the face of one was deeply pitted as if from the smallpox, though that disease is not known to exist in New Holland.[*] A very great difference was observed in the comparative cleanliness of these savages; some of them were so abominably beastly that it required the strongest stomach to look on them without nausea, while others were sufficiently cleanly to be viewed without disgust. The beards, which are remarkably bushy in the former, were allowed to grow, while in the latter they were cut close, apparently by a sharp instrument, probably a shell.

The only covering they make use of, to preserve their persons from the winter's cold, is a square of opossum skins, neatly sewn together, and thrown loosely over their shoulders; the fleshy side, which is worn inwards, is marked with parallel lines, forming squares, lozenges, &c and sometimes with uncouth human figures in the attitudes of dancing.

[*] Smallpox had in fact appeared in Sydney in 1791.

DAVID COLLINS
Stating My Deficiencies

Lieutenant-Governor David Collins had a back-up
option if Port Phillip should prove unsuitable for settlement: he could try again in Tasmania. After abandoning
the tented encampment in Sullivan Bay near present-day
Sorrento after just a few months, the lugubrious Collins
went on to establish Hobart.

The soil from Arthur's Seat to Point Calcutta, at the entrance
of the harbour, is light and mixed considerably with sand.
Even the few patches of black vegetable mould which are here
and there have been met with abound therewith. I have, nevertheless, opened two acres of ground for a garden, and am
preparing five acres for Indian corn. Of the success of the latter I
do not entertain much hope, but I find it some employment for
my people. They, I am happy to say, conduct themselves most
perfectly to my satisfaction, wading the whole day long up to
their middles in water, with the utmost cheerfulness, to discharge
the boats as they come in.

The bread, flour and salt provisions for their support I have
stowed in large piles in the open air, while the bale goods, wine,
spirits and other articles of value are deposited under three large
elaboratory tents, which I have guarded well as my small military
force will allow...were I to settle in the upper part of the harbour,
which is full of natives, I should require four times the force I
have now to guard not only the convicts, but perhaps myself,
from their attacks...

The season of the year when I arrived there, as well as the soil
of Port Phillip not admitting any of the corn to be sown, I was

only able to try some of the garden seeds, when I was concerned to find that, of eighteen or twenty different sorts which were put into the ground, not one succeeded...

I am sorry to state that many of the articles of ironmongery were totally unfit for use, owing to the badness of the materials of which they had been made. Specimens of these I shall send to the Transport Board by Captain Woodriff. The axes in general are so soft that the commonest wood will turn their edges...In the medical department, the surgeon has represented to me that most of the instruments had been in use before they were put up for us...As we have neither glue, borax, resin or a bar of steel, articles that are indispensably necessary, I hope a supply of each may be sent by the next conveyance.

But while I am stating my deficiencies I must do justice to the people who packed the provisions, as better meat can nowhere be found, for it is better than any I have seen in New South Wales...

I am at a loss to know how to dispose of the settlers, this place not holding out any prospect for their succeeding in agricultural pursuits. Sixteen having signified their wish of remaining here, I have placed them in a valley close to my encampment, where I have allowed them small portions of garden ground. I imagine the excellence of our provisions, than which none can be finer, has induced most of them to remain here; but, if I am not to remove, I shall look out for situations whereon to place them, and ease the government of the expense which they incur as speedily as the circumstances, in which I find myself, will admit of. I am sorry to observe that in general they are a necessitous and worthless set of people.

The ration which I at present issue is to each male convict for seven days: seven pounds of beef or four pounds of pork, seven pounds of biscuit, one pound of flour, six ounces of sugar. The one pound of flour formed no part of the ration which I received from the treasury, but it was given to the first convicts who landed at Port Jackson, in addition to the seven pounds of biscuit, and I thought it would enable my people to make a pudding on Sunday, which is the use to which they put it, and find thereby a grateful addition to their salt meat on one day in the week. When the biscuit is expended, which it soon will be, I shall then issue seven pounds of flour.

I have issued, since my arrival, a complete suit of clothing to each male convict, a comfort that the majority of them stood much in want of, for the wretched apparel with which they embarked was completely worn out long before we had reached the most trying part of the voyage. During the progress of this, I had made up and issued to them about sixty suits from the materials which were put on board to be made upon the passage, and these were distributed to men who were falling ill for want of clothes...

The people for the three weeks which succeeded our debarkation continued healthy and well-behaved, but since that time we have never had less than thirty under medical treatment and a desertion rather alarming has taken place among them. I am concerned to state that twelve of the convicts have within the last week left the camp and were at first said to be gone for Port Jackson, but I have since been informed they are proceeding to a bay upon the coast which they have been told is at this time of the year the resort of the South Sea whalers.

I had received information that these were to be followed by five others, who I caused to be seized a short time before the hour at which they purposed quitting the settlement. I have them now chained to each other, with an assurance from me that they shall remain in that state upon two-thirds allowance of provisions until they will either give me such information as may lead to the apprehension of the others or that those others return.

WILLIAM HILTON HOVELL AND HAMILTON HUME

A Little Better Understood

The arduous and protracted journey of Hamilton Hume and William Hovell overland from the Sydney district to Port Phillip in 1824–25 is one of Australia's notable early explorations. They were the only documented white visitors to the bay between 1803 and 1835. This account of their journey was edited by Sydney doctor and philanthropist William Bland and was first published in 1831.

16 December 1824 — This morning they crossed the river or creek without difficulty, the water not taking the cattle more than chest high. Mr Hume named this stream the Arndell*, after the late Dr Arndell, the father of Mrs Hovell. They now proceeded SW by S through the plains about six miles, when they were struck with an appearance, respecting which they could not decide, whether it was that of burning grass, or that of distant water. They now proceeded S and at four o'clock, had the gratification satisfactorily to determine that the appearance which had just now created so much doubt, was that of water; and which, leaving the river a short distance, and directing their march from SW to SSW they soon ascertain to be part of the sea — the so long and ardently desired object of their labours. They now again alter their course to SW, and travel six miles in that direction along the shore, over excellent land, but quite clear of timber.

On the downs or plains today, they had seen several flocks of emus, and wild turkeys. The kangaroo, however, was seldom met with. Indeed this animal is not generally found in so open a tract

* Werribee River.

of country, as that over which they have been passing the last three days.

The water near the shore was covered with waterfowl, of various descriptions, some of which were new to them. And by the time they had halted for the night, they had procured an ample supply of black swans and ducks…

17 December…This morning, one of the men, James Fitzpatrick, having proceeded a short distance up the creek, to shoot wild fowl, was suddenly surprised by a couple of natives who were lurking behind some reeds; the man no sooner perceived them, than he began to retreat, and they to advance, throwing off their cloaks, and with their arms in their hands; perceiving this, he turned and snapped his piece at one of them; but as it missed fire, he had no resource left, except flight, and which also would have been unavailing, had not his shouts for assistance brought him timely aid. About two hours after this occurrence, as two of the people were employed in procuring firewood in a small clump of trees not far from the tent, two natives sprung towards them from behind the trees. These, however, on the men presenting their muskets at them, made signs of peace. Mr Hume who was at hand now approached, when laying down his arms, and beckoning to the men to do the same, the natives followed the example, and after much conversation, but of which not a word was understood by either party, they proceeded with Mr Hume to the tent. These people by degrees began to be a little better understood, when they seemed to wish to describe that a vessel had been in that bay, and that the people had landed; and to imply that both the master and the people were continually in a hurry. They also appeared to point out where the vessel lay, and suiting 'the action to the word', endeavoured to explain that they had seen men felling trees in that direction, and this was all done with a gesture and grimace, evincing that these people were at least not bad mimics.

These natives, who were soon joined by a third, it was

discovered were inquisitive, troublesome, and great thieves, cunning and treacherous. They made a laugh of the circumstance of one of the people having been pursued, though there could be no doubt as to the hostility of their intentions on that occasion. Messrs Hovell and Hume had been desirous of taking their horses in the direction of what they supposed to be Port Phillip, but the conduct of these people, and the numerous fires which were being made around them, apparently as signals among the natives, made them conclude, that it would be unsafe for the party to separate.

The natives here, in their form and features, very much resemble those about Sydney; their manners and customs appeared very similar, and they have the same kind of weapons. The language however seemed totally different, as to words, from that of the Sydney natives, or those about Jarvis's Bay, though in sound, it is much the same.

They did not seem astonished at the horses or bullocks, though evidently very much afraid of the latter, and even dreadfully alarmed, if the bullocks, although at a considerable distance, were looking towards them.

JOHN BATMAN

The Greatest Landowner in the World

John Batman was an ambitious Australian-born grazier and the motivating force behind the Port Phillip Association. Widely hailed as the founder of Melbourne, he sailed without official sanction for Port Phillip in 1835. Upon his return to Tasmania with 'treaty' in hand, the press proclaimed him 'the greatest landowner in the world'. Batman seems to have had genuine affection and respect for the Aborigines and even suggested that the Tasmanian natives be relocated to Port Phillip. Three years after signing the treaty Batman was in terminal decline. His once muscular physique was wasted by syphilis; his nose was rotted away and he was unable to get about except with the assistance of a rush-work perambulator. His death on 9 May 1839 was a merciful release, for his wife had deserted him and returned to England. He was tended to the end by a group of Sydney Aborigines who had been in his employ since the 1820s. Included here are Batman's historic diary entries, recording his negotiations with local chiefs, the deed for Melbourne land and a letter to John Montagu, the new colonial secretary.

6 June 1835—After some time and full explanation, I found eight chiefs amongst them who possessed the whole of the territory near Port Phillip. Three brothers, all of the same name, were the principal chiefs, and two of them men of six feet high and very good-looking; the other not so tall, but stouter. The other five chiefs were fine men. After a full explanation of what my object was, I purchased two large tracts of land from them—about 600,000 acres, more or less, and delivered over to them blankets, knives, looking-glasses, tomahawks, beads, scissors, flour, etc, etc, as payment for the land; and also agreed to give them a tribute or rent yearly. The parchment the eight chiefs signed this afternoon, delivering to me some of the soil, each of them, as giving me full possession of the tracts of land...

7 June—Detained this morning some time drawing up triplicates of the deeds of the land I purchased, and delivering over to them more property. Just before leaving, the two principal chiefs came and brought their two cloaks, or royal mantles, and laid them at my feet, wishing me to accept the same. On my consenting

to take them, they placed them round my neck and over my shoulders, and seemed quite pleased to see me walk about with them on.

I had no trouble to find out their secret marks. One of my natives (Bungett) went to a tree, out of sight of the women, and made the Sydney natives' mark. After this was done, I took with me two or three of my natives to the principal chief and showed him the mark on the tree. This he knew immediately, and pointed to the knocking out of the teeth. The mark is always made when the ceremony of knocking out the teeth in the front is done. However, after this I desired, through my natives, for him to make his mark; which, after looking about some time, and hesitating some few minutes, he took the tomahawk and cut out in the bark of the tree his mark, which is attached to the deed, and is the signature of the country and tribe.

About 10 a.m. I took my departure from those interesting people. I think the principal chief stands six feet four inches high, and his brother six feet two inches and as fine looking men as ever I saw...

8 June—The wind foul this morning for Indented Head. We tried, but could not get out of the river. The boat went up the large river I have spoken of, which comes from the east, and I am glad to state, about six miles up found the river all good water and very deep. This will be the place for a village—the natives on shore.*

> Batman drew up two deeds, one for the Geelong
> area and the other for Melbourne. Here is the latter
> document.

Know all persons that we, three brothers, Jagajaga, Jagajaga, Jagajaga, being the three principal chiefs, and also Cooloolock, Bungarie, Yanyan, Moowhip, Monmarmalar, being the chiefs of a certain native tribe called Dutigallar, situate at and near Port

* Batman was on the Yarra River near where Queen Street now terminates.

Phillip, called by us, the above-mentioned chiefs, Iramoo, being possessed of the tract of land hereinafter mentioned for and in consideration of twenty pair of blankets, thirty tomahawks, one hundred knives, fifty pair scissors, thirty looking-glasses, two hundred handkerchiefs, and one hundred pounds of flour, and six shirts, delivered to us by John Batman, residing in Van Diemen's Land, Esquire, but at present sojourning with us and our tribe, do for ourselves, our heirs and successors give grant enfeoff and confirm unto the said John Batman, his heirs and assigns, all that tract of country situate and being at Port Phillip, running from the branch of the river at the top of the port, about seven miles from the mouth of the river, forty miles north-east, and from thence—west, forty miles across Iramoo Downs or Plains and from thence south-south-west, across Mount Vilaumanartar to Geelong Harbour at the head of the same and containing 500,000 more or less acres, as the same hath been before the execution of these presents delineated and marked out by us according to the custom of our tribe by certain marks made upon the trees growing along the boundaries of the said tract of land, to hold the said tract of land, with all advantages belonging thereto, unto and to the use of the said John Batman, his heirs and assigns for ever, to the intent that the said John Batman his heirs and assigns may occupy and possess the said tract of land and place thereon sheep and cattle. Yielding and delivering to us, and our heirs or successors the yearly rent or tribute of one hundred pair of blankets, one hundred knives, one hundred tomahawks, fifty suits of clothing, fifty looking glasses, fifty pair scissors and five tons of flour.

In witness thereof, we, Jagajaga, Jagajaga, Jagajaga, the before mentioned principal chiefs, and Cooloolock, Bungarie, Yanyan, Moowhip, and Monmarmalar, the chiefs of the said tribe, have hereunto affixed our seals to these presents, and have signed the same. Dated, according to the Christian era, this sixth day of June, 1835.

Signed, sealed, and delivered in the presence of us the same having been fully and properly interpreted and explained to the said chiefs.

James Gumm
Alexander Thompson
Willm. Todd

Jagajaga
Jagajaga
Jagajaga
Cooloolock
Bungarie
Yanyan
Moowhip
Mommarmalar
John Batman

★

30 November 1835—I beg to acquaint you, for the information of his Excellency the Lieutenant-Governor, that on Thursday last I arrived at George Town, in the barque *Norval*, from Port Phillip, after a passage of about thirty hours (the same space of time having been occupied in my passage there).

On my arrival at the station of the Association of Indented Head, where only two white men with two Sydney natives are now staying, I was happy to find that a most friendly feeling existed between them and the Aborigines, between sixty and seventy of whom were also there, in proof of which feeling I need only acquaint your Excellency that my party had been for many days without rations; but, by the kindness of the friendly natives, had been well supplied with the roots on which they chiefly subsist, and which my people assured me they found nutritious and agreeable. It is gratifying to know that should supplies at any time fail, nature has provided that which will secure them from want.

I then proceeded to the north-east part of the port, where the settlement is formed, where I landed the cattle and sheep, and found everything progressing in a way beyond my most sanguine expectations; so favourable are the soil and climate to vegetation that we found the people well supplied with vegetables of the finest growth and quality, the produce of seeds sown only about ten weeks before, and they were able to supply the ship with potatoes and a variety of other vegetables for our return voyage. The wheat was looking most luxuriant, the people all well satisfied, and not one wishing to return. The country affords them an abundant supply of fish and wild fowl, and as regards stock, all which were taken there ten or twelve weeks since had improved beyond description; and incredible as it may appear, the change for the better, which took place in the condition of the stock taken down by me, during the four or five days that I remained, was so great that I must myself have witnessed it to have believed it.

The intercourse with the natives had gone well. Once since our establishment as many as 400 natives were assembled for the purpose of settling some ancient quarrel; and, although so many different tribes were collected together, uniform goodwill was by all of them towards the white people, and the dispute they had met to settle ended without any more unfortunate result than a slight wound in the arm, which one of them received.

Shortly after, 270 of them left the settlement, and were at their own request ferried across the river in our whaleboat. Here I cannot refrain expressing my thankfulness to that good Providence which threw 'Buckley'* in our way, for certainly he has been the medium of successfully establishing between us and the natives an understanding, which, without his assistance, could never have been effected to the extent it has been, and which now leaves no room to doubt the most beneficial results in proof of the present favourable state of intercourse with them. I may mention that for the trifling gratuity of a piece of bread they are always ready to perform any useful service as far as their ability will go.

During my stay there Buckley explained to several chiefs

---

* William Buckley, who lived with the Aborigines between 1803–35.

our motives and intentions in settling amongst them and the consequences which might arise from any aggression on their part. He also explained that any ill-treatment on the part of white men towards them, if reported to the heads of the establishment, would meet with its proper punishment. With this understanding they were perfectly well pleased, and promised to act in conformity with it. In fact, however sanguine I may previously have been as to the complete success of the undertaking, I feel now infinite reason to be much more so; and doubt not but the settlement now formed will be useful, not only to all immediately concerned, but to the mother country as well as to this colony.

P. S.—I take the liberty to forward through the commandant a portrait of 'Buckley', which I consider to be a very correct likeness.—J. B.

JOHN PASCOE FAWKNER
Mutton and Potatoes

John Fawkner was born into lowly circumstances in Cripplegate, London, on 20 October 1792. When his father was convicted of receiving stolen goods and was transported on the *Calcutta* in 1803, bound for Collins' ill-fated settlement in Port Phillip, young Johnnie and siblings followed. Also aboard was William Buckley. The Fawkners went on to settle in Van Diemen's Land. Fawkner's party entered Port Phillip Bay in August 1835, two months after Batman, with Fawkner himself following in October. He published Melbourne's first newspaper and, although a teetotaller, ran a hotel. He was not a pleasant person—'half-froth, half-venom' according to a contemporary—but he rose to a position of considerable wealth and influence. Fawkner's first house, written about here, was located near the corner of Flinders Lane and Market Street. We encounter him in 1836, railing in his diary against Henry Batman, John Batman's brother. It is interesting that Fawkner signed his letters as from 'Phillippi' while Batman located his 'Bearberp' in deference to the Aboriginal name for the place.

6 February—Jem at the bark chopping machine and the rest at work in the garden, put the tar casks in the earth.

Ferguson, sent to him the iron bar he ordered, weight 24lbs 24. Charles this day found part of an iron pot about eight inches deep in digging to make my garden, I think it must have been left here by the first person who escaped here*, and that seems more likely as it was found near the falls.

7 February—Found myself very unwell today, pains in my chest and head ache. Shoulder of mutton and potatoes for dinner, quite a treat. Charles William, Mrs F. and Amelia took a walk over to the garden, today some more blacks came in, about twenty here now. Paid Winberry through Mr Henry Batman the remainder due him for woodwork of chopping machine.

8 February—Charles, James, Scott and Maloney, went out barking down the river. Messrs Gellibrand** and son, Malcolm, Gardiner, Leake, Robertson, Dr Cottar and Buckley returned from their excursion; Gelli had bought Robertson's share for £400, they state the country to be an open and fertile one but

---

* William Buckley.

** Joseph Gellibrand was attorney-general of Van Diemen's Land until dismissed from office in 1825. He became involved in the Port Phillip Association and disappeared during an expedition in 1837. Fawkner also refers to him here as 'Gelli'.

that the best land lies out of the boundaries which the Company have taken at present, all but Leake highly praise the country in general. More blacks came in, Batman invites them to let Mr Gellibrand see them.

9 February—Heard a cannon fired at midnight last, and one at 5 o'clock in the morning When the mist cleared up saw vessel at anchor in the bay. I shot two woodducks, four spurwinged plover, and one woodpigeon. Captain Symors of the *Caledonia* came up from the vessel in the bay. Brought 1005 sheep for Solomon, and lost thirty-one on the passage; had very bad weather was driven into Western Port, the whole of the sheep would have been starved (having only twenty trusses of hay) if the captain had not fortunately had a quantity of paddy on board which he fed them. Ferguson highly offended with captain about the thirty-one lost.

10 February—Ed Ferguson hired my boat and men to land sheep from the *Caledonia*—landed all the sheep by about 2 o'clock. Batman and Ed Ferguson quarrelled on board the vessel both ¹/₂ and ¹/₂. B. went away, I left with the captain about one hour after, ordering Charley to take charge of the boat, it appeared that after we left Ferguson got blind drunk and would not give the necessary receipt, the boat did not arrive here till midnight. Batman had refused his boat and men to Ferguson because he, F., had made the men drunk the overnight and got the boat aground several times. A vessel seen coming in thought to be the *Adelaide*.

11 February—Scott and Maloney had behaved so bad last night that I found it necessary to tell them that they must alter or I would not keep them. Scott went away and hired as steward of the *Caledonia*, but I told the captain he was a drunkard, he said he would not employ him. Captain Symors, Dr Cottar, Mr Gardiner and Jem Gumm, went out this afternoon on foot to survey the country and return tomorrow. The vessel seen yesterday proved to be the *Mary Anne*. Hesketh and Lancy, they came up in the

forenoon, Lancy and me exchanged a few angry words. He declared that he would take away his daughter even if he took her to Spencer's Gulf. A boat came up with goods to Ed Ferguson but he was too drunk or too idle to unload it, so the men had to watch the boat all night in the rain.

Mr Batman sent out to call in as many natives as possibly could be induced to come, or could be found in a reasonable time in order to exhibit them to Mr Gellibrand. Very little provisions and scarcely a single article of clothing has been issued to the blacks by Mr Batman.

12 February — Mr Henry Batman went down to the *Mary Anne* with his friend, Lancy. Brought back some spirits, had from Lancy or Hesketh. He also had some rum from the *Caledonia* as did Mr Edmund Ferguson likewise. This morning, Captain Symors, Dr Cottar and Mr Gardiner returned from their excursion, they looked fagged and very wet.

Arrived this evening late, the captain of the *Adelaide* reported his vessel at the landing place for sheep, and that he had 505 on board for Mr Henry Arthur all alive and well. Lent Mitch Moloney to Mr Ferguson either to keep him altogether and pay half his expenses down or return him in one week this was to enable him to bring down his men for examination on a charge of violating a native woman.

13 February — Batman went down to unload the *Adelaide*. Messrs Gellibrand and company returned this morning highly delighted with the country. I delivered a demand to Mr G. for twenty acre town allotments and also for a section of land on The Company's grant, agreeing to relinquish my title on those terms, and to have an answer as early as possible…Mr Gellibrand examined two men of Ed Ferguson's on a charge of violating a native woman, the woman said (as interpreted by Buckley) that they were present but they did not touch her. Mr J. B. Ferguson gave me a check on Mr M. Connolly for £3 — three being the amount of

his account to this date. Lancy and me parted friends, and he said no more about his daughter. I put Bait-Bainger and Merap* onto his boat but Batman brought them both up afterwards.

15 February—Jem and Charles at work at the garden preparing ground for seed. Mr Ed Ferguson gone to fetch his man Saunders down to be examined touching some injury said to be done to a native woman, some of the natives preparing to go away in consequence of no provisions being given to them: after Mr Gellibrand went away, they were put over the river by me and Dr Cottar. This day I complained to Mr Henry Batman that John Scott, my servant, was harboured on his premises and I claimed him, he promised to send him away but did not do it. Attended to see if the native woman recognised Saunders as her violator; Buckley interpreted and declared she charged Saunders with the crime. Ferguson at first refused to send him up but after consented.

16 February—Jem, Charles, me, and part of the day Jemmy at work at the garden over the river. Mr Batman complained of Jemmy being away, but has not yet sent Scott from his employ. I sent him a note this evening to that effect. I learn this day that he, Mr Henry Batman, has applied for the ground my house stands on.

18 February—This morning Dr Cottar and Captain Flett started in my boat, Scott and Taylor as their crew. Mr Batman, Jem Gum and Mackay went with them some distance to look for land on my side of the river, and this when the work of the men is so very much wanted here. Grog Glorious Grog and visions of large salary and great fortunes just at his fingers ends. Thus the world wags when even at *Phillipi*. Mr Henry Batman showed Captain Flett the point where I project to form a township and was present when 'Flett' put his initials on a tree, Mr B. Gum and Mackay returned at night and brought home three or four snappers.

* Bait-Bainger and Merap (Merrap) were local Aborigines.

19 February—Sent Jem and Charles to look at the bark on the point, and found it very safe considering the weather we have had, at work myself preparing to put a porch to my house. Charles and Jem fell three trees for plates and drew one home. Intend to put up a skilling and raise the roof of my present dwelling. Charles shot two mountain ducks and brought home. Jem Gum and Mackay sent over by Mr Henry Batman on my side of the river under the pretence of fishing or pig hunting. Mr Henry Batman informed my servant Jem that I might build as much as I liked but that I should only receive the price for my house which Mr Gellibrand put on it!!! Pray who is to turn me out and by what title does Mr Gellibrand fix prices for others houses without the consent of the party or any second person to assist the assessment? Copy of letter to Mr Henry Batman:

19 Feby Sent 20
Phillippi

Sir, I cannot account for the manner in which you act towards me, I do not deserve to be treated as you continue to use me. Only a few days ago you shot one of my dogs close by your mens fire; the day before yesterday you would have shot my bitch, and that not near your sheep, only your piece missed fire (I suppose that is in return for my kindness in finding you in powder and shot). Yesterday you went to show my land to Captain Flett, and was present when he marked the trees with his name; and this day *you* tell *my servant* that *you* intend to have *my house* over my head, at some value (said to be) fixed by Mr Gellibrand. Now, I only ask you if you think this is manly conduct towards me; or is it like the way I acted towards you from the first? I have borne a great deal, but I assure you I will not be trampled upon; I can point out land to newcomers as well as others, and I beg leave to tell you that if I had thought proper to act towards your brother, as you seem inclined to act towards me, I could have injured him very much, for most of your men are ready to leave *you*. But on the contrary I have borne a great deal without saying much; But depend upon it, that I shall no more sit down quietly and let *you* turn *me out* of *my house* (particularly as I have as good a title to the land as even your brother has)...

20 February—Sent yesterday's letter to Mr Henry Batman and received in reply an unique specimen, I preserve it and place also a copy here below; preparing porch for my house and Jem employed shoeing. Jem Gumm and Mackay came home. Two other of the blacks sent out over the river this day. Copy of Henry B's letter to me:

Bareberp. Feby 20—1836, Sir—You say my piece missed fire at your bitch, it is a damned lie and so is the whole of your letter.
Henry Batman

21 February—Mr Henry Batman sent blacks out to get parrots, got Buckley to abuse W.W. for buying squirrel skins for me, and I find that he is forbidding the natives to sell us any skins or birds. He wants them all himself.

Mrs F. James Gilbert, W.W., Mr Carr and old Jemmy went over to look at our far garden, pulled some french beans, found the corn, the pumpkins and melons doing well. On their return in the evening, Mr Henry Batman quarrelled with Old Jemmy, a man old enough to be his grandfather, and struck him more than once and knocked him down. I think Batman was drunk, for he began to abuse my wife until James Gilbert answered him, he appeared half mad, I think with rum. After this although on Sunday he gave a bucket of beer to the men and set them a-singing songs. Mrs B. sent for Mrs F. desiring to be friendly with her, as she said, although her husband had offended me, but this is only a cloak.

22 February—This day killed a suckling pig. Had roast duck and pigeon for dinner. Jem planing boards, Chas and me putting them on the porch and bringing boards and rails over from the other side of the river. Two of B.'s blacks came back today, from my side of the river. Batman wanted to grog Old Jemmy today to make friends. Mrs B. fell out with Mary, Jem's wife, because he had the spirit to repel B.'s bad language yesterday. Mrs B. sent us word that one of our hens had killed her swan—this is fudge.

2 March—Jem and Charles gone down with a load of bark to the schooner, and to stop and load her. Took from this for the vessels use—four pieces of pork and bag about five pounds of fine biscuit. Found one panel of my paling had been pulled down in the last night, was informed that Mr Batman had set the Sydney blacks to it, by giving them grog and by telling them that I intended to come at night and burn them in their huts. Batman *and* wife both drunk this day. Carpenter and me at work on the framing of the new house. Mrs Batman this day set one of the dogs they have at their house upon the calves that are tied up and it bit it severely and threw it down and broke its leg. Mr Ferguson set it, and Carr kindly made a snug place for it to rest in all night—this woman is cruel as well as a drunkard. She says we can't hurt her stock, why?

Thursday 3 March—...Batman and wife not quite so drunk today. I think their grog was short. Could not work, my mind too ill at ease from the lying villainy of Batman. I think a man that will tell lies as he did to the blacks and also the whites about me would not scruple much to swear to them...

9 March—Charles at fowlhouse and then at fence. James Newman refused to agree for his wife to serve as well as self so I tore up the agreement. He offered to work week-work but I would not agree. I offered to take him for ½ year [but he] did not accept it; he would, but the wife overruled. He proposes going

on his own resources. Derrah-Mert and Bait-Bainger went out shooting for me, brought home only one bird, gave it to them. Began to boil rice for the blacks—Mem: they will not eat it without sugar. Report brought in that three women have been shot by white men at Western Port. Sent in my bill today to Mr Batman £20 odd and to Dr Cottar £2.

10 March—…Great numbers of blacks about—just heard 5 p.m. that a vessel is seen in the bay—by Pigeon* from the lookout tree. Proves to be the *Adelaide* with sheep for Mr Wedge**—Mr Batman after all his bluster took Mr Wedge into his own dwelling and gave him his own bed. I believe Mr W. to be as false as Batman 'sure such a pair were never seen, so truly formed to meet by nature'.

19 March—Went on board the *Caledonia* to bring up Dr Thomson's goods. Me and Jem and Messrs W. Headlam and man and my two blacks, brought up sugar, rice, biscuit, pots, cask beef &c. Batman's two boats also came up loaded for Dr Thomson got up just at night, brought up 4½ galls of rum from the *Caledonia*. Charles at work on the house all day, this day Mr Reed returned from his bush excursion I put him across the river he seemed very fagged. Batman was drunk when he came and said to be abed with a bad headache. He is a complete deceiver. Found Mr Darke on board the *Caledonia*. He came from the Barra-Bool Hills to bring the account of Mr Swanston's two men Moran and Gunshenah being reported to him by one of the blacks as having been speared to death near Indented Head and also that another man who ran away had also been killed. Buckley refused to believe the account and affronted Mr D. and when he told the affair to Mr Batman (who was half drunk) he also said it was false, this is out of spite to Mr B. J. Ferguson. Batman is utterly

* Pigeon appears to be a Sydney Aborigine in Batman's employ.
** John Helder Wedge moved to Port Phillip in 1835 to help survey the land Batman had acquired that same year.

unfit to hold office here, for he is devoid of intelligence, a mere bore who goes about with a short pipe in his mouth and always drunk when he can get the liquor and is very brutish in his address those times—when sober he is a specious hypocrite.

4 June—…A black man, by name Wir-ar-bill died this day. The natives appeared to lament his death very much, the women set up dismal cries and his wife and all the women present belonging to the tribe tore their hair and faces till the blood ran down in streams. In the evening the men tied up the deceased's knees to his neck with cord, put his blanket and rug round his body, put his pipe, spear, and all kinds of weapons along side of him, put a pillow of grass under his head and grass under him for a bed. They then covered him up with grass and bark and wood, they lighted a fire at his head and feet and so left him. This was near my hut in the garden. Mem: his wife broke her water bucket, made with great labour of a tree knot, and laid it near him.

5 June—…Mr and Mrs Diprose and Mrs F. went to take a walk—a very cold day, the wind felt piercingly cold, the man left unburied by the blacks near my hut at the garden begins to become offensive. Told them they must remove the body and either burn or bury it. They promised to do so tomorrow.

6 June—…The blacks, with Negremoule at their head, dug a good grave and interred the dead man. Mem: put a lump of earth for his pillow, his shield, spears, rug, blankets, pipe &c put in the grave, the women then set up a dismal howling and face scratching he was then covered up and a good fire left burning by him.

29 June—Me and Messrs Gellibrand, Simpson, Wedge, Thomson and Dr Cottar and Tom Armytage went to select a church, as also a burial ground (Goodman having applied to me to inform him where he may bury his infant son, which died this morning at 1 o'clock). We agreed to locate ten acres for burial ground and that at the Prospect Hill where the harbour is visible from, and another site for a church and schoolhouse. Messrs

Simpson and Wedge refused to become parties to building the church, that is to say, at the expense of The Co.; so then it was agreed to build it by subscription. Mr Gellibrand commenced it by a donation of £10, Mr Jno Batman £10, Mr Jas Simpson £2, J. P. Fawkner £5, Wm Diprose £2, Dr Thomson £5. Mr J. H. Wedge meanly refused to contribute, although it is well known that he is a wealthy man.

31 June—Went with Goodman and marked out the first grave in this infant colony. Mr Wm Diprose made the coffin a very pretty cedar one.

1 July—Charles and Gibbs with cart to sawpit. Dr Thomson's team, Diprose and Jem went with them to make a bridge and mend the road where required. Diprose and Jem returned about 3 p.m. Mr Gellibrand about ½ past 3. Dined and prepared for the child (Goodman's) funeral. The funeral started from the house of death at ½ past 4 p.m. Attended by the undertaker, Mr Wm Diprose, two carriers one man to carry shovel &c and J. P. Fawkner, Joseph Tice Gellibrand, Dr A. Thomson and the father of the child. Upon arriving at the burial ground found Mrs Thomson and daughter there. Buckley, Mr Batman and a black boy. Dr Cottar came there. Dr Thomson read the funeral service, I acted as clerk.

The funeral gave rise in my mind to many serious thoughts: on looking into the grave (about 6 feet deep) the wet and cold appearance caused my flesh to revolt at the thoughts of the cold, damp, dark, doleful depository of the body when the mortal spark has fled. Here is only one grave in a burial ground of ten acres, the first natural death in this new settlement commenced by me on the 31st of August, Monday, which day my people and horses landed. Having been ten days exploring the river and getting vessel up. One death in just ten months, our present population is 179. Eight persons landed then and the schooner's crew were five, this eight had already rose to 180, one consigned to the tomb. How many more would there be committed to the dark house within the next five years, how many will strong drink hurry there prematurely, I fear a great many. Well I hate the grave, let my mortal remains be placed on a pile of timber and reduced to ashes, this will prevent the loathsome worms from preying upon me.

9 July—Went down to receive cargo for Ross & Co., found that Mr Gellibrand had been to the point in the night and reported that Mr Franks and his men were missing as also their sheep, and that the hut was partly destroyed and he could not find either of the persons although he repeatedly called as hard as he could…and being in the night he left the cart and bullocks and ran away. He says from the way the goods lay about the place has been plundered and both the men killed.

10 July—Resolved in full meeting that something must be done to protect ourselves, so we enlisted as many natives as would consent to go and agreed to send them out to deal with the murderers as they think according to their rules they should be treated.

11 July—The bodies were brought in, Taylor (the brute) refused to lend his cart for this purpose. Diprose making the two coffins. I was down today at the vessels.

12 July—The bodies of Mr Franks and his man were buried this day. They had been killed by repeated blows on the head with a tomahawk. Franks had received one deep and deadly cut on the temple and one on the back part of his head and two or three contusions. The brains were cut and beat entirely out of the man's head.

GEORGE LANGHORNE

A Snapshot of Vanished Tribes

In 1836 Governor Bourke appointed George Langhorne to head a mission school for the Aborigines, to be based on the Yarra. It opened in 1837 and at first attracted students, but by 1839 the school was closed—just one of many disruptions to the tribes. Langhorne the mission-ary gives us a snapshot of the true locals as they were when he first encountered them.

In this year the Aboriginal population in a circuit of say thirty miles around Melbourne numbered at least 700 men, women and children. They were divided into three tribes, the Waworong, the Bonurong and the Watowrong.

The Watowrong tribe inhabited the district extending from the Yarra River to Westernport as far as the Dun Fin Bear Creek (now I believe the Ginger Beer Creek).

They were (I say 'were' for I hear this tribe is now extinct) the most peaceably and well affected towards the settlers and seldom exhibiting the same hostile feelings manifested by the other tribes.

The head or chief of this tribe was Jika Jika, a tall manly figure and withal very intelligent. It was with him that a treaty for the purchase of land [occurred] in exchange for blankets and toma-hawks, a proceeding by the bye that somewhat excited the ire of Sir Richard Bourke, the then Governor of New South Wales, when His Excellency was informed of this offhand cessure of His Majesty's territory without his permission.

Jika had a family of several sons and daughters (after the

former such as Jika Jika, Keelbundora, two of the parishes, are named).

Next in command to Jika Jika was old Tukulveau, an aged man, but who had great influence with his people.

It was with this tribe, the Waworongs, that I had the most intercourse, and as soon that they had learnt the object of my coming down from Sydney, and that I was to live among them and in charge of them, this old chief assumed my Christian name, and I was ever after known by his, and was always addressed by it.

The Watowrongs inhabited the Geelong district. Fiercer and more warlike in their habits than the Waworongs and I considered more numerous. The dialect they spoke was very different from that of the Waworongs—the former giving a harsh nasal pronunciation, and what impressed me most was the dissimilarity in the personal pronouns and other words in frequent use.

It was with this tribe that William Buckley, who had been among the blacks thirty years, chiefly dwelt, and as I had only intercourse with them occasionally when they made their visits two or three times a year to the black station at Prahran, my knowledge of them was principally derived from him.

The Bonourongs spoke the same dialect as the Waworongs—a small tribe which Buckley informed me had been greatly thinned in number by a cruel onslaught made on them in the night by the Waworongs, on which occasion they murdered men, women and children. As the coast about Westernport was their principal location, and for years they had been in contact with the sealers from Van Diemen's Land, it is not improbable that an occasional affray with these men might have also tended to thin their numbers.

PHILLIP PARKER KING

Inundated...with Sheep

Phillip Parker King was one of the first Europeans to be born in the Australian colonies—on Norfolk Island in 1791. The son of Australia's third governor, he became a hydrographer in the Royal Navy, and surveyed large portions of Australia's northern coast. At the time this diary entry was written, King and Richard Bourke, governor of New South Wales, seem to have been on good terms. Just two months later, however, King was refused a seat in the New South Wales Legislative Council, which created a breach that remained until Bourke resigned from office in January 1838. King died in North Sydney on 26 February 1856.

3 March 1837—We arrived here the day before yesterday, having had a tolerable passage. The night after parting with the *Lady McNaghten*, we had a foul wind for three days, and then two most delightful smooth-water days, with a fair wind, which brought us to the entrance of this place, anchoring three miles within the Heads for the Governor to select a spot whereon to build a Custom house, as well as a lighthouse.

This having been done, we sailed yesterday at noon, and arrived at the mouth of the river, eight miles from where the settlement is situated. We found here two vessels from Van Diemen's Land, each having brought 500 sheep. The whole country hereabouts is inundated with them, but unfortunately not with water. A very dry season has been experienced, and stock are very badly off for feed, so much so that the Governor is obliged to land hay to feed his horses.

Captain and Mrs Lonsdale and an officer of the 4th Regiment

(a Mr King) are here. The country in the vicinity of the shore is very low, and rises very gradually towards a range of distant mountains, perhaps thirty or forty miles off. In the space it appears to be a succession of undulating grounds, interspersed with woods and open plains, now looking quite burnt up...

5 March—Yesterday we landed in due form. On our way up the river our boat was joined by a motley procession of whale-boats and other kinds, some cheering and others popping off musketry all the way in honour of His Excellency's visit. At the wharf the detachment of the 4th or 'King's Own' saluted and, joined by the gentlemen present, we walked up to the small tents which had been erected by the Governor's suite the day before. A small tribe of natives, headed by Buckley, were drawn up on the roadside, who stared with all their eyes at the 'Gubernoz'. Compared to Buckley, they appeared to be of diminutive size, but are fine-looking men, and by no means so short, for Buckley measured 6ft 6in. He acts now as interpreter for the commandant, and is a very useful person in that capacity.

On the Governor reaching the tent, he held a *levée* to receive the heads of departments and the settlers, and then mounting his horse he rode round the township, and marked its boundaries, which embraces about a mile of river frontage. At 5 o'clock he received a deputation of the inhabitants, who presented an address of congratulation, etc, replied to it, bowed them out, and we sat down to an excellent dinner in a very nice tent, well furnished with furniture, eatables, and other comforts, for which we were indebted to Captain Westmacott's (the Governor's *aide-de-camp*) activity, for he had arranged everything.

One part of dinner must not be forgotten. Mrs Westmacott had sent Mrs Lonsdale a goose and a gander, a valuable present considering the infancy of the establishment. They were landed in the boat that took the Governor's things. No sooner was the poor goose brought up than His Excellency's cook knocked her down, cut her throat, and dished her up as a second course at dinner. The gander was rescued, but now bemoans his fate as a widower. Mrs Lonsdale was, as you may suppose, much mortified, as was also Captain Hobson, for he had taken great care of them.

I was very much pleased with the settlement. After pulling for eight miles through a tea-tree scrub, which impenetrably clothes the low banks of the river, the settlement suddenly burst upon our view. It is scattered, of course, at present, but consists of perhaps thirty or forty huts. Some are of sods, others framed and weather-boarded, other wattled and plastered. The framed houses have all been sent from Sydney or Launceston. Were it not for the burnt-up appearance of the place, the scenery about the town would be beautiful. The ground undulates, and between the houses and the river is an alluvial flat of good soil, in which good gardens may be formed, and very productive too. We called upon the ladies of the place, and found them enduring great discomfort, some living in mud hovels, others in tents, and others just entering their new abodes formed of 'wattle-and-dab'.

ROBERT HODDLE

Fixing the Boundaries

Robert Hoddle was appointed assistant to surveyor-general and explorer John Oxley in 1823. He was regarded as superbly competent, but Thomas Mitchell, on taking over from Oxley, formed a low opinion of his assistant. It was thus probably with some relief that Hoddle accompanied Bourke to Port Phillip in 1837. Controversy surrounds the issue of whether Hoddle designed Melbourne's distinctive city grid or just insti-tuted plans drawn up elsewhere. He acted as auctioneer at the first land sale, buying two allotments for himself and building a house at the corner of Bourke and Spencer streets. The wide thoroughfares he instituted for Melbourne continue to be key assets of the city.

3 March — Rowed over to Gellibrand Point to fix a site for allotment and reserve at Point called Williamstown.

4 March — Left ship for encampment at settlement…Received orders from the Governor to take charge at Survey Department. Accompanied the Governor around the Settlement.

6-7-8 March — Fixing the boundaries of the corner lots and sites.

9 March — Governor requested that it would be desirable to commence marking the sections from the West of Melbourne on both sides of the Yarra Yarra River.

21 March — Marking allotments in town of Melbourne; also in Williamstown. The Governor returned from the interior.

26 March — Memo received to take levels of the streets and inform inhabitants that they are to build to those levels — Notice to be given to the inhabitants that so many feet will be required to be taken off the road, in order that they may regulate their buildings. The same to take place in June.

Streets to be confirmed between Flinders and Lonsdale…were named by Sir Richard Bourke.

RICHARD BOURKE
Affixing Whig Names

Sir Richard Bourke was a son of the Emerald Isle, born in Dublin in 1777. He was a great supporter of democracy and protector of native peoples. From 1831 to 1838 he served as governor of New South Wales, during which time he travelled more widely than any of his predecessors. In 1837 he sailed to the settlement of Port Phillip where he delighted in commemorating the names of fellow liberal thinkers throughout the district. In this extract from a letter to his son Richard, we see a relaxed man, enjoying his role in giving the new settlement name and structure.

14 April—...I am just returned from refreshing myself in exploring the new settlement at Port Phillip. Six weeks under canvas enlivened me a good deal, and I have had the satisfaction of offering Whig names in the bush.

Melbourne is a *beautiful* site for a town and there will soon be a very pretty one erected. In laying it out I have avoided the cross into which my predecessors fell in establishing Sydney and the people of the new town will not have to go over this work a second time as we are now doing in Sydney Flats. My party consisted of Harten and Holden and we were joined by Captain King who very kindly acted as our geographer and has made a very correct plan of one sort and the portions of many of the hills and other features of the country are accurately laid down. We have corrected this plan with Major Mitchell's map having taken points again from a hill which he ascended for the same purpose. This hill, what he called Mount Macedon, we made 3500 feet above the level of the sea and so steep and stony I found it a tight job to get to the top. I went from hence to Port Phillip in the *Rattlesnake* ship of war and returned by the same. I would have wished to have gone or returned over land but had not time to spare...Upon the whole the expedition has I think benefited my health and I am sure it has rendered an important service to the Phillipians where settlement has been considerably accelerated by the visit. I went once [through] a great deal of fine country both for grazing and cultivating and we recommend any emigrating agriculturist to try his fortune in the new country.

EDWARD EYRE

Arrival of the Overlanders

Edward John Eyre is well known for his heroic explorations of the Australian inland, and particularly for the discovery of the vast salt lake that bears his name. In April 1837, however, his thoughts seem to have been more with livestock than exploration, for he was about to set out with 414 sheep, seventy-eight cattle and horses and oxen from Sydney to Port Phillip. Eyre arrived in July, in advance of his party, then set out again to help guide the animals into the township on 2 August. The beasts were sold at such a profit that he immediately determined to become the first overlander to travel from Sydney to Adelaide.

15 July—We passed several stations but called at none of them pushing steadily on for the township of Melbourne where we arrived at about eight in the evening, very weary and very hungry. Finding a small but clean and comfortable hotel kept by a Mr Fawkner we took up our quarters there. Having got our supper as speedily as possible we tumbled into bed and soon forgot all the miseries of a long and exacting journey.

Upon getting up the next morning we found food laid for a good many—a sort of *table d'hôte* being kept, presided over by the host and hostesses. The guests were chiefly parties from Van

Diemen's Land who had come over to settle in, or look at, the recently occupied district of Port Phillip. The township of Melbourne is beautifully situated on slightly undulating ground abutting on a fine freshwater river called the Yarra. The houses were not very numerous and were a good deal scattered. They were built chiefly of mud, turf or wattle and dab. There were also a good many tents here and there which gave a pleasing and picturesque effect to the whole, particularly as the contiguous country was very pretty and lightly wooded with casuarinae, mimosa and banksias...

On 21 July, having completed my arrangements I set off with the two black boys to meet my party...[Several days later and after a number of mishaps] I eventually crossed the track and got to my party, with the animal quite safe about eight in the morning, fully determined, however, never again to attempt on foot to drive a bullock over a mountain range in the dark.

Having been twenty-four hours without food and undergoing no little amount of exertion all the time I was very glad to get some breakfast as well as to enjoy the luxury of a comfortable wash and clean linen.

After seeing the drays move on, I walked across the country about six miles to see Mr Hamilton, with whom I remained for the day. The following day he walked with me into Melbourne. Passing our teams encamped within two miles of the settlement, we arrived there ourselves about seven in the evening, very tired and very hungry. As dinner was some time in preparing we imprudently drank a glass of wine each before taking any food, whilst over-fatigued and still fasting, and having taken the same quantity at dinner, and a single glass afterwards, we were both as much affected as we should have been under other circumstances after taking a very considerable quantity. The way I discovered our state was by noticing that my friend, who was himself a very clever artist and draughtsman, was greatly admiring and descanting on some beautiful engravings, but that he had them turned the wrong way up...

2 August—Early in the forenoon my whole party entered the township of Melbourne after a journey of sixteen weeks during which we had traversed about 470 miles of country. As the drays, sheep and cattle passed along through the scarcely defined streets the inhabitants flocked to their doors to see the novel sight. I halted my party and pitched my tent on the banks of the Yarra, just above the falls, where we were scarcely encamped before we were visited by half the population, most of whom had all sorts of questions to propound, which the overseer invariably answered as wide of the mark and as incorrectly as possible. Some wanted to buy the boat, some the sheep and some the cattle—in fact we appeared to have come to a very good market for all we had to part with. I soon made many acquaintances and even the first day I received several hospitable invitations to dinner.

The day after our arrival we swam all the cattle and sheep across the Yarra and boated over our baggage. On the following day I removed the whole party about three miles further to the station which I had selected for them on the north-eastern side of the harbour. Here my tent was carefully pitched so as to be square and neat and securely fastened, lined with green baize, the floor being covered with tarpaulin. The tables and other articles of furniture were fitted with appropriate covers, books were put out and the whole interior thus looked neat, clean and comfortable, quite like a little sitting room in which I was not at all ashamed to see my friends.

Having established ourselves we at once commenced putting up yards for the sheep, milking bales for the cattle and sheds for a dairy...The boat I took down the river and anchored in the harbour opposite my tent. It was of great use to me in obtaining a supply of fish with which the port abounded and also in travelling up the coast round the harbour to examine the country and look for a larger station should I hereafter require one...

Being located within three miles of the township everybody called on me and I received the greatest kindness and attention from all. Captain Lonsdale, the commandant of the settlement, and his estimable and charming wife were most friendly and kind to me…The general society was not very large but it was very united and social, comprising many intelligent well-educated and agreeable persons of both sexes. Nor were young ladies wanting to add grace and attraction; for Port Phillip even at this early period of its history was able to boast of its belles who might well vie with those of the older and largest settlement of New South Wales.

Parties of some kind or other were given almost every day, and I more than once received two or three invitations for the same day. There were dinners, lunches, little dances and picnics up the Yarra, ending in singing and dancing on the smooth turf by the light of the numerous fires, and a walk home by moonlight through the picturesque scenery along the banks of that pretty river…The township at this time was so little defined, cleared or occupied that in returning home late at night from these little parties I often ran up against the stumps of trees or fell over logs or tumbled into holes.

Dirty Irish Women, Axework and Bestiality

To peek into the early pages of the Melbourne Court Register is to immerse oneself in the sordid swaddling-rags of infant Melbourne. The place seems to have been awash with all species of criminal activity.

Melbourne Court Register, 20 July 1837

John Moss, being sworn, states:

I am the son of John Moss, publican residing in Melbourne. Yesterday morning between 9 and 10 o'clock I went from home with Joseph Hodgson to find our horses. We were out somewhere about an hour making the search when we went up near the old burial ground at the back of the town. I was going towards Hodgson, driving the horses, when he put up his hand making a sign to me. I went to him and he pointed out the prisoner now before the court.

Upon looking I saw that the prisoner was behind a calf. He had the tail of the calf in one hand which he held on one side. He had the flap of his trousers down and I saw his private parts close against the calf under the tail and from the position of the prisoner he was having connection with the animal. From a noise made by Joseph I suppose he saw us and he sat down on the tree. We then left and went to another place where I remained only a short time and left. Hodgson then went after the horses and on coming back I saw the prisoner going towards the town. I cannot be mistaken about the man. I am quite positive the person I now see is the same man I saw with the calf, and from what I saw, am sure he was having intercourse of an unnatural sort with the calf.

Committed for trial at the criminal court. John Moss and Joseph Hodgson bound in £50 to appear.

*

Melbourne Court Register, 18 September 1837

Thomas Bullock, being sworn states:

Last Tuesday I bought some fish and took them over to Mrs Mooney's house to cook about 4 o'clock in the evening and upon her assenting to do so I returned to my work till dusk when I went to my place which is about fifty yards from Mooney's.

About half an hour after, Mrs Mooney sent her two children to say the fish was ready if we were to go over, that is William Winberry and myself. Winberry is living with me and we went and we had not been ten minutes in the hut when the defendant William Mooney came in. We were at the table. Mooney ordered Winberry to go out, he said he would when he had his tea and refused to do so until then. Mooney said if you don't I will lay your head open with an axe. Winberry immediately went out and as he was passing the door Mooney struck him with an axe and cut him slightly on the thumb. Winberry took up a frying pan to defend himself. I had followed Winberry out of the house and as soon as Mooney saw me he ran after me with a broad axe in his hand. Winberry prevented him doing me any harm when he struck at me and threatened me.

William Mooney, in his defence, states:

The witnesses Winberry and Bullock have been in the habit of coming to my house contrary to my wishes and encouraging my wife in habits of drinking and having them in my house. On the day in question I was so much exasperated that I acted in the manner sworn to, except the extent.

Fined 10*s* 0*d*.

★

Melbourne Court Register, 26 September 1837

Judith Croaker, being sworn, states:

I am the wife of James Croaker a private in the 80th Regiment. On Saturday evening last I was standing at the door of my hut when I heard the defendant Jane Gibson, who was standing at the door of her hut, call me a dirty Irish woman. I went up to her and we had some words together. Her husband came up and put her into the hut and shut the door. A short time after she threw the jug I now produce at me, which struck me on the side of the face which still bears the mark of the blow. There was nothing in the jug and I am positive the defendant intended to strike me with the jug when she threw it at me. I was not a dozen yards from the window at the time.

No penalty was recorded.

★

Melbourne Court Register, 3 October 1837

William Mooney, being sworn, states:

I am a labourer at present in the employ of J. Hawdon Esq. On Saturday evening last on going into the hut in which I live I found my wife was absent from it. About two hours after she came home drunk. I tried to put her to bed but could not from the interference of some persons who came in the hut. On Sunday afternoon I saw my wife in the hut occupied by the defendants William Winberry and Thomas Bullock. I ordered her to come out, but she would not come out, and upon going towards the hut to insist upon it, the defendant Bullock struck me. Some other people were present, my wife among the others. When Bullock struck me they all set on me and knocked me down and abused me very much. I cannot say that Winberry was present.

Mathew Collins, being sworn, states:

I am living as a servant in Melbourne opposite where the defendant Winberry lives. On Sunday evening last I heard a disturbance at the hut occupied by Winberry and Bullock. I saw Mooney shoved out of the hut in attempting to take his wife from it. He repeated the attempt and was again shoved from it. Mooney, upon his being shoved out the second time, struck Bullock who returned the blow and upon Mrs Mooney seeing that Bullock was likely to get the worst of the scuffle that ensued, took his part and attacked her husband with a long stick. Mooney fell three times during the scuffle. There was another woman present who kicked Mooney when he was on the ground. Winberry was looking on but did not assist. I saw no other weapons used except the stick in Mrs Mooney's hands. Mooney was drunk at the time.

Case dismissed.

WILLIAM LONSDALE

Arson, Escape and Inebriated Gaolers

The earliest penitentiary built in Melbourne was none too secure. No wonder it was replaced with the resplendent and forbidding Old Melbourne Gaol, followed by Pentridge, that palace of a penitentiary in Coburg. In this series of letters to the colonial secretary, William Lonsdale outlines the deficiencies of existing arrangements.

10 October 1837—I have the honour in reference to my letter of the 25th ultimo to report for the information of His Excellency the Governor that I have suspended the gaoler, Thomas Smith, from his office, finding that his conduct is such that a longer continuance of his holding it would be prejudicial to the public service.

The grounds upon which I have thus acted are the following:

On the evening of the 6th instant Constable Hooson reported to me that he had been to the gaol to place a man he had apprehended in charge, when he found the gaoler quite drunk and the keys of the gaol in the keeping of the scourger, Steel.

I immediately sent the chief constable to ascertain if this was the case and if so to place one of the constables in charge. Upon his going there he found the gaoler asleep on his bed and upon awaking him found that he was drunk.

The next morning the gaoler sent to me saying the chief constable had been to the gaol the previous night in a perfect state of intoxication. This I knew was not the case, and I went accompanied by Captain Fyans in the course of the day to the gaol to inquire into his conduct, when I found him again quite drunk, and immediately suspended him, and directed Constable Hooson to take charge of whatever he had in posession, but having since been obliged to send Hooson in search of some prisoners of the Crown who had absconded, I have placed Constable Rogers in charge till he returns.

I beg to take this opportunity of stating that the number of constables is not sufficient for the duty of this place, in fact I should now be without any for the routine duty required, had I not been able to borrow one from Captain Fyans.

The constables are at present disposed of as follows: one sick (inflammation of the lungs), one on escort to Sydney, one in charge of gaol, and one in search of runaways. There is the total for the duty of the district, besides those sent from Van Diemen's Land to apprehend runaways from thence, one of whom I have included above, which number was sufficient upon the first establishment of this place. But now that the duty has very much increased, the force is but barely sufficient for the town alone.

6 December 1837—I am sorry to be obliged to report that I have been prevented placing James Waller in charge of the gaol of this town according to the appointment which His Excellency Sir Richard Bourke was so kind as to bestow on him, for on the day I told him of his appointment and immediately after making me the most positive assurance of being most particularly in his conduct

and attentive to his duties, he went to the lowest public house in the town, got very drunk and made a public exposure of himself.

I am the more annoyed as after a considerable period of the most regular conduct I was induced to recommend him for the situation.

I have now the honour to request he may be removed, and I shall continue the gaol in charge of a constable until someone is appointed.

26 April 1838—I have the honour to report for the information of His Excellency the Governor that the gaol and government store were consumed by fire last night.

I was at first apprehensive that some of the blacks had set the gaol on fire (as it was there that it originated) for the purpose of liberating the two who were confined, but to ascertain what I could on this point I went, as soon as I was satified that the stores and prisoners were temporarily disposed of after their being taken from the buildings, into the different camps of blacks, of which there were three in the neighbourhood, and felt satisfied that the blacks there had taken no part in the burning, in which opinion I was afterwards confirmed by the prisoner black Jin Jin.

Describing how the gaol was set fire to, he says that the other black who was confined with him got a long piece of reed which he thrust through an opening in the partition between the place he was confined in and the guard room, and after lighting the reed by the guard's candle he drew it back and set fire to the thatch roof.

Fortunately the prisoners were all got out, and I believe but very little was lost in the store.

The two blacks got off but one was afterwards retaken, viz. Jin Jin.

This affair is much to be regretted, keeping up as it undoubtedly will the public alarm and agitation regarding the blacks.

Port Phillip Gazette

The *Port Phillip Gazette* first hit the streets in late 1838, as a weekly, then as a twice-weekly paper. Its editor, the eighteen-year-old George Arden, hoped that it would 'assist the inquiring, animate the struggling, and sympathize with all'. Indiscretion and court cases ruined Arden, and he relinquished control over the paper in late 1842. Included here is an anonymous paean to the growing city.

December 1838—Melbourne, the present capital, is a remarkably fine place for a township, and is surrounded with a truly delightful country...

Society in Melbourne is much better than that of Adelaide, being entirely destitute of half swells, loungers &c., so prevalent in Adelaide; nor is there any nonsensical party spirit, with caviling for office by a few individuals sent out under the patronage of titles men, and whose salaries will neither find them in shoes to tramp their barren wastes, nor turn their pretty bright button threadbare coats into new ones.

When the word hotel was announced to me on my way to Melbourne, I pictured myself in a little weatherboarded house, or a bark hut, or some such as I had seen in Adelaide; but judge of my surprise when I looked at a building something like the Bush Hotel, Piccadilly—the fittings up are certainly less costly, but upon the whole, there are two or three houses in Melbourne capable of entertaining noblemen. Buildings generally are very much superior in Melbourne than in Adelaide; in the former place there are neither canvas tents nor wigwams—in a few words I beg to say that Melbourne is to Adelaide what gold is to dross.

★

26 January 1839
MELBOURNE
Melbourne! Unclassic, anti-native name!
And yet, as by Magician's spell up-sprung,
Thee have I chosen, subject fit for song.
No antique relics, pyramids sublime
May be thine to boast. But who thy hist'ry
Knows? Whether primal city, embattled
Tower, or imperial throne on which have
Sate tyrant Czars, a long succession, the
Muse informs me not. No seer am I, nor
Doth my vision scan time past; sufficient
'Tis the present to describe. Then aid me
Austral Muse, if such exist.
                          The swarthy
Tribe appear'd, remov'd, or with force of arms
Into the interior driven back;
(For power, the law of right, too oft o'ercomes)
A savage to a civil race gives way.
                    At first, selected, is large patch of land
Deem'd suitable, and for water standing
Well. A weather-boarded hut is rear'd, or
One of turf; shingled or thatched, not to rain
Or penetrating winds impervious,
Or against the sweeping storm secure; round
It the electric fluid fork'd or sheet
Is seen terrific; while above is heard
Of thunder loud, peal after peal: Meantime
The lonely hut shakes at its very base,
If base it may be nam'd. The affrighted
Inmates now, their isolated thoughts, in
Turn express and other neighbours wish. They
Wish not long. Man must not dwell alone. So

Hut unites to hut, to acre, acre.
A site thus fixed, a town is plan'd; the streets
At angles right are then divided off,
And Anglicised. The whole a Statesman's name
They give, and call it Melbourne. Its fame now
Sounded far; emigration's tide rolls in,
And population swells. Lot after lot
Is sold. The lonely weather-boarded hut
Is lost. The turf-built house is taken down.
Now brick to turf succeeds, and stone to wood.
Now spacious stores, and dwellings palace-like
On every hand are seen. Enacted now
Are laws and magisterial rod, the
Rights of each protect. Tis thus men form the
Future empire; the central city build.

      Melbourne! Thy rise an Austral poet sings;
But who thy fall shall see and thus record?
I leave thee now, and distant be the day,
When 'Here stood Melbourne', shall the traveller say.

WILLIAM WATERFIELD

The End of the World?

The Reverend William Waterfield was a Congregational minister who spent four years at Port Phillip. Melbourne's first recession, largely brought about by avaricious land speculators, brought Waterfield such financial woes that he resigned in 1843, returning to Tasmania where he died in 1868. Here in his diary he records a remarkable natural phenomenon.

1 January 1839—On the first of January last year I had not lost sight of the old England, for I lay in the Margate roads. Now I am in Port Phillip in the vast continent of Australia. How mysterious are the ways of Providence. The Lord enable me to see His hand in all things. Today the Reverend Mr Grylls and I walked to Mr Gardiner's and spent the day there. We had a pleasant walk home. This day was ushered in, I am grieved to say, in the most shameful manner possible. Firing of guns, shouting, cursing and swearing, drinking and singing, breaking of windows and bursting open of doors. Where the police were, what were they doing, I know not: but the whole town was disturbed. May the Lord destroy the folly and the sins of men. Today I had the Governor's approval of the selection of the allotments in Block No. 10...

29 January 1839—Most of the morning at home and my first letter to the editor of the three P.'s*: subject, Dust. Immediately after dinner today we were visited with the most terrific hurricane I ever witnessed. It came on gradually till the whole atmosphere was completely darkened with dense clouds of dust. We could not see each other in the rooms, though but a few yards distant from each other. In the midst of this a fire took place and a house was burnt down, besides several brick buildings fell. Some thought an earthquake was to follow, and others that the end of the world was come. Very many persons were so terrified as to cry out for fear and some left their houses, not daring to keep within. Many trees were torn up by the roots and branches dashed to the ground. Altogether it was frightful. May such a visitation be sanctified. It was a beautiful evening. We had no rain...

12 April 1839—This morning while at breakfast, we were again dinned with another disturbance with the natives. It was a repetition of last night's sparring only there seemed more

* *Port Phillip Patriot.*

determination. It came to nothing. Spent the day variously, wrote an article on education for the P.P.P. Paid Mr Fawkner's bill and Mr Arden for his paper. Each informed me of their intention to publish twice a week. Wars and rumours of wars among the civilians, alias duellists. Purchased a secondhand copy of Hone's works for 30s. Went upon the hill tonight, to see a corroboree. There were two. The breaking up of the last was caused by a spear being thrown into the midst. We all moved off as quickly as possible. It was supposed to be thrown by one of the Barrabool tribe.

PATRICK EDWARD CUSSEN

A Chronic State of Tribulation

An Irish doctor, Patrick Cussen arrived in Australia in 1837. He was appointed assistant surgeon at Port Phillip and evidently expected the respect that such a post might have offered elsewhere. In this letter, written to William Lonsdale in January 1839, he vents his spleen at the ingrates he is forced to deal with. His proposed cure certainly seems a formidable one, to which any mother may well have objected.

On Saturday night the 8th of last month, I was disturbed from sleep about midnight by a loud knocking at my door. On inquiry I found it was a messenger from the overseer of roads here, Mr Lewis Pedrana, requesting my immediate attendance on his child. I dressed myself hastily and on reaching the house of the overseer (which I did as quickly as possible) I found his child labouring under one of the most alarming diseases (spasmodic croup) to which human nature in childhood is subject.

I endeavoured to explain to the parents (both of whom I must here observe were considerably under the influence of liquor at the time) the very dangerous situation of their child. I told them that its only chance of life depended upon the most prompt and active measures. I mentioned to them the different means I intended to adopt, but that the remedy I attached most importance to was a blister applied to the throat. The moment I made use of the latter expression, the mother told me in the most offensive terms that she would allow no blister to be applied to her child, as she considered it (the child) too weak.

I said, 'If you imagine you are a better judge than I am, why send for me?' Her reply was that she knew the case of a child of a friend of hers in Scotland for whom a doctor had ordered a blister, that the blister was not applied and that yet the child recovered. I observed that may have been the case but I would assure her that if she did not do as I advised she would most probably lose her child.

After still further expostulating with both parents on the necessity of attending to my directions, but without effect, I left the house saying that I had done my duty but they would, I was certain, regret their obstinacy, adding that I would never again prescribe for a member of the family, as my advice was not then attended to.

I reached home with some difficulty as the night was excessively dark, and was a second time aroused from sleep (in about two hours after my return) by knocking which proved to be another messenger from the overseer again demanding my attention. I sent word that as my advice was not attended to in the first instance, I saw no use in my visits and that I would not go. I again went to bed, and in about two hours more was for the third time awoke by a knocking which proved to be a messenger from the same person saying that if I then sent the medicines I recommended my directions would be attended to.

Although I considered I would have been professionally and officially justified in refusing them after the insolence I had received in the first instance, the refusal to be guided by my advice and the time which had elapsed (which was almost death in such a case) yet through a motive of humanity that should not allow me to leave anything undone that afforded a chance of saving the child, I sent the necessary matters.

I visited the infant early again in the morning and prescribed for it, but found that the mixture to which I also attached much importance was not given as I ordered, as I could perceive by the vial it was untouched. On speaking to the mother on the subject she again told me she considered her child too weak. Though disheartened by the total inattention to my advice, I still continued to attend the infant (generally twice a day) for several days, during which time I found its father (the overseer), on two occasions particularly, lying so stupidly drunk on the bed of his almost expiring child (and at periods when his duty required him being on the roads) that he was quite insensible of my presence.

During my attendance of nearly a fortnight, which nothing but an anxious desire of saving the child could have induced me to continue, I met with repeated insults and instances of conduct such as above alluded to.

I shall detail one other instance of the difficulty I had to contend with and the insults I received. On a particular occasion I ordered a medicine in the form of a powder to be given at night and some castor oil the next morning. On visiting the following day the mother told me she had not given the castor oil as (again) she considered the child too weak, and on my meeting the father in two or three days after (I had visited the child repeatedly in the meantime) he told me, on my inquiring for the infant, in the most grossly insolent manner that the child was never the same since they had given it the powder above alluded to.

On reflecting on the different insults I received, I now feel surprised how I could have continued my attendance, yet such was my anxiety to be if possible useful to my patient, it outweighed every other consideration, till Friday morning the twenty-first ultimo when on visiting it on that day I found the child's dissolution fast approaching.

On making some inquiry relative to the case the mother told me in a tone surpassing all former insolence that she had sent for another doctor and that the child should have been bled in the first instance. I observed that I deserved such treatment, for after the conduct of herself and her husband to me the first night I visited her child, I ought never to have returned to see it again.

The overseer who was in the adjoining apartment came in on these words, in a state of extreme intoxication, and asked me in a most insolent menacing tone what row I was kicking up. I said, 'I am kicking up no row,' but irritated by his manner I added, 'I was a damn fool to have continued my attendance after the repeated insults I had received.' He repeated the words (damn fool), when I said in making use of that word I was wrong and I exceedingly regret it, but I will say I was a great fool, he then in the most ferocious menacing language said, 'Quit my house instantly and never dare attempt to put your foot into it again.'

I cannot express my feelings at such gross and unmerited insult, never in the whole course of my professional life did I receive such treatment. On the evening of that day I did myself the honour of addressing you a letter respectfully calling on you to institute an inquiry into the man's conduct and to afford me the protection from a repetition of such treatment in future.

It appears more occasion than I then imagined existed for such protection, for in a few days after (27 December) I received instructions to attend a punishment in the prisoner's barrack yard, on going to which the overseer, who saw me approaching at a considerable distance, hastily went up and placed himself in the doorway (a narrow one) so as completely to impede my entrance. Seeing the man's intention of insulting and impeding me, and wishing if possible to avoid any intercourse with him, I stopped at the door in the hope he would make way for me. Seeing he was determined not to do so, I at length said, 'Allow me to pass, sir,' when he dropped one of his arms, both of which he had akimbo, scarcely allowing me room to get through, turning his face to me at the same time with a most insolent and contemptuous leer. The moment I had entered and he had obtained his object of insulting me, he turned on his heel and walked off. I here must observe that his duty did not lead him in any way to this yard.

In a day or two after this additional insult, I again, Sir, did myself the honour of addressing you on the subject. You have heard my complaint of this man's conduct in his presence, and in obedience to your desire, I now, as I said before, in this mode state all the particulars, and have to apologise for the extreme length of the communication.

I now, Sir, most respectfully call on you and the government through you to afford me such redress for such a tissue of unmerited insults while in the discharge of my official duties, and such protection from a repetition of them as the government and you may consider I am entitled to.

I must add that since I laid my complaint before you, I have heard from so many different sources that I have no doubt of the fact that this man has frequently boasted of the grossness of his insolence to me and of his intention of continuing the same line of conduct, and also of the little attention he was positive would be paid to my complaint. I imagine I perceive, in consequence I am certain, a falling-off in the respect of the prisoners generally towards me.

JANE FRANKLIN

Not People of the
First Respectablity

Lady Jane was the wife of Sir John Franklin, who was
appointed lieutenant-governor of Van Diemen's Land
in 1836, and who perished in the Arctic in 1847 while
leading an expedition to find the North-West Passage.
She was the first European woman to climb Mount
Wellington and the first to travel overland from
Melbourne to Sydney. Less esteemed was her attempt
to drive all snakes from the Apple Isle by paying convicts
a shilling for each reptilian head brought to her. In the
1850s she organised several expeditions to find her lost
husband, one of which located the wreck of the expedition in 1859. Jane Franklin died in 1875.

April 1839—We landed in a mud bank on our left, (ascending
the river) and found ready to receive us the same gentleman
we thought we had left behind but who had taken a shorter cut to
land…

Capt. Lonsdale informed me he had one room in his house at
my service; but having learnt in my way that there was an Hotel
with respectable accommodation I begged to prefer the latter as
we could then be all together, a proposition which met with no
opposition, and we accordingly drove to Mr Fawkner's hotel
where we were expected. Mr F. formerly kept the Cornwall Hotel
at Launceston, and is the son of a man who came out in the first
convict ship to Port Phillip thirty-six years ago. They are not
people of the first respectability but are doing well in this money-
making place. He is the editor of a newspaper, the *Patriot*, and his

printing press is in the room adjoining my bedroom…

On arriving at the inn, Capt. Lonsdale asked me when I would like to receive visitors, and I told him at three, expecting thus to have an hour of quietness. Mrs Lonsdale, however, immediately arrived and sat down with me above an hour before anyone else came in. Then they came in, one after another for an hour and a half, when finding myself and poor Sophy too, quite ill and absolutely unable to go through any more of it…

About eight or nine o'clock we went out to see a Coroberry of the natives who are encamped in the outskirts and who, consisting of the tribes usually frequenting this port and of several more distant ones, are supposed to amount just now to about four or five hundred.

The Coroberry of one of the stranger tribes was over before we arrived on the ground. After a long delay during which the men were painting themselves the home tribes began their dances. For this purpose they had thrown aside their skins or blankets and were perfectly naked (except bundles of heavy fringes hanging round their loins like aprons) their breasts, arms, and thighs and legs were marked with broad white belts of pipeclay and borders of the same were traced round their eyes. Round their ankles they wore large ruffs of the gum-tree branches and in each hand they held a piece of hard wood which they were constantly employed striking against each other. The leader of the band was an elderly man, dressed in a blanket who stood with his face towards a group of women squatted on the grass, and who beat time with their hands on some folded opossum skins, thus producing a dull, hollow accompaniment. They sang also the whole time, in the style of the Flinders Island people, led by the old man. With the exception of these songs there was little else which reminded us of the exhibition at Flinders.

The principal feat performed by these savages was quite indescribable, it was performed by stretching out their legs as wide as possible, and making them quiver with great rapidity, and as if they didn't touch the ground, a deception aided by the boughs round their ankles. One would have thought the trunk of the body a prop on which to rest, while the lower limbs were thus shaking, apparently without touching the ground. They did not all commence simultaneously, but rapidly advanced one before the other, never clashing and constantly coming forward, and reminded me in this and in the manner in which they addressed themselves in face to the spectators of the kickers and jumpers and spinners on the Opera Boards. At last they formed a line close to our faces, changed their posture and measures, kicked up the dust with tremendous vehemence, in the way of a salute turned half round and with bent bodies and with extreme rapidity slank away...

We have had the greatest difficulty to make Mr Fawkner agree to take any payment for the accommodation, &c. he has afforded us. 'The honour was everything.' This would not do, and at last Capt. Moriarty has made him promise to make out his bill, but this is only on condition that I will honour his 'library' with a visit. I suppose I must subscribe to the good man's paper in return, but as the other one is said to be the best of the two, this is a pity, and perhaps should lead to a double subscription or not at all. It is not probable that both will last.

JOSEPH ORTON

A Great National Question

Joseph Orton was a Wesleyan Methodist missionary who arrived in Australia in 1831. He preached and travelled widely and, on 24 April 1836, was the first clergyman to preach in Melbourne. Here we find Orton on a visit to the Melbourne tribes in 1839 where, aside from his condescension towards the Aborigines, he becomes acutely aware of their extraordinary relationship to the land.

19 April 1839—This morning I was induced to walk about the town (Melbourne) to visit some of the friends, when I was struck with amazement at the rapid progress and vast improvements which had been made. When I was here three years ago there were but two houses of any note whatever, and they comparative hovels. Now I find a town occupying an area of nearly a mile square, on which are some hundreds of houses, and many of them spacious and well built edifices; with a population of about 2000 inhabitants enjoying all the comforts of domestic life—encouraged by the most flattering prospects of worldly prosperity—and living under the protection of an excellent political and civil economy.

There is a vigilant and effective police establishment (much required), sessions court, and a plentiful supply of legal professionalists. There are also two weekly newspapers to interest and inform the community by circulating the local and foreign intelligence of these eventful times. Nor is this vastly increasing community destitute of the means of religious instruction, and it would afford me pleasure to be able to state that the moral and spiritual improvement of the people were commensurate with the advantages and opportunities with which they are favoured, but unhappily I regret to have to say that the reverse is the case.

There are in the town an Episcopal clergyman, a Presbyterian and an Independent minister, each having their respective congregations; and last though not least, may be mentioned the Wesleyans, who maintain a prominent situation among the religious communities of this town, though they have not a stated minister among them...

Assisted by my friend the Protector, I held an imperfect but interesting parley with some of the natives on this occasion—particularly with those belonging to the tribe who consider themselves more immediately attached to our mission which has been temporarily conducted at Geelong, fifty miles to the westward of this place.

Mr Tuckfield, who has been longer among them than Mr Hurst, appears to be much beloved by them. When I caused them to understand that I was Mr Tuckfield's brother, they surrounded me—embraced me—and clapped me on the back and exclaimed 'Merrijik' (which is a barbarism introduced among them meaning very good) 'Mr Tuckfield Merrijik you Mr Tuckfield brother. When you gego (go) Mr Tuckfield's mya mya (home)?' I replied 'By and by'. They said 'Merrijik you merrijik Mr Tuckfield, plenty sing Mr Tuckfield.' This simple incident was to me as gratifying as encouraging, as it discovered a grateful recognition of the missionaries as their friends, and that the missionaries had successfully conciliated and secured their friendship.

They are certainly a deeply degraded race of our fellow men, but they are notwithstanding an interesting people—having minds quite capable of comprehending and hearts susceptible of feeling. O that at least some few of them knew and felt the truth as it is in Jesus. The influence of the example and precept of some of them becoming true converts to Christianity, would no doubt be very great among the respective tribes. My daily prayer is 'Lord give us some one or more of these souls'. I say 'us' identifying myself with my brethren who are more immediately called to this great and arduous work—though I am but a sojourner to assist, to carry into operation the wishes of the committee towards a class of my fellow men, among whom it would be my honour and happiness to offer myself to labour more permanently were it not for the situation in which providence has placed me at the head of a large and rising family, whose interests have a demand upon me, which could not be met while peregrinating the wilds of this country, which must be a considerable part of the duty of those missionaries who labour among these heathens with any hope of success.

There are difficulties connected with the prosecution of our mission to the Aborigines which nothing but self-denying perseverance in simple and firm trust in the declarations of divine truth can encourage the labourer to hope for success.

The migrating habits of these natives is not the greatest difficulty to contend with. The government is fast disposing of their lands—in addition to which an Act has been passed by the local Legislature, commonly called the 'Squatters Act', under which settlers may establish themselves in any part of the extensive territory of New South Wales, and no reserve whatever of land is made for the provision of the natives, neither in securing to them sufficient portions of their own native land as hunting ground, nor otherwise providing for their necessities. The result of which is that the natives who remain in the neighbourhood of the settled districts become pilfering—starving—obtrusive mendicants, and after enduring incalculable deprivations, abuses and miseries will gradually pine—die away—and become extinct, leaving only an eternal memento of a blot upon the justice, equity and benevolence of our Christian government, for no adequate provision is made for them.

The design of the scheme of protectorship may be good, but it is cramped in its operation for want of a well digested, liberal and extensive plan. The means to carry such a plan into efficient operation might and ought to be furnished by the local government—one tithe of the revenue from the sale of lands would accomplish the object—which would only be an act of justice, to the credit and interest of the country.

On the other hand those natives who may be driven back to the interior must encroach upon the boundaries of other hostile tribes, by whom they will be murdered and exterminated.

Thus as enterprising settlers extend themselves, under the sanction of government, the great object of missionary enterprise will be defeated unless some measure be speedily adopted by the government to prevent the evil. It certainly must become a great national question; to regulate over-extending colonisation, and to make suitable provision for the Aboriginal nations and tribes.

JOHN HUNTER KERR
Jump Up Whitefella

As John Kerr discovered to his dismay, entering the bay by ship was an uncertain undertaking before a channel was marked. His *Glimpses of Life in Victoria by a Resident* was published many years after these events took place in the late 1830s. It offers insights aplenty about early Melbourne and its Aboriginal inhabitants.

The fourth day after our passage through the Heads dawned, and found us still at the entrance of the bay. A small craft had passed inward the preceding day, but too far from us to allow of any communication. We now encountered a schooner, outward bound, whose captain presented ours with a rough chart, on which the principal sandbanks in the bay were marked. Furnished with this talisman, we confidently hoped that our difficulties were all past, and once more set sail, gliding smoothly through the water, till, to the consternation of us all, and the unutterable vexation of the captain, we felt again the well-known bump, and then a short dead stop. We were aground for the third time.

At the same moment a large vessel, with all her sails set, swept triumphantly past us through the opposite or eastern channel.

The captain swore tremendously, and stamped the decks in futile rage, as he wildly looked at our successful rival. Another minute, and she too staggered and stopped.

'By Jove! she's aground too!' shouted a score of voices simultaneously, with a feeling very like exultation, at seeing the envied ship reduced to the same condition as ours. This circumstance soothed our captain's ruffled temper not a little; but when we had succeeded in working off the ship once more, and had regained a safe anchorage, he announced his intention of trying the treacherous bay no further.

That afternoon we observed a whaleboat steering towards us, and were shortly afterwards boarded by the skipper in command, an old whaler, known as Captain Boden. He was the proprietor of a small public house at Williamstown, in Hobson's Bay, and volunteered to pilot us to our destination the next day…

The lions of this primitive locality did not require much time to be thoroughly examined, and having returned to our good ship for the night, we quitted her next day, and rowed across the bay to land at Sandridge, the port of Melbourne, which lies three miles to the south of the city, at the mouth of the river Yarra…it was a silent wilderness, where tea-tree scrub grew close and thick amid the tall gum forests, while the native grasses waved rank and high. We followed a well-defined track, which was the only visible path through the wilderness of sober-coloured verdure; but it led straight to Melbourne, and there was no risk of missing the way. We had not proceeded more than a mile when we could hear distinctly through the still atmosphere the sound of hammers and axes at work in the town two miles distant.

At length we emerged on a large cleared spot by the river's side, where houses dotted here and there proved that we had arrived at our destination. The wild woodlands around were slowly yielding to the blows of the woodman's axe, but savage and civilised life were still strangely blended together. Here we saw the mia-mias and campfires of the Aborigines still lingering among the trees on the banks of the river, and their dusky, gaunt figures, loosely draped in scanty opossum skins, stalked about among the new population like spectres of the past...

After a short residence in the bush I was joined by a friend of the name of D——. He was rather a delicate youth, and not equal to hard work, and, being of a contemplative turn of mind, he frequently elected to do the shepherding of one of our flocks. He was a lover of the fine arts, and especially of music, and spent many an hour playing on the Scotch bagpipes, of which he was enthusiastically and patriotically fond. His favourite instrument was his frequent companion while shepherding, and he would pour forth many a stirring pibroch or plaintive lament on the profound stillness of the primeval wilds.

It happened that about this time there was an outlaw among the Aborigines, a big powerful fellow, who had more than once attempted murder. The police had been for some time on the lookout for him, but he had contrived to evade all pursuit. With a companion after his own heart, 'Jacky-Jacky' roamed over the country, a noted character, dreaded by all men, and committing depredations wherever he could do so.

One day D—— had gone out as usual with his flock, and at noon he collected the sheep in a convenient place, where a few large trees offered a pleasant shelter. Here, according to his general habit, he intended to take his frugal midday meal, but the musical inspiration was strong upon him, and having completed his simple preparations, he stopped to finish a favourite tune before proceeding to satisfy the calls of hunger. A sad disappointment awaited him. Hearing a slight rustle behind him, D—— looked round and saw, standing close by, the redoubtable Jacky-Jacky, with his trusty companion. A pair of formidable-looking scoundrels they

were, and well-armed, having contrived to provide themselves
with a couple of guns in addition to their own spears and other
native weapons. They felt their power, and evidently enjoyed the
situation.

Squatting down coolly on the grass beside D——, they began
by demanding his stock of '*baccy*'. This was grudgingly given,
for D——, being quite unarmed, was completely at their mercy.
Presently they spied out his dinner, which D—— had deposited on
the ground, and which peeped temptingly out of the half-opened
paper by which it was enveloped.

'Give it that ow?' said Jacky imperiously, in his jargon. And
when D—— hesitated to comply with his request, he unceremoniously helped himself to the provisions, which he generously
shared with his companion. D——, who was a very plucky and
rather hot-tempered little fellow, looked on, fuming with rage;
but the cup of his humiliation was not yet full.

Jacky pointed to the bagpipes, whose long-drawn notes had
pleased his ear as he approached; evidently music had charmed the
savage breast, though its effects upon him did not appear to have
been very humanising. 'Merryjig that fellow!' was his sapient
remark. 'You go on; play him.' D——'s eyes flashed with impotent
anger; in vain; he must needs obey, for two loaded guns, which
might be levelled at him at any moment, had an eloquence of
persuasion which he dared not resist. So the dinnerless man was
obliged to play for the delectation of the savages, whom he
watched with suppressed wrath while they consumed every
morsel of his dinner. It can hardly be supposed that his instrument
brought forth gentle strains under such circumstances.

At length Jacky and his friend thought it prudent to retire,
and D—— returned home in a state of mind very far from peace-
able, vowing vengeance on the insolent black fellows. Next day he
sallied forth, gun in hand, fully resolved to punish Jacky, but the
latter was too wary to cross his path again.

As a general rule the prestige of the white man in the early days was very great, and the blacks looked upon him as some sort of glorified being. They believed that after death they would commence a fresh existence with a white skin, or, as they expressed it, 'jump up white fellow'. That belief, like the superstitions of more civilised races, has long faded away; for since death has laid so many immigrants low, the black man has ample proof that his white brother has no immunity from the common lot of mortality. Very shortly before I settled among them, one of their number, known by the name of Bowen, had died in consequence of a spear-wound in his foot. Happening to bear the scar of an old cut on one of my feet, it occurred to me, as a frolic, to test the well-known superstition of the natives, and, showing them the mark, I gravely informed them that I was Bowen, 'jumped up' again from the grave. To my surprise and amusement this statement was implicitly believed, and I immediately became an object of much interest. Many came to see me, and begged to be shown the scar, which they examined with great curiosity, and pronounced to be on the exact spot where Bowen's death-wound had been.

Seeing them completely convinced of the truth of my story I did not venture subsequently to undeceive them; yet it is strange that they never expected me to become one of them, but treated me with great respect, and seemed to think it natural that one who had 'jumped up' could not return to his old ways...I was told that two women from one of the tribes desired to see me. They were sisters of the departed Bowen, and had travelled a long distance for the purpose. I felt considerably dismayed, and began to repent of my joke. How would they greet me? Perhaps they might be very affectionate. The idea of being folded in the embrace of two black greasy smoke-dried beauties, and of perchance receiving from their lips the kiss of chaste sisterly love, made my hair stand on end. But I dared not refuse them an interview, and they came.

Two poor swarthy withered creatures they were, with eager agitated faces, and tears of genuine emotion streaming down their cheeks. They were greatly moved, and when I saw them thus my heart smote me for the deception I had practised. But it was too late to undeceive them now. I therefore received them with a stately and frigid dignity, for I feared they might otherwise become demonstrative in their affection. They seemed disappointed, but evidently acquiesced in the promotion of their departed brother to a higher sphere, where he could no longer be to them as of old. After a brief conversation they left me, and I watched them departing with a sense of relief. My assumed character was long remembered by the natives. Years after, when I returned to Australia after a visit to Europe, grown older, and bearded—when my own name had been forgotten, the single word 'Bowen' was a talisman which never failed to recall me to their memory. They could not even then quite cast off the old superstition, and ever retained a kindly feeling for me...

On one occasion Mr T——, the native protector, invited me to accompany him to the blacks' camp, where he prepared me to expect a strange scene. It was a dark night, and when we reached the camp we found a large number of the natives seated on the ground, silent and motionless. Not a word was spoken; not even the bark of a dog was heard. There was no light but that of the campfires, which threw a lurid gleam over the dark figures as they squatted on the ground, and over the background of high trees behind them. There was something inexpressibly weird and uncanny about this dark, silent assemblage, in which even the youngest child had been hushed into an unnatural stillness. In the centre of the group, close to one of the fires, lay stretched at full length a man who appeared to be very ill. His chest heaved visibly and hurriedly under the opossum rug which was thrown over him; the perspiration stood out in big heavy drops on his brow, the whole expression of his face was one of unmistakable anguish and terror. Mr T— explained in a whisper that the man thought himself bewitched; he believed that some secret enemy had by supernatural means robbed him of his kidney fat!

This part of the body was by the Australian Aborigines considered among the most vital of their frame. When they killed an enemy, his kidney fat was carefully extracted; sometimes it was eaten, but more generally preserved as a charm. No threat could terrify the savage more than that of depriving him of this important substance.

On this occasion the terror and distress of the man who believed himself to be so deprived were so intense that I am convinced he would have died had not his mind been set at rest. The medicine man belonging to the tribe had retired to a distance from the group, and was invisible in the darkness. He was supposed to be engaged in a struggle with the supernatural power that had afflicted the sufferer; and his hoarse voice was audible through the deathlike stillness, as it rose and fell in a kind of wild chant that was alternately pleading and menacing in its tones. Once he came to the camp to look at his patient, and bade him take courage, as he hoped to prevail over the evil spirit, then retired again and was lost in the darkness, where he resumed his incantations. Finally he came back, with a triumphant air, making a feint of concealing something in the folds of his rug. Stooping over the recumbent form of his patient, he pretended, with many gesticulations and other ceremonies, to restore the missing fat to its place.

The effect of all these incantations was magical, and instantaneous in its operation. The sick man, who had the moment before been trembling and shivering in the most abject fear, presently rose steadily from the ground, his distorted countenance recovered its serenity, and about five minutes later he was squatted among the group, smoking his pipe with the rest, and perfectly happy.

Port Phillip Gazette

17 April 1839—On Thursday last, one of the fishermen living on the banks of the Yarra Yarra, reported at the police office. Having found the body of a man floating on the water opposite his own hut, he had secured the corpse with a rope to the nearest tree, and come up to town to dispose of his fish, the announcement of the above facts seeming to be quite a secondary consideration.

The medical officer of the settlement immediately repaired to the spot, and on examination stated the man to have been dead some time; the cause of death intoxication, the cavity of his stomach being full of spirits and beer. Subsequently to this the body was allowed to remain the rest of the day and the next night without any covering. On the following morning the body presented a mass of loathsome putridity, the swine of the town had been on the spot, and preyed upon its remains. Such was the drunkard's end.

*

27 April 1839—We have been authorised to announce that the overland mail for Sydney will be made up on Tuesday morning next, arrangements having been entered into for the weekly conveyance of the same. The intelligence has come from such a quarter as almost to persuade us to be a believer, but the inhabitants of Melbourne have been so often disappointed that we would not but at all wish to meet the first brunt of their vexation if again deluded, especially if credence had been yielded upon the strength of any representation on our part. When we see the mail bags delivered, opened, and have ocular demonstration of the result by the receipt of unexpected newspapers, then and then only will we be persuaded that a weekly mail has been delivered.

*

30 April 1839—To the Editor,

Sir—It is well known that of the free emigrants recently arrived in our port, a very considerable proportion are natives of the Highlands of Scotland with large families—the women and children composing which, are frequently unable to speak, or even understand, a single word of English. When these 'Sons of the Mountain Glens' 'take to the bush', one obvious, but most lamentable consequence is that their interesting offspring are debarred from entering instruction, in even the simplest and most elementary parts of education...

An uneducated population will neither be virtuous nor loyal, neither good members of society nor good subjects; and to import large numbers of young children, only to grow up in ignorance and barbarism, would be to defeat the great end and object of emigration, *viz*, the infusion of pure materials into the corrupt and depraved body politic of the colony.

The force of these considerations is not unfelt by the High-landers themselves. Not a few have remained in Melbourne, in preference to proceeding into the country, avowedly with the view of obtaining *schooling* for their children...Even those now resident in Melbourne have not availed themselves of the means of education, happily at their command here, with the alacrity that might have been expected. This has arisen partly from the eagerness with which the services of even very young girls are sought after in town, and the inducement thus presented to poor people to send their children to service, when they ought to send them to school, and partly from the inability of parents to pay school fees, whilst a highly laudable spirit of independence will not allow them to seek or even to accept instruction graciously.

GEORGE HAMILTON

Flood on the Wattle

George Hamilton was an early overlander, driving 350
cattle from Port Phillip to South Australia in 1839. From
his vantage point atop the Melbourne Club he got an
extraordinary view of the settlement before departure.

It was about the middle of the wet winter of the year 1839 that
I made preparations to take 350 head of mixed cattle from Port
Phillip to Adelaide...When all preparations were completed—the
cattle mustered and ready to start—I stood, on the evening before
my departure, on the roof of the house occupied by the lately
formed Port Phillip (now the Melbourne) Club, and contemplated the scene below me. The house was situated on the west
end of Collins Street, and from its roof I looked down on the
Custom House flat, and saw the Yarra at full flood submerging it.
This club house was at that time a building of some pretension, as
it was one storey high and peered over the ground floor cottages
which surrounded it like a black swan among a flock of teal.

A great quantity of rain had fallen during the day, and the
Yarra was grumbling, roaring, and splashing on its way to
Hobson's Bay as if the weather was behaving badly towards it.
This river was then ornamented by the beautiful wattle trees
(*acacia decurrens*) which grew on its banks. They were now bursting into flower, and their golden-tufted blossoms appearing here
and there in large rich masses, mingling with marble-like trunks
of the glorious gum trees which reared their lofty heads
among them, might have hinted at the golden metal which
was then sleeping undiscovered in the soil. If such was the
case the hint was thrown away upon me, for as I looked forth

on the wet landscape I brooded over the sloppy nights and moist days in store for me for many weeks to come, and the idea of so much moisture was not a pleasant one.

As night closed in I left the roof, and, going into the coffee room, sought consolation in hot brandy-and-water. One of the members of the club was seeking consolation in the same way, and when I sat down near him he exclaimed, 'I say, old fellow, you are not going into the bush in such weather as this is, are you? By the bye, they say you are going to Adelaide by the same route that Bonney took when he got into such a mess for want of water, and only saved his life by killing a bull and drinking his blood. What will you do if you get into such a mess as that?'

'Why, drink blood too.'

'Bah!' said he, 'what is the use of tempting Providence?'

Port Phillip Gazette

June 1839—On Sunday last, during the morning, seven whales were seen in the harbour. Mr Harding, chief officer of the brig *Emma*, and an old whaler, procured a whaleboat, and for want of harpoon or other instrument, borrowed a bayonet from the Tide Surveyor at Williams Town, and fixing it in the manner of a lance gave chase; after a short run he succeeded in striking a fine sperm whale off Gellibrand's Point, and hauling it alongside, another was subsequently made fast to by a boat belong to the *William Bryan*, but from want of skill in the harpooner or deficiency of gear, the fish got off. Mr Harding's prize was, when measured, found to be fifty-five feet in length. It was bought by Messrs Campbell and Woolley for eighty pounds.

It has been generally supposed that Port Phillip would never offer any chance of success as a whaling ground, the present instance, however, is a proof to the contrary; since the fish has been struck. The inhabitants of Williams Town recollect having before seen several fish in the bay at different times; this capture, and the chance of its repetition will, we have no doubt, induce some of our enterprising citizens amongst whom we could point out one who has proved successful in the pursuit, to form a whaling establishment at the port, and thus open another source of wealth and credit to the number which we already possess.

★

28 August 1839 — Matrimony.

'L' abstinence de plaisir est un grand peche.' — Bernier

In quoting the above the writer begs most humbly to intimate to the Fair Sex of Melbourne and its vicinity that there are lately arrived in Australia Felix (happy Land!!! may it prove so to them), two or three young Gentlemen (the writer among the number) whose greatest wishes, are, to become respectable members of society, *viz* — Married men. And it is to be hoped that no prudish fears will withhold Ladies from answering this appeal to Cupid, but will joyously come forth in all their pristine purity to meet half-way those who will be but too happy to link their fates together in the hallowed bonds of holy matrimony. All letters addressed A. B. & Co, at the Gazette Office, will meet with the greatest secrecy and attention.

Edward Curr

Town Allotments at a Price

Almost from the time of first settlement a mania for speculation had taken hold in Melbourne. Edward Curr saw the hysteria gain momentum during a visit in 1839, but by the time he returned in 1842 with his family, a recession had severely upset future prospects for many of the investors.

The community seemed urgently bent on ascertaining, by the test of auction, the value of every horse, house, and acre in the colony. I was the more confirmed in this view by observing how few persons seemed to have any idea of retaining permanently any property purchased, as it was no sooner acquired that the new owner seemed to set himself to calculate what it would fetch when put more advantageously on the market, and resold at the expiration of a week or two. This seemed to be specially the case as regarded the town allotments, and the people were always arguing that the value of that commodity increased in proportion to its subdivision, and hence buying large lots, subdividing, and reselling was constantly going on.

In connection with this business I remember that there was a grey-haired old man who was quite a character about the town. Mounted on an old white horse, this individual might be seen daily perambulating the streets between the hours nine and twelve a.m., ringing a bell, and carrying a red flag elevated on a staff, a few feet above his head, on which appeared in large letters the word *Auction*; whilst two boards, on which were posted bills of the sale to which the old man drew attention, dangled at his back and chest. As he rode down Collins Street, I often noticed that the board which hung in front rested on the pommel of the saddle, and, coming under the rider's chin, elevated his line of vision far above the horizon. As he could see little of what was passing around him, and hear nothing for the noise made by his bell, his look naturally became abstracted, if not solemn. Somehow this old man, always gazing upwards, apparently at some distant hills, with banner upreared and locks floating in the wind has become mixed up in my mind with Longfellow's Alpine hero...This old man with horse, flag, bell and board served, it might be, more than one useful purpose; and I certainly, as a result of a limited experience, came to consider that, at the auction announced by him, the beer and champagne would be found cooler and more choice than anywhere else; indeed, I often led to debate in my mind whether he did not carry out a hospitable device of the jovial dwellers of the town for letting strangers know where the principal commercial spread of the day would be, at which, *sans façon*, their company was expected.

The Melbourne Club, which at that time occupied the corner of Collins Street and Market Street, was another object of note. The number of its members seemed considerable and it was at the club door—which stood at what I may call three-quarters face to the street—that the orderlies and horses of the Commissioners of Crown Lands (the former in spruce uniform, and the latter be-holstered and be-cavesson) were to be seen in attendance several hours daily; their masters being probably engaged with brandy and cigars within. Those were the palmy days of Commissioners, when licences for runs, the settling of disputed boundaries &c., depended on their *fiat*. They were also in command of the mounted police, and in some instances, at least, displayed in their costume and manner decidedly military proclivities...

I was present at, I believe, the first land sales at Pascoevale and Sandridge, or the Beach, as the latter was then called. To arrive on Sandridge the Yarra had to be crossed on a punt...Arrived with a friend at the future Sandridge, we met as usual, hams and turkeys, beer and champagne. I do not recollect seeing any land sold. It might have been that the company had only come to view the allotments, which were shortly to be offered for sale in Melbourne. What I do remember is that the gathering was a very pleasant one; everyone seemed in the best of spirits, and several tents had been set in a prominent position, in which the company lunched as they arrived. That important preliminary over, we broke up into twos and threes, some strolling on the beach with the ladies, some examining the surveyor's lines in the future township, whilst others sat down to enjoy their cigars in the shade. Altogether, anything more like a picnic, and more unlike the usual routine of business, I never saw.

CHARLES JOSEPH LA TROBE

Arrival of 'The Gov'nor'

By the time Charles La Trobe was made superintendent of the Port Phillip District in 1839 he had published a book of poems inspired by a continental tour, a book on Switzerland and a travelogue of North America. He was, according to a contemporary 'a man of a thousand occupations…a complete virtuoso'. La Trobe coped well with his responsibilities while Victoria was small, but his administrative abilities were severely tested by the gold rush, during which he lost control of the budget and much of the populace. He proffered his resignation in 1852, and was relieved of duty two years later. Although he lived until 1875, for the last years of his life he was blind, unable to complete his planned, great work describing his Australian experiences. Here we find him in happier times, writing to George Gipps (Bourke's successor as governor of New South Wales) in October 1839 about his arrival in Port Phillip.

M y dear Sir George,
The first scene of the first act of the drama is over. The welcome which the good people of this portion of your territories gave me was as the papers would say *enthusiastic*: that is to say, the grave amongst them got up grave addresses and received grave answers—the gay made bonfires, put lights in their casements and fired off fowling pieces—and the lower class got jovially drunk and were fined—all in my honour.

The second scene has now commenced. The newspapers (I understand for I have not had time to read them) begin to give me a great deal of very excellent advice—every man in the street thinks (as I must now have rested sufficiently from the fatigues of the voyage) that it would be both improper and impolitic to pass the door of my temporary residence without stopping to do business with 'His Honour'. One steps in to ask after my health and how I like Australia Felix; another to request I would give him a government appointment; a third to inoculate me with his opinion on some subject of public interest. Official men have all some arrears of some kind or another to fetch up: having modestly kept them in the background till *'His Honour' should arrive*: so that I am led to suppose that everybody within the district (the Hentys from Portland Bay even have been at me) thinks that he does the state good service in assailing me: and all this at a time when I have neither a roof over my head, nor a single shelf upon which I may arrange my papers. However, I do not complain, on the contrary I take it as a matter of course that I must pass through this ordeal in common with other honourable men. They will soon find that the lemon has been squeezed so often there is no longer any juice in it, and then I hope to have a quiet life. A quiet life it may be, but I have no idea that it will be an idle one. I am sure you will give me time to recollect myself and to get to understand my business, and then I will send you a full report of what is doing and what is to be done in this part of the colony...

As to my own private arrangements—they are soon stated. Upon my arrival here, I fixed upon a suitable spot in the government paddock, next to that in which Capn L. resides and took measures to put up my portable cottage and whatever offices were indispensably necessary. I know that I am there on sufferance and not of right, and that whenever circumstances may oblige you to tell me to remove I must do so at all risks.

Nevertheless I have been obliged to spend so much even in putting up these temporary erections (for such they may be called) from the exorbitant price of labour (10/- to 14/- per diem) and materials, that this alone would make me unwilling to move for some time unless it were necessary. But other considerations impel me to ask you to sanction my remaining where I am proposing to live, till the public good or other circumstances require my removal, and that is my utter inability to cope with the speculators of this town in buying land within any reasonable distance, and my determination to seek from you no advantage or indulgence in selecting and purchasing what might suit me, beyond what you might accord to any other.

Were there no land fever in the district, and were land selling in a natural way; plentiful as it is, there might have been no impropriety in my asking you to sanction my purchasing a given plot of ground conveniently situated at an elevation; or to allow it to be put up to auction at one of the land sales that I might become the purchaser—and none in your yielding to my request. But as matters are, I can do neither with propriety and so little hope have I of procuring land at present within a few miles of the town at any reasonable rate that I have taken measures to dispose of my permanent house which I expect daily from England, even before it arrives, as, to keep it warehoused here is out of the question—I believe the position I have chosen is not likely to interfere with anyone. The paddock is railed in, and is part of that reserve which was set apart by Sir Richard Bourke's orders for the use of government cattle and horses. The mounted police have their barrack in one corner of it and I have modestly placed my cottage &c near another.

Mrs La Trobe is well, thank God, in the midst of all our discomfort and confusion for we have not yet been able to get into our quarters. She requests me to present her kind regards to Lady Gipps to whom I beg to offer my respects.

JONATHAN BINNS WERE

No Place for a Poor Gentleman

The shipboard diary of Jonathan Were lay in a locked chest for nearly 125 years before a curious descendant discovered it and realised its value. Were sailed from Plymouth on 25 July 1839 bound for the new settlement of Melbourne where he hoped to set up business as a merchant. He was accompanied by wife Sophia, daughter Sophia Louisa and son Jonathan Henry, who was just a year old and narrowly escaped death on the voyage out. Jonathans snr and jnr were to be spectacularly successful in their new home, founding the stockbroking firm of J. B. Were & Son.

We had expected to have entered the harbour of Port Phillip on Thursday 14 November 1839 but it was late in the afternoon when we approached the entrance, which induced our Captain to lay too till the morning, which proved to be fine and soon after 7 a.m., we rapidly approached the Port Phillip Heads, Arthur's Seat on the east being a distinguishing landmark of the greatest height of any land in this neighbourhood...

We had supposed on our voyage out that we should be the first arrival to this hardly known or heard of place in England, but you may guess my perfect astonishment when on nearing Hobsons Bay one mast after another opened to our view, and when we cast anchor we were as completely in a little fleet at the mouth of the Yarra Yarra as if we had been in Plymouth Sound. Three ships, eight barques, five brigs and two schooners lay at anchor round us, and more astonishing than all, the whole of these vessels had or were delivering their goods and passengers for Melbourne.

During the succeeding ten days, the number of vessels were increased by new arrivals from eighteen to twenty-five!! I was perfectly astounded and selfish enough to be disappointed for I well knew if all these vessels had come, there were ways and means and merchants to receive them.

When had Plymouth with her naval port, and all the enterprise which her merchants possess, twenty-five sail of vessels (and most of them averaging above 300 tons) delivering cargoes in her port?...

On looking round from the poop, about one mile over the indigenous foliage and the varied hues of the forest, was seen curling sundry wreaths of smoke, and on attentively looking through the trees some indescribable masses of brick which proved to be some of the senior and half-finished buildings assisting to found the noble city of Melbourne.

I soon landed, and as my friend Dr Cooksworthy told me, the best way to give information respecting a place was to describe things and persons exactly as I found them, I shall endeavour to give you as well as I am able some account of how I found this place.

The ship lying eight miles from Melbourne by the Yarra Yarra River, we landed, two friends and myself, at the beach nearest to where the smoke indicated the town. We landed on a fine sandy beach of reddish colour to which the brush came close upon high water mark. We found a good road through the wood which is here formed of the blue gum and red gum principally but the mimosa, cherry, myrtle and bay tree occasionally lay in our way. The distance was near two miles to the river where you cross to the town and our walk much pleased us, varied as it was by open clear land through clumps of trees.

Arrived at the river, we got into the ferry boat which was rather more than half full of water, but we got safely landed on the city side and on tendering payment some coppers, the man said he had not seen such a coin for a great while before...Here and there one, two and three good-looking and substantial buildings of brick were erected, interspersed with wood houses of less attractive size, while others of the same material were very modestly attached to its more prominent counterpart.

Melbourne is built or rather building on the side of a gently rising hill facing the south and runs along parallel with the river for about a mile and back about three-quarters, and has a most picturesque appearance with the lovely (as it is here called) Yarra Yarra gliding beneath it...

We found good shops with drugs, groceries, haberdashery, ironmongery; indeed each shop seemed to be quite an emporium. But what struck my fancy was the many young men we met, dashing-looking fellows, all with trousers lined with yellowish leather and having large riding whips in their hands; no braces on but with coats of the most fantastical shapes and colours, and their bearings being that of gentlemen, young and handsome. Their speech, as free as their appearance, was careless and their *tout ensemble* declaring them to be true English-born Britons, residing in the wilds of Australia, under the title of squatters.

The place most attractive after a voyage is the inn, to where we bent our steps and refreshed ourselves. What we partook of I will give you the items as it was the first bill I ever paid in Australia. There were three of us.

Lunch, Bread, Cheese and Butter	£-10 6
Bottle of Ale	3 0
Bottle of Porter	3 0
	£-16 6

and when I gave a 1/- to the waiter he looked at me as though he was surprised and I found afterwards 2/6 was their usual fee.

I went to nearly all the shops to take something green and fresh on board for the children and Sophia to eat, but not a single article of fruit was to be obtained, and I was content to give 1/2 for 1 lb. broad figs.

I returned the way I came and plucked many beautiful flowering shrubs, the wild geranium among them. I observed but few birds yet those few gave forth some pleasing notes, which alike with the shrubs gave lie to those who have stated that the flowers were without scent, and the birds without song.

The excitement on board to see what we brought and to know what we had seen you cannot conceive, but every little matter connected with the shore became of importance. I was however pleased with my day's trip and very much surprised to find Melbourne had progressed so rapidly as she had done.

Not having determined where I would sit myself down, the next morning after our arrival I went to Williams Town to find out her prospects and survey her situation. A few, some half-dozen, houses were built. The land is low and the water shallows to some distance as you approach the shore, which I considered objectionable in as much as vessels could not approach within a hundred yards of high water mark. There was no fresh water to be had, it being all taken and brought down from above Melbourne. (A beautiful well of fresh spring water in great plenty has since been obtained.) And on inquiring I found land to be supposed to be equally valuable in proportion as I had found in Melbourne, two hundred pounds being asked for a quarter of an acre in the centre of the proposed but laid out town. I took the boy who helped me on shore and gave him a glass of beer for which I had to pay 9*d*.

On returning on board, I found some fish had been taken. They resembled very large bream, tasted like them, and are here called snappers. It was now my business of course to get a piece of land a few acres I intended in the town of Melbourne and to place my house on it, but what was my astonishment to be told that only a few days before I arrived, land had been sold at £33 (not per acre, but per FOOT) with only fifty feet frontage to the street with a depth of ninety feet back.

Of course I would not believe that this could be a fair average price, and I supposed the gents of Melbourne were making game of me. But, on delivering some of my letters of introduction, I was seriously informed that the price of land had risen in a most extraordinary and almost unaccountable way. But there were two causes assigned for it and I think with much propriety.

The first was the government having put up such a limited quantity it had all been bought up by the Sydney speculators who doled it out to you as sparingly as if it had been purchased at a heavy price. One half acre which was bought for £46 in March last was cut up in small frontages and sold at auction the following November a few days before we arrived for upwards of ten thousand pounds.

These prices of course did not agree with my finances, but I still hoped to get (and tried for many days) a place near the wharf where I could put up my house and commence business. But at last, found this impracticable also, as there was no land to be had under £10 per foot.

At last I tried leases, but 25/- per ft was asked as a rental upon the supposed value of the land. I was then obliged to turn my back upon the water towards the bush and after many anxious and seriously troublesome days, got a quarter of an acre which is 57 feet × 132 feet and a building lease to pay £12/10/- annually for ten years and to insure all buildings erected thereon, which are to become the property of the owner of the land at the termination of the lease. Insurance here on wood houses being £3/3/0 per cent you will at once see I am paying a handsome rental, but it is still thought advantageous terms for the place and it was the only way for me, who had no capital to take out of my business to sink in land…

Our tents one after another had been upset in the middle of the night. On two or three occasions, the wet had come through the top of the tents with running streams passing through the centre. Our furniture was drenched, blown down and broken. Sophia and the children were repeatedly unwell and to add to our dilemma the weather prevented the workmen from erecting our cottage and it was quite out of the way to think of endeavouring to find house room anywhere, single small rooms letting from £1 to £2 per week bare wooden sheds. Added to this, I had enough to do to attend to my family and was unable to commence business.

But as all things changes so did the season and weather, and on this 1 January 1840, we first slept under our own roof.

I had found it absolutely necessary to have a chimney in our cottage and for erecting this and laying a brick foundation, I had to pay £46/10/- and the carpenter for putting it together and making the necessary alterations attendant on the chimney being put up, I paid £31, so that by the time I had added first cost, freight, landing etc. my little box stood me in near £200—but, I am still thankful I have it, as I can let it at £80 a year or sell it for upwards of £400.

I had stored the merchandise I brought with me and sold some of it to good account. I eventually hired a room for 14/- per week which I have converted into a counting house and still retain. I do assure you that at first I was quite broken down, and disappointed, everything being so very dear. The loaf with you at 7*d*, is here 2/4, beef and mutton 6*d*. per lb., potatoes nearly as dear as bread 23 to 25/- per cwt., and with a family such as I had with me, the matter became so serious that I believe I once expressed a wish to Sophia that I had not come.

Under this feeling I refrained from writing, but I still think it right to tell you exactly how I felt and was situated. But, now that the rough is passed and things take their regular turn and business being *abundant and profitable, I feel differently* and see with different eyes and am now very thankful I am here and well assured it is with a prospect of ultimate prosperity...

I do not know of any articles so cheap as you have there, if I except tea and sugar. Milk is 6*d*. to 9*d*. per quart. Wine is pretty reasonable, but spirits which are subject to an import duty 10/2. (Brandy and rum, Geneva) is now selling in bond for 12 to 15/- per gallon, but a most expensive fashion is adopted here of drinking ale and porter which cannot be bought in the cases of three dozen for less than 1/- per bottle...

There is no coal used—all wood, 6/- a load which will last a fortnight, but I have bought none yet and still have enough around me to last a couple of months longer. But it takes time and breaks tools in converting it. All our water is brought us from the river by carts which carry about 100 gallons for 1/6 to any part of the town. I have suffered much annoyance from the mosquitoes. They attack newcomers for their first two or three months very fiercely and on Christmas Day I could hardly see out of either eye. The poison from the bite lasts twenty-four hours, then gradually subsides, but now a couple of hours after the bite, there is no appearance left of it...

Millar (from Kingsbridge) has a situation in the Customs. Good, the butcher, will do well if he be steady. Indeed, every active and industrious working man or woman can secure constant employment, at such wages as will permit them with frugality to put by one to two pounds per week. But this is no place for the poor gentleman, I mean a man of limited means who wishes to live upon his income, but if he be a professional man, tradesman, or an assistant willing and active, or a man of some calling or trade, he *must do well*.

Where everything is so very dear, it seems almost incompatible with the idea of saving, but the payments and profits are in proportion and no more is thought of giving £150 a year rent of a house here which in England or in Plymouth would not bring £15.

You may remember I bought three tents of Davies and just to shew what some things sell for, I will tell you what I made of them after 6 weeks use.

Large one cost	£10/15/-	Sold for £40
Small one cost	1/15/-	Sold for 8
Smaller one cost	1/10/-	Sold for 5
	£14/-/-	53

which leaves only £39 profit!!!!

You must not make this article public, as it will be matter for correspondence in my business letters. If you can find an active *labouring* lad who can write and spell a little, I should be glad to have him out if he could be bound to me. I would pay his passage or refund it to his friends. See if you can get one about fifteen years, make the best terms you are able and send him out.

We have three banks, the Union Bank of Australia, Bank of Australasia and the local Port Phillip Bank, the latter just established. They all do business on the same terms *viz*., for a running account they allow 4% per annum, for deposits 5% per annum and charge for overdrawn accounts 12% per annum and for discounts at the rate of 10% per annum. But, paper to run longer than three months is objected to for discounts. Bills on England vary. When I arrived they were at 3% discount and now at 1% premium.

Money should be paid to either of the agents or branches of the above banks if intended to be brought here so that when you arrive you are at once in cash without further trouble.

It appears to me that I have spun out rather a tough yarn but I dare say that some part of it will be read with a little interest. I was unwilling at first too hastily to form my opinion of the colony. Now that I have left it till nearly the departure of the vessel, I have scarcely time to give the opinions I have formed. Certain thus much it is that Port Phillip is peculiarly situated and favourably so, inasmuch as that not only she has great natural advantages of situation in a commercial point of view but that the country, soil and native grasses possess in themselves qualities totally different from either the Sydney district or that of V.D. Land, putting out of comparison altogether South Australia.

The inhabitants of Australia Felix are considered to be the pick from her sister colonies who have been disgusted with the convict system in the neighbourhood on the one hand and of the unproductiveness of the western settlements.

To those who are active and wish to better their condition, I have only to say—Come hither.

Patrick Edward Cussen

A Miserable State
and Total Inadequacy

As Dr Cussen made clear in this January 1840 letter to
Charles La Trobe, Melbourne's new hospital was, if
anything, worse than the first. The building combined
infirmary, gaol and police station, and was located in
what is now Flinders Lane. It was here that Cussen
performed the first surgery in Melbourne—the amputa-
tion of an arm.

I do myself the honour respectfully to represent to you the very
miserable state and total inadequacy of the small fragile building (of one apartment) used here for the reception of the sick.

Independent of the prisoners in the service of government,
amounting (including Geelong) to over 180 persons, a great
increase has taken place in the number of the assigned servants in
the district. Our beds, as Your Honour is aware, are only seven
and these do not afford accommodation (if such a term may be
used) for half of the applications under the head of convicts alone.
The consequence is that I am occasionally obliged to have two or
three patients on the floor, besides having frequently to dismiss
persons far from being convalescent in order to make room for
the more urgent cases.

From the situation of the hospital it is, during the greater part
of the year, exposed to the exhalation of stagnant water, a part
of which at least eighteen inches deep lies under the very floor,
fortunately raised high enough to prevent its rushing through.
What its effects on the human constitution are, may be supposed
from the fact of the bedding (not many months in use) being

generally damp and rotten. One of our prevalent diseases here is rheumatism, such is the state of affairs I need not express affords justice neither to the patients (warm bathing from the numerous draughts of air being nearly inadmissible) or to the efforts of the Surgeon. Many persons who come in with other diseases have gone out severely imbued with the just mentioned.

I need not, I am certain, say more to prove to Your Honour its general unhealthiness, but especially to show its total unfitness for diseases requiring the administration of mercury, such as syphilis and dysentery, both also prevalent here.

Independent of the exhalations through the floor, the roof is far from being weather-proof, and the wind rushes through the innumerable crevices in the boards (being neither bricked or plastered) forming the sides. The cold at night is frequently intolerable in consequence, so much so that sleep is occasionally a stranger to its inmates. The want of a separate apartment for patients labouring under ophthalmia (also very common here), where the glare of light may be diminished, is much required.

The loss to the public service from protracted recoveries, exclusive of the sufferings of the patients, has been in many instances, I am certain, very great indeed from the causes above mentioned.

Severe as the cold is at certain seasons, the heat is nearly equally distressing at others, the shingles (there being no ceiling) and the boarded sides, affording little protection against a burning sun. Cooking also (having no kitchen) being obliged to be performed in it, contributes at such times materially to the increased temperature, besides rendering the place dirty and uncomfortable. The want of a *Necessary* I need not detail the disadvantages of.

While on the subject of the many inconveniences we labour under, I beg to mention to Your Honour that I have been obliged ever since my arrival here to convert (for the want of any other accommodation) two apartments in my own house to the public service, one for surgery, the other a store, a circumstance which has added materially to my own private expenses, rent being so exorbitantly high here. With one other observation on our present hospital I shall have done. Its immediate proximity to the convict barracks is such that all my endeavours (besides many other disadvantages arising from the same cause) cannot prevent the frequent introduction of rum.

Port Phillip Gazette

25 January 1840—The number of dogs that are everywhere to be met with in the streets on our infant city during the moonlight nights is incredible. They roam abroad not only in parties of three and four but 'in battalions'; and it is remarkable that the 'bonny Lady Moon' seems to exercise some mysterious influence over their motions and conduct. This, to people ardent in their pursuit of animal history, &c., may be all extremely interesting, but to us who have arrived at that easy stage of existence when a night of calm and undisturbed repose is more prized than any abstruse investigation into the principles of metaphysics, whether canine or otherwise, it is altogether the reverse. The following programme of the nightly concert of these animals will, we believe, give a tolerably faithful idea of their proceedings: the first intimation is given by the master of the band in a long low prolongation of a howl, which seems peculiar to the species in these colonies. This is answered by some impatient reveller in an adjacent street, who calls to him aloud. Immediately crowds of yelping curs of all degrees congregate from the neighbouring thoroughfares, and, uniting their voices in all varieties of dissonant tones, combine to produce such an infernal commingling of sound, as no mortal tympanum can withstand…In their career they attack every spec-

imen of animated nature that crosses their path, until to their own dismal and discordant notes are now added the bellowing of cattle, the squeaking of pigs and the baaing of goats.

*

5 August 1840—Little Collins Drain. We would beg, with all due deference, to suggest to the authorities the necessity of having a bridge thrown across this *drain*, with as little delay as possible. We have been told that some of the inhabitants continue to apply to it the original name of *street*; but upon referring to the latest edition of Walker, we perceive that a street is defined to be 'a properly paved way', and that a *drain* is 'the channel through which liquors are gradually drawn'. We leave common sense to decide which is the most appropriate.

*

24 October 1840—There are certain boys (or fools) who are frequently annoying the inhabitants by discharging firearms at all hours of the night and morning, not perhaps being aware that they are liable to a penalty for such conduct. A few nights since, between twelve and one, some person alarmed the residents of Lonsdale Street and that neighbourhood by a constant firing of a gun, which might have been attended with very serious consequences, as a female in a very delicate state of health was thrown into the most alarming state of mental as well as bodily suffering, being impressed with the notion that the blacks were besieging the town. This nuisance gives rise to another; as a sudden explosion in the dead of the night fails not to arouse all the dogs in town, who keep up a concert of howling generally until the break of day.

*

5 January 1841—The river Yarra, on the purity of whose waters the health of the inhabitants of Melbourne depends, is made the receptacle for the dead bodies of all animals that die within a mile of its banks. To the deleterious effects of its brackish water, is thus superadded the abominable and poisonous qualities communicated by putrescent carcases. The compound thus formed is of a kind the most noxious which it is possible to conceive. People are allowed to deposit dead bodies in the river at any part below Batman's Hill— at least such an order was at one time foolishly made, and is not yet, so far as we are aware, rescinded. Even this qualification is not adhered to; and even if it were, would it be of much use since the influx of the tide immediately floats them up to and beyond the town. On this point as on all others, those fortunate individuals who reside beyond high-water mark, have the advantage over us, since once objects have flowed past them in the current, they cannot be, as with us, floated backwards and forwards until putridity has dissipated their constituent elements and mixed them with the stream from which the supply of a whole community is drawn. In the majority of instances it would be quite as easy to dig a grave and inter these animals, as to drag them to the banks of the stream; and we all expect that an order to this effect will not only be immediately given, but rigidly enforced.

★

30 January 1841—The number of cattle at large in the streets is a disgrace to the constabulary force, whose duty it is to attend to and endeavour to put a stop to such nuisances. We know of a gentleman who having lost some working bullocks for some time, and sought all over the country for them in vain, found them upon his arrival in Melbourne walking very quietly down Elizabeth Street.

★

Port Phillip Patriot, 18 February 1841—Swine of all descriptions, shapes and sizes have been permitted to stray about the streets of Melbourne, until they have become a public nuisance. Not long since a child was dreadfully mangled by a ferocious sow in Little Flinders Street, and more recently a child has had its ear torn off by a pig at Newtown*, yet as far as we can understand, the police have made no effort to abate the nuisance or to punish the owners of pigs allowed to stray about the streets.

★

20 February 1841—We beg to caution the public against the artifices of a set of impostors who wander about the town exhibiting subscription lists, which they pretend to have got up for the relief of individuals deprived by some unforeseen disaster of their accustomed means of support…A few evenings ago, one of these compassionate relievers of the distressed called at a certain shop in town, and after announcing with a most lugubrious visage, and in tones suited to the occasion, the sudden death of a certain tradesman, exhibited a subscription list, the proceeds of which he pretended were to be devoted to the purpose of bestowing on the remains of the deceased the honours of a Christian burial, and the residue to be applied to the relief of the distressed widow and famishing children. As the party appealed to chanced to have known the tradesman in question, he did not fail to contribute largely for the charitable object of interring his remains, although he could not avoid remarking the suddenness of the fate which had befallen the deceased, whom he had seen only a few days previously in the enjoyment of robust health, and also on the destitute circumstances in which one whom he had known to be a sober and industrious man had left his family. The sanctimonious collector of charity uttered a few pious ejaculations and remarks

* A suburb of Geelong.

having reference to his own disinterested exertions on the occasion, pocketed the shopman's booty and retired. About an hour afterwards, while sitting quietly in his shop ruminating on the precarious tenure by which our mortal existence is held, our informant was not a little confounded when the individual mechanic, for the celebration of whose funeral obsequies he had so lately contributed, burst into his shop in a state of unusually high excitement, and in the familiarity of long-established friendship fairly upset him in the ardour of his salutation.

*

14 April 1841—The healthiness of the town, we would venture to prophesy, would be almost insured by the clearing away of the forest which covers the swamp and sand between Melbourne and the beach; and yet, much to the public surprise, it is bruited about that Mr La Trobe is anxious to save the huge and ungainly mass of trees which obstruct the sea breezes reaching the town, and mainly contribute to that unsufferable heat and healthlessness of atmosphere which afflicts us during the summer months.

GEORGE GORDON MCCRAE
Magenta, Blue and Gold

George Gordon McCrae was only seven years old when he, his three siblings and mother Georgiana arrived in Port Phillip in March 1841. His father had emigrated two years earlier.

L ittle Lonsdale Street in the early forties barely existed except on paper, and, although we certainly had opposite neighbours, they were a good way beyond the narrow limit of the street of today. Next beyond us to the west was a brick cottage belonging to a very clever artisan named Landells; beyond him again, a yard in which was erected a large windmill. Whether the mill had been built on the spot, or merely put together as the parts were imported from the old country, I think it might safely have claimed to be the very first windmill that ever aired its sails in Port Phillip, though Sydney had many windmills years earlier.

Our first new (and opposite) neighbour was a settler of the name of Minifie, who pegged out his ground, established a fine cabbage garden, and, after having erected a skillion house in frame, carted in loads of tea-tree cut on the bank of the river, and we soon had the entire mystery of 'wattle-and-dab' at our fingers' ends—as also that of the laying of a lime and earthen floor, first of the kind we had ever seen. The shingling and door and window hanging did not appear to interest us quite so much as there was no novelty about it. A little to the east of Mr Minifie a foundryman established himself for a while, but, very shortly after he had commenced operations, something went wrong, and the whole place was suddenly blown to pieces. He escaped with his life and none of his neighbours were hurt…

Nearly all the country to south, north and west of us was at this period in a state of nature, with just a few cottages dotted over it here and there. On our side of Batman's Hill (then a beautiful green knoll thickly covered with round-headed she-oaks) stood the white tents of a detachment of the 26th Regiment, producing a very pretty effect as relieved against the verdant and flowery mead on which they were pitched. To the west of us and just a little to north, stretching away from beyond the base of the Flagstaff Hill, lay a beautiful blue lake…a real lake, intensely blue, nearly oval and full of the clearest salt water; but this by no means deep. Fringed gaily all round by mesembryanthemum ('pigs-face') in full bloom, it seemed in the broad sunshine as though girdled about with a belt of magenta fire. The ground gradually sloping down towards the lake was also empurpled, but patchily, in the same manner, though perhaps not quite so brilliantly, while the whole air was heavy with the mingled odours of the golden myrnong flowers and purple-fringed lilies, or ratafias. I often used (this was 1841) to visit this lake along with my father on his shooting expeditions, in the early mornings, surprising the numerous wildfowl that frequented its margin or waded about unconcernedly in its waters…

Lower down towards the south and west spread some scattered trees and patches of bushes; behind these again, a dense wall of tea-tree scrub that marked the course of the Yarra, and above which daily curled the smoke from the *Governor Arthur*, then the only steamer on the river; while, to the southward and eastward of the Blue Lake, gradually rose a pretty green hill of a gravelly formation and known to all the world of Melbourne as the 'Flagstaff Hill'…We were not long in becoming *au fait* at flag talk, and could readily determine from the respective positions of the bunting and great wicker balls on mast or yard whether the vessel 'spoken' was a steamer or sailing vessel, whether coastwise or from a long sea voyage, whether intercolonial, man-o'-war or foreigner, and so on.

RICHARD HOWITT

Port Phillip Is Infinitely Best Off

The three brothers Howitt—William, Richard and Godfrey—left an impressive legacy in the Port Phillip

District. William was a writer, Godfrey a physician and Richard a poet. Although he only lived in Australia between 1840 and 1844, Richard's *Impressions of Australia Felix* was widely regarded as the most author-itative description of Australian colonial life then available. Here we find him enjoying Melbourne and surrounds at the height of the Austral summer.

The objects which in the town first attract the stranger's notice are the flags—not the flagstones—though of these there are some, but more dirt; flags flying about auction rooms and the ever-lasting jingle of auction bells. Some dozen of such rooms there are: there is a constant gleam of crimson flags, and distressing is the clang of bells. These auctions serve instead of English pawn-brokers' shops. Here are disposed of whatever almost in the shape of merchandise can be mentioned, paid for by insolvent merchant schedules; and therefore, as they cost little, are sold amazingly cheap.

Next to the bell-noise-makers, what strikes us as quite colonial is the immense numbers of drays, many loaded with wood drawn by four, six and eight bullocks: few drays drawn by horses in proportion. There is not so much variety in the shops as in old countries, necessity having, whilst there were few, compelled the shopkeepers to deal in almost everything. Thus 'General Stores' are common. Another peculiarity: you see many people not to be mistaken; hard-face grim-visaged dry-countenanced workmen— and women too—whom at a glance you recognise to be convicts. Even amongst the richer folk there are some, not disguised by dress or wealth. The dresses of the people are peculiar too; light colours, and of lighter texture. The houses are roofed with wooden shingles—not inelegant covering—and the heads of the human creatures with straw.

Walking along Collins Street, you see of shops kept by Jews very many—Levi's, Lazarus's, Nathan's, Soloman's, Simeon's, and Benjamin's. There is no lack of Liverpool, Manchester and London Marts—grand shops (one of them the smartest in Melbourne) all kept by these people.

Other peculiarities there are, quite Australian. On our first arrival we frequently met walking about on the Eastern Hill— tame of course—two emus. Parrots, the gorgeous native parrots, abound in cages; cockatoos also, but generally at liberty. On lawns and grass-plots, hop about or bask in the sun large tame kangaroos. At one of the inns a pelican stalks in and out very leisurely. Nor is it anything extraordinary to see tame opossums and other animals of the country, tame exceedingly.

But of all objects the wild, grotesque, painted, feather-ornamented, tea-tree-besom carrying natives, with their singular costumes, war implements, and their wild gestures, grouped and scattered over the town, and with the shaggy accompaniment of dogs, give its most original feature to Melbourne...

What are we to do till dinner? The iron kettle is on the fire, and preparations are making for that meal. Meanwhile I commence this journal, and then stroll down to the Yarra. There the kingfisher, a beautiful creature, is skimming to and fro over the surface of the river. The mosquitoes are, confound them! keen as death. Look at the bellbird's nest, admire the two spotted salmon-coloured eggs. Wonder that, as the nest is so flimsy and gauze-like, the old bird does not, hung as it is so lightly on the tea-tree, press it from its place and entirely ruin it.

Noon—Burningly hot. The thermometer 100° at least. Everything Australian in extremes; the weather at least, wet or dry.

Get peas for dinner. Even about so simple a thing as gathering and shelling peas, what household associations are awakened! Link after link, the mind passes unconsciously through the vicissitudes of many years, and the period to these reflections is, a sigh. Beef, peas, suet-pudding with raisins in it, for dinner; homely food, yet healthful, and to the temperate, sufficient...

7 December — Up at the usual time. Go to Melbourne; leave my brother a quantity of peas on the premises before they are up, and return home.

Longing ardently for rain; not able to do anything in the garden, owing to its dry-as-dust condition. Hot winds blowing steadily from the north, from some inland sandy desert no doubt. We feel dusty all over. So intensely dry is the atmosphere that wood shrinks, and books have their covers curled up as if you had been reading by a hot fire; whilst the butter, hard in the morning, is melted to the transparent resemblance of olive oil before noon. Out in the sun all vegetation droops and withers, as though it would never revive. In fact some of it never does, but turns black and dies as though it had been seared with a hot iron.

8 December — No rain. Nothing to be done. Go again to Melbourne. Much amused today by the ceremonious politeness of a native woman. There she stood in a perfect state of nudity, a little way from the road, by her miam, smiling, or rather grimacing; for there is nothing of heart or intellect in that movement of the black countenance. She waved her hand and head to me, not ungracefully: the trick imitated from some Melbournite. The blacks are admirable mimics, catching up to the life of civilised speech and action. 'Good morning, sir!' say the piccaninies with the utmost gravity. 'Where you go?' asks another…

Today, soon after my return home, being alone in the house, I heard the most melancholy noise in the bush, not far off: I thought someone had met with a serious accident, and ran out terrified. It proved to be the fore-running announcement of three coming black fellows. Two women, one with a piccaniny at her back, had turned down to the ford below. Three men came forward. One of them had on a short white sailor's frock, and common black-wool hat. The others had brown blankets wrapped round them loosely. Their hair was ornamented with white cockatoo feathers, and profusely with kangaroo teeth. Their object was to beg white money. When I turned one of my pockets to show them I had nothing, they laughed in their loud manner, and felt at the other. So away they went, dissatisfied; and they, with the woman and child, busied themselves in crossing the ford. Soon they disappeared in the bush on the other side of the river. The men were armed with spears and waddies.

9 December—Rise at four o'clock; the Australian jay laughing away the darkness, and the magpies with their rich warblings welcoming the light.

No rain. Nothing to be done. The same day after day. The sun intensely hot. The cicadas in millions, making the very air dizzy with their dissonance. Ten thousand spinning-jennies could not match them. The noise is the most wearisome imaginable. This is the cicada year. Last summer there were, owing to what cause I know not, very few of them.

Picked up half an old *Weekly Dispatch*, containing extracts from two letters, each from Sydney or its district, giving miserable accounts of that part of Australia. There is a great deal of truth in the statements, though many in England, whose minds are quite of a glow when they think of these warm pastoral altitudes, would fain disbelieve them. I daily hear worse and worse accounts of these colonies, and do honestly think (God help us!) Port Phillip is infinitely best off, both in its natural position and climate; being warmer than Van Diemen's Land, freer from frogs and frosts in winter; free too, from Van Diemenian summer frosts: and better watered by rain—scattering westerly winds, than Sydney.

JOHN HENRY HOWITT

I Enjoyed It Exceedingly

John Howitt, the son of physician Godfrey Howitt, was eleven years old when he penned this letter to his cousin Alfred, who was still in England. The little Johnny Were referred to in the letter is Jonathan Were, the son of J. B. Were. Alfred Howitt, the recipient of the letter, was to go on to an illustrious career, recovering the bodies of Burke and Wills, and recording much valuable information on the native tribes of south-eastern Australia.

1 March 1842—My dear Alfred, Are you alive and well, this and fifty other things I want to know about you; Anna Mary's letters to Mamma did not say one syllable about you, I never thought I could have been so angry with Anna Mary who was so kind to me at Esher and in London, I felt very much inclined to wish her letters into the candle. I hope she will never again forget to write about you and I will forgive her this once. And I think you deserve a scold too, for you promised you would write to me as soon as you were at Heidelberg and give me a long account of its famous castle. Mamma has often told me when I wanted something to do to begin you a Journal but I thought I would wait till your letter came but I am at last tired of waiting. Today is very hot, the thermometer 96 in the shade, just the heat that suits me. I was very poorly all last winter and kept almost entirely to the sofa but the hot weather has at last began to do me good, though I do not sit out of doors as I did last summer I get plenty of fresh air for we keep all our windows and doors open.

4 March—Our dear little poet Charlie has many times been ill, he is cutting teeth; now he is lying quite still on Mamma's lap and takes very little notice of us so different to when he was well.

Oh what a fat merry little creature he then was; he has never been so ill before and Papa is very much afraid he will not get better. I don't know what we should do without him he is such a very sweet entertaining little creature.

13 March—When I began this journal I had no idea I should have such a sorrowful subject to write about Our darling little Charlie died on the 9th at 5 in the morning He is buried in the garden. I shall put this by till we feel cheerful again.

17 March—I have had such a pleasant drive to day, down to the Beach. The very sight of the sea did me good, it was extremely green with just the tops of the waves tipped with foam. Many ships, schooners &c were lying at anchor at Willams Town. Three miles beyond, the *Manlius* was in quarantine, the *Pathfinder* with many of her sails set was tacking out of the bay; the *Corsair* steamer from Launceston was coming up, some boats close to us were pulling out to sea and famously they were rocked up and down. It was altogether a beautiful sight; I did long to be on board the *Pathfinder* for I believe another journey would do me good...

12 April—I have been staying thirteen weeks at the Plenty with Mamma and came home yesterday—I enjoyed it exceedingly, all but the drive there and back which shook me too much. Uncle Robert made me a little carriage to ride in, and took me several short drives in it. I went to see some trees that Willie had felled when he was there as thick as himself which he had made a famous boast of. Uncle Robert has a very nice garden, it is down in a flat you go to it by a zigzag walk; his vines were fourteen feet high. They have abundance of melons, the pigs are regularly fed on them; while we were there the dray and four bullocks brought up a load out of the garden, for the rats had taken a fancy to them there. The bellbirds sing all day long at the Plenty; I like to hear them much better than the laughing jackasses. I read *The Talisman*, *Old Mortality* and *Ivanhoe* while I was there which delighted me exceedingly and I

am now reading *Quentin Durward*. As we came home we called at the Yarra to see Uncle Richard. The river winds there very prettily, I had just a peep into the cottage but it did not look very clean I assure you. Mamma got out but I took my notes sitting in the carriage.

29 April—All the talk lately has been about the bushrangers who have [sic] in the Plenty district, the first there have been in Australia Felix. They are a party of four well armed and mounted, who have robbed more than thirty stations beside highway robbery, but their reign of terror did not last more than a week. They commit their daring deeds in broad daylight. Would you not think it extremely pleasant to be bailed up in a corner with someone standing over you with a pistol threatening you with instant death if you stirred; this they do while other bushrangers ransack the hut of what they want and then are off to the next station. Two parties of gentlemen and a few of the mounted police went in pursuit of them, one of the party five in number at last got on their track and at Mr Hunter's the bushrangers were interrupted just as they were going to sit down to a breakfast of roast ducks. The gentlemen of the house having been ordered from table to make way for their superiors. When they saw the party in search of them they called out stand to your arms men, they then rushed out and fired a volley but in retreating to the hut the ringleader got separated from the rest and after a very desperate resistance, three of the gentlemen having been wounded, the man was shot in self defence. The other three after firing sixty shots at last surrendered and are brought in for trial. Uncle's escaped a visit from these bushrangers and only heard of them the night before they were taken.

Edith has been a week at Brighton and is to stay two more. It is by the seaside. There is a nice firm beach. I dare say she will be fonder of running about on the beach than attending to her lessons, though Miss Ascham, a lineal descendant of Roger

Ascham, is the teacher at Mrs Were's. Little Johnny Were is a very funny boy, he says he does so wish he was married his Mamma is so cross to him. He is only four years old.

Edmund Finn

The Corporation

Irishman Edmund Finn arrived in Melbourne in 1841. In 1845 he joined the *Port Phillip Herald* and three years later was appointed clerk of the papers of the Legislative Council—an excellent position from which to document the development of the colony. His first anecdotal history of Melbourne was published in 1880 titled *The Garryowen Sketches*; his *nom de plume* was from Owen's Garden on the outskirts of his native Limerick. Finn relied on documents or older residents' recollections for the period prior to his arrival, but thereafter his own witness was more than adequate to support a marvellous and detailed account.

The Melbourne Corporation Act of 1842 brought the first semblance of democratic government to the city. Its first mayor elected under the Act was Henry Condell, the son of an Edinburgh wine merchant whose fondness for 'a drop' was renowned. Condell's greatest difficulty lay in persuading the citizenry to pay rates, and his reign lasted just one year.

The returned twelve were almost beside themselves with the new-blown honours showered on them by public suffrage, and lost no time in making the most of their novel situation. In private conclave they decided upon organising an imposing 'turn out' in the shape of a public procession through the town, on the occasion of the swearing-in of the mayor before the resident judge. Mr Justice Willis was consulted and was only too glad of an opportunity of airing his 'little brief authority' before the *oi polloi*. Had he descended to modern times he would have vegetated into the most inflated 'plebiskiter' known to Victorian history. The preparatory arrangements were put *en train*, and included the adoption of a particular uniform or livery, in which the 'corporators' were to make 'dons' of themselves, and this was of very easy adjustment. According to sumptuary regulation, each alderman and councillor was to be decked in a 'belltopper', white shirt, and 'choker' to match, blue cloth coat with wide swallowtail (the breast and tail lined with white satin), and the coat-front to be starred with the blaze of large VR gold-gilt buttons, black doeskin trousers, white Marseilles vest, snow-kid gloves, and high-heeled Wellington boots polished to a shine in which a monkey might shave himself...By special favour, the mayor was permitted to be 'unbelltoppered' on this august occasion, and under circumstances yet to be described...

The 13th December was appointed for the demonstration, and there was a very general turn-out of the inhabitants to behold the exhibition. An invitation to the Masonic body was accepted, and as the mayor had no official gown to put on, he borrowed a Masonic robe of crimson silk, arrayed in which he appeared as if clad in the morning dress of some obese dowager. A town band rattled away during the forenoon, and the 'stormy music of the drum' beat up all the washed and unwashed urchins in Melbourne to headquarters.

The chief constable, and such rank and file of the constabulary as could be spared, were drawn up as a guard of honour outside the door of the Royal Hotel, and an old half-cranky customer named Hooson, afterwards appointed 'street-keeper' was acting as unattached marshal or conductor, waving a short staff, to which he fastened a square of red calico. As noon approached, the mayor, aldermen and councillors appeared at the rendezvous and, in the phraseology of one of the newspapers, 'they looked quite gorgeous'. They paraded in the long-room of the hotel, and when the mayor had indued 'purple and fine linen', he reappeared in the hall, marched to the front door, and looked around him with all the turgent vanity of a pompous turkey-cock...

The movement progressed without interruption until near William Street, when the ensign-bearer, who was some yards in advance, made his appearance. A man was driving a bullock past St James' Church, on his way to the slaughterhouses, and the animal's eye caught the mad fluttering of Hooson's ruddy streamer. Hooson looked round, became alarmed, and executed a figure of serpentine posturing which would have done credit to a bandelero in a Spanish bullfight. Now, a man waving a red flag as a danger signal on a railway line may, perchance, succeed in stopping a coming train, but to shunt a half-wild bull by whirling a red rag in the air, is about the very last thing to succeed.

The bullock at length made a plunge towards the standard-bearer, who ran for his life, followed by his pursuer. The runaway howled nearly as loud as the quadruped bellowed, and an only, though not a pleasant, chance of safety offered for Hooson. There was then at the junction of William and Little Flinders streets, near the Custom House Reserve, a chasm nearly brimful of thick slush, and into this the future 'street-keeper' plunged head foremost, carrying his banner with him, and burying himself all but his head in the muck, came to grief in a slimy, instead of a gory, bed, with the red drapery as a martial cloak around him. The bullock did not follow him, but with a parting snort of contempt at the almost invisible signifier, started away in the direction of the Yarra falls...

Meanwhile the civic display had gone its way as if nothing had happened, and in due course arrived at the courthouse, corner of King and Bourke streets, when further progress was impeded by the immense miscellaneous crowd…After some delay and difficulty the mayor marched in with head erect, his hair stiffened as with starch and likened to a crown of long bristles. Condell, followed by his colleagues, strutted forward in his trailing red vestment looking like an ancient flamingo…Mr J. D. Pinnock, the deputy-registrar administered the necessary oath to the mayor, who kissed the greasy, insanitary-looking Bible with a solemn face and loud smack…The company [then] retired, and the procession, considerably shorn of its attractive accessories, re-formed and proceeded to interview Mr Superintendent LaTrobe.

At his office on Batman's Hill where the magnates were received by the sub-treasurer (Captain Lonsdale) and by him ushered into the august presence of the superintendent, who sat in state, arrayed in the uniform of a lieutenant-governor, and wearing the 'hat and feathers' which in after years were so ridiculed by the *Argus* newspaper. Captain Lonsdale announced them seriatim by name and official designation, and the superintendent met them with a cordial courtesy. A lengthy and interesting conversation ensured, confined mainly to topics municipal…

After the interview the remains of the procession, with the mayor leading, commenced its return trip along Spencer Street to Lonsdale Street via Elizabeth Street back to the Royal Hotel, where the mayor was given three cheers, and the fag-end of the day's pageantry quickly disbanded.

LUCY ANNA EDGAR

Among the Black Boys

From 1845 Lucy Edgar spent six years of her childhood at the Aboriginal Institution on Merri Creek, where her father was superintendent. The institution housed Aboriginal boys who had been gathered by the 'Black Protector' from around the countryside. The children were kept there in order to educate, protect and 'save' them through Christianity.

I was but a little girl when my father was appointed Super-intendent of the Aboriginal Institution at the junction of the Yarra Yarra and the Merri Creek near Melbourne. How well I remember our first introduction to the place that was to be our home for three years! The great rough, heavily laden cart, the only vehicle fit for the fearful state of the bush road, amid the contents of which grandmamma, mamma, and I were packed more closely than was convenient, laboured slowly along, whilst papa aided the carter in his ever recurring difficulty with the panting horse.

Our three miles' journey from Melbourne—only *three* miles, and it seemed endless—was not completed before the darkness overtook us; the rain poured drearily; the cart wheels seemed to take turn about in going up and down like a seesaw; and to complete our discomfiture, papa, who had been residing at the schoolhouse for some weeks, and was now our pioneer, announced that the last bit of the road was 'the worst' and that we had better 'hold on'. And we did hold on in silent terror, while the horse plunged suddenly down a miniature precipice, rushed down the hill with the carter hanging on at his head, staggered and stumbled through the Merri Creek, and as suddenly began to climb the opposite hill, which, in spite of his struggling efforts, could not be surmounted.

We were obliged to leave the cart where it stood and plod up the muddy steep to the house, where one light twinkled at us through the darkness. Holding on to one another, papa coo-eyeing and shouting at the top of his voice, 'Charley, Jackey, Jemmy, bring a light!' We at last saw a door open, and half a dozen black faces peering out over a lantern, and in another minute we were introduced to the kitchen, where nothing struck me but a yawning cavern of a fireplace, a roaring fire, and a sloppy earthen floor. Then up two steps into a passage, through a door, and we were in the parlour...

We were too thankful for shelter and warmth just then to find fault with our accommodations, and immediately approached the blazing wood fire. This fireplace was not so cavernous as the kitchen, but I noticed that the jambs and even the floorboards adjacent were in some parts blackened with burning. We looked around for seats and discovered a rough three-legged stool, not a sign of furniture besides; so contented ourselves with pulling off our wet garments, whilst papa and the black boys helped the cart up to the door, and disencumbered it of that part of our luggage we had judged sufficient for the first day or two.

In a short time our parlour was furnished with a table and chairs; some bedding and change of raiment was huddled into another room, which had no door, and by the time we were re-dressed and re-entered the parlour, it looked quite cheerful, with the kettle steaming energetically over the fire; while two or three boys who were helping to lay the table tried to hide shyly behind each other at our approach, stealing wondrous glances out of their lustrous black eyes, and finally, when mamma addressed them, vanishing with a great display of ivory into the kitchen, where they kept up an incessant jabber-jabber, diversified by unrestrained laughter, during the whole of our first meal at the Merri Creek.

The next morning, child-like, I was up with the lark—I should have said the swallow, for we have no larks in our part of the world—poking and peering into every nook and cranny where a little girl could possibly push herself. The house (I magnify it by that title) was really pleasantly situated. The Yarra flowed only a few yards in front; beyond the river rose a thickly wooded hill; behind the house, at a rather greater distance, murmured the Merri Creek, now a fordable stream, in flood-time a mighty torrent. On one side, some hundred yards further, the two streams joined, and at their junction on low ground stood Dight's Mill, a three-storey building, above it was Dight's House, a very nice residence: these were our nearest neighbours. On the other side of our dwelling were the stockyard, paddocks, and then the bush.

Our habitations, for there were two, were composed of 'wattle and dab'; they had no ceilings, and only our parlour and two bedrooms had floors. The walls were unpapered, the boards uneven, and seemingly intent on having as little of close quarters as possible. But our three best rooms had french windows, and the front of the house boasted a verandah; a primitive one certainly, the posts being stems of young trees, and the floor earth.

The kitchen was a long low place, dirty, damp, and miserable; you needed to pick your way between the little pools that gathered as rain dripped off the roof. There was another great barn of a room adjoining the kitchen, which made a capital storeroom after some renovating.

The other building stood apart; just one large room with three or four windows, which was afterwards divided; one half being made the boys' sleeping apartment, the other dignified by the title of schoolroom, and used accordingly…

The first day of our arrival was of course a scene of bustle. The weather cleared up, goods and chattels were unpacked,

kitchen utensils displayed, and their uses explained to the wondering assistants, who had never beheld most of the articles before,
and began timidly to inquire their names.

Of course their stock of English words was very small, and
they mixed so many native words with their English that it was
difficult to comprehend their meaning. Their pronunciation was
different to that of any coloured people that I ever heard. They
laid great stress on the vowel sounds, sometimes giving the full
and accurate expression to words that we are accustomed to
shorten; such as potato, which they rendered po-ta-to, laying the
utmost stress on the first and last syllables.

But in most cases they added to and extended their words to an
outrageous length, putting two or three vowels in the place of one.
It is almost impossible to give an idea in writing of the peculiarity of
their pronunciation; they sounded *big*, *be-eg*, and if they wanted to
give greater emphasis, and convey the idea of the superlative of
size, they added yet another vowel, and made it *be-e-eg*. 'Plenty,'
was another word that they murdered in the same manner; it was
always, if used in the mildest term, *planty*, that was the positive
degree; to make it comparative, they put in another *a*, *plaanty*, and
to express the superlative, three *a*'s were requisite.

It will be noticed that in almost all native names the vowels
abound, though there are not generally enough of them employed
to give an accurate idea of the native pronunciation. Very little can
be said for the euphony of their language; they talked generally so
fast and so loud that it just sounded like the unmeaning jargon
known by the title of 'High Dutch'.

Never were boys more anxious to learn, or quicker in picking
up the first elements of a language. 'What this fellar?' one would
ask, pointing to a cup; 'What call this fellar?' indicating a saucer;
and much amused they were at finding that cup, saucer, and
spoon belonged to each other; or, as they phrased it, 'Him belong
to him.'

Everything was handled and admired; a pair of bellows particularly. After learning their name and use, they employed them
for several minutes blowing into each other's eyes, and down
their mouths, stopping now and then to indulge in contortions of
feature that might have set Job a-laughing…

The kitchen was wind and water tight; the floor made level,
and a cellar entrance formed in one corner; the cellar itself being
under the house, dug out of the earth. A great convenience it
proved in the hot days; for butter, meat, milk, everything edible
and drinkable could be preserved there cool and solid, even at
times when the butter ran to oil if allowed to stand five minutes on
our parlour table. We sometimes took a candle down in the cellar,
and buttered the bread, or cut the meat there; and when the atmosphere above ground was like the breath of a furnace, the cellar
was my refuge; I could sit there as cool as a watermelon, whereas
in our rooms I could not bear my frock on my shoulders, and a
pinafore was altogether dispensed with.

As for the boys, they were used to it. They did not dislike the
heat half so much as the cold; but it was always thought excusable
for them to be lazy on those days of burning heat; and they generally took advantage of the holiday to bathe and dive in the river.

Our garden was made and fenced in by this time; it extended
round both the buildings, with the exception of a plain surface,
several yards; in width, left clear in front of the schoolhouse for
the boys' playground. The garden was planted with various
vegetables, native shrubs, fruit trees, and all the flowers we could
obtain. Many a begging expedition was organised to get more
flowers; great was the labour bestowed before some of them
flourished; others took kindly to the light sandy soil and flaunted
their colours gaily in the sunbeams. Round the verandah's ugly
posts we twined creepers and roses, until the front of our bush
cottage looked as we may suppose 'my cottage near a wood', did
in the olden time. Before our front windows bloomed our gayest

flowers; but few of them were the dear old English blossoms mamma so dearly prized; the polyanthuses certainly vindicated their claim to be noticed; and the cowslips—oh! there were never such cowslips, so large, so yellow, and the bunches so full of bells, as our cowslips at the Merri Creek; we have counted a hundred bells on one stalk. The native shrubs grew fastest and largest. The wide carriage path from the playground to the stockyard gate was lined with them; little tiny roots when planted, they sprang up in a few months to the height of a man, and when they put forth their white or lilac blossoms there was no sight prettier.

Gooseberries and currants would do nothing but wither just as we expected to enjoy the fruit; but the delicious nectarine, the grape, and watermelon, flourished with little trouble.

Outside the garden fence, enclosed by a high palisading, was the stockyard, so called, though all our livestock consisted of two cows, a calf, and Dora, our good little mare, and servant of all work; cart, carriage, or saddle, nothing came amiss to Dora, and she was in requisition for each alternately. A capital and substantial coach-house was built of logs adjoining the schoolhouse, and thatched with straw; there the plain little carriage we used for our journeys to Melbourne was safe and dry, let it rain ever so heavily. Papa could not always find time to drive us, nor could a boy always be spared either; so mamma learnt to use the reins herself; and such is the change effected by the habit, that she could soon drive as rapidly up and down our hills and over the creek, as on the level road, even when it was growing dusk; whilst I, who had been so terrified at first sight of the place, sat fearlessly by her side.

Pigsty, fowl yard, goose yard, and goat shed, all compact little places, and all behind our house, bounded by the Merri Creek, were filled with plump and noisy creatures, the delight and pride of our boys; whose love for dumb animals was always expressing itself in acts of attention to their wants. Ducks, chickens, turkeys, guinea-fowl, and our splendid tribe of geese, at one time one hundred in number, all these excited the admiration of the boys in consequence of their various forms and habits.

They were so delighted to watch the long flights our geese took sometimes, circling the paddocks, and coming down in a body on the bosom of the Yarra or returning home in slow and stately march of an evening, in long single files, with a gander at the head of each detachment.

The boys gave names to all their pets, but only two come up to remembrance now; these were a most hideous little whining dog, called 'Bobby', a shaky-legged, puny-bodied, shivering little imp of a thing, that Tommy loved as the apple of his eye; and a hollow-backed, plump-bodied pig that they called 'Publican'.

The manner in which the creature got his name was this: at the earlier stage of their school days, papa brought home an illustrated alphabet to amuse them; and when they came to 'P for Publican', a very corpulent man, with more body than his legs seemed able to carry, they roared till the house rang again.

'What for him eat so much?' asked Charley. 'Black fellar never eat so much, black fellar never beeg one fat.'

'What call him?' asked another.

'Publican.'

'Him publican keep house sell rum?'

'Yes, keeps a public house.'

'Him beeg one drink, beeg one eat—beeeg one publican'; and they all relapsed into merriment.

After this there was no hesitation as to what term they should apply to anything or any person over-corpulent; 'publican' was the universal word. Of course the fat pig was a 'publican', and their conversation of an evening would run on in this way: 'Bobby got him supper,' 'Me milk him goat tonight,' 'Publican ran away today,' or 'Publican got beeg one belly tonight.' And it sounded rather strange some time afterwards to hear Charley, coming in with a knife in his hand, say 'I killed him; I killed the publican!'

Anonymous

Melbourne As It Is and As It Ought to Be

Few in early Melbourne seemed to give much thought to the planning of their city, but the anonymous author of this pamphlet, written in 1849–50, indicates that the citizenry were not entirely without sentiment on this front.

Whatever is done *now* in planning towns, laying down lines of road, selecting sites for townships, &c, receives augmented importance from the impress it must give to the future. The main streets and approaches of a new town are, so to speak, the skeleton to which everything done subsequently must be referred and adapted. Collectively they form the *rough sketch* of the future city. If your first sketch is defective or deformed, not all the depth of Rembrandt, nor the splendour of Titian's colouring, can hide or compensate for the original blunder: and so, if your first plan for a new city is defective, you may adorn, and alter, and contrive, and patch, but you cannot rectify the fundamental error...

Surveyors and systematic improvers have ever been as devotedly attached to straight lines and right angles as artists have detested them. They seem not to have been daunted by the fact—or more probably never thought of it—that throughout the whole range of nature, amid her unnumbered and matchless beauties, you can extremely rarely find a straight line—never a right angle.

What then are the true principles of which a town should be planned? What are the requirements to be fulfilled? Those requirements will be modified somewhat by climate and the national habit of the people, yet are they to a great extent the same in all ages and among all nations. Thus in all the western nations, convenience has dictated, the desirableness of forming an open space in the centre of the town, for public resort and traffic—whether called a *Forum*, a *Piazza*, a *Platz* or a *Market Square*...During the heats of summer and the rains of winter they equally offer an agreeable promenade, a pleasant rendezvous for the purposes of business and pleasure, a kind of public exchange for commerce, politics and news.

On one side of the square should rise the 'local habitation' of municipal dignity—the town hall—mixed up with, and recalling all the historic associations of the place, and throwing its long shadows over the paved square; its clock being the public time-keeper, and its great bell commemorating every occasion of public rejoicing and public sorrow. On another side of the square should be an establishment more closely identified with our own times—the post office, the focus of international and provincial inter-course, the colonial centre of a system extending its ramifications over the globe. In the midst of the square a fountain should throw up its sparkling column, cooling the air and refreshing the ear with the music of its falling splash; or if a fountain should be impossible, an equestrian statue or monumental column, or monolithic obelisk, might supply its place; though far inferior in beauty, as indeed everything must be, to a fountain, with its silvery jet, and its shower of falling brilliants, and its melodious murmur.

The public buildings next claim attention. Their sites should be determined by the natural levels of the town, by their respective uses, and by the public convenience. Elevated positions, easily accessible on all sides, are the most proper. Wherever placed, they should be united with each other by broad streets, twice the width of ordinary ways; and access should be given to them from all parts of the town, by means of similar great arterial streets, capacious enough to receive the living tide of men that will occasionally roll along them, to witness imposing spectacles and solemn ceremonials. Other similar main streets, diverging from the heart of the town, like the rays of the spider's web, should give ready approach to the city from the suburbs and the surrounding country. The intersection of these principal streets will form open spaces of irregular form, which may be enlarged at pleasure by cutting off the corners of the converging masses of buildings. Whoever has seen such spots, when the slant rays of the rising or setting sun just catch the summits of the buildings, must have been struck with the magic effect of lengthening vistas and strongly contrasted light and shade. Such places or squares, in conjunction with the main arterial streets opening upon them, serve to ventilate and purify the most crowded quarters; the broad streets acting as tubes to convey the fresh air from the country into the heart of the town.

Our ideal town should have a noble river, margined with massive quays and public and private buildings, which, sweeping round with the windings of the stream, should charm the eye with all the beauty of evanescent lines and ever-shifting perspectives; while the massive stone bridge, contrasting with the gossamer delicacy of the suspension, should unite the opposite banks. Finally, *Boulevards*, or wide open roads, with rows of trees here and there, and broad footways, should encircle the town, and separate it from the suburbs, serving at once as streets and promenades.

Such is our ideal of a city. Now turn to Melbourne; look on this picture and on that! It may be objected that it was impossible to do all this in a new country; that we had neither money nor labour to do it. Very true: but have we done what we could? Have we laid out a noble plan which might hereafter be worthily filled up? Have we drawn our rough sketch aright, leaving it to time to complete the picture? Have we laid the foundations of a great edifice which might hereafter grow into an august pile? Alas, we have done nothing of all this. Melbourne boasts no large central square, possesses no main arterial streets, conducting to the heart of the town, ventilating its back lanes, and carrying health to its crowded quarters; has no broad suburban roads, giving easy access to the country, no boulevards, no great lines of communication uniting the public buildings. It has its river; but the lines of the houses on the banks, instead of gracefully sweeping round with the stream, run off at a tangent from it. In short, the only skill exhibited in the plan of Melbourne is that involved in the use of square and compass. We have planned our metropolis as we should plan a coal pit.

Georgiana Huntly McCrae

Separation!

Georgiana McCrae's journals were published through the influence of grandson Hugh McCrae in the 1930s. She had a wonderful eye for incongruity. Here she takes us into Governor La Trobe's residence on the morning the Port Phillip District's independence from the colony of New South Wales is announced.

11 November 1850 — At dinner Mr Harding was telling us about plantain leaves used for plates in India, when there came the sound of wheels grating on the carriage-way followed by the noise of at least two sticks hammering on the door. Mr La Trobe sent his servant to answer the summons, and, while he arranged his neckerchief, hinted at the possible arrival of a new governor in search of a night's lodging! Enter the mayor, Nicholson the grocer also, the

ex-mayor Augustus Frederick Adolphus Greeves...Nicholson, with one of his fingers tied in a rag, holding an Adelaide newspaper.

'Your Honour, allow me to draw your attention to the fact that the Separation Bill has passed through both Houses. The news is spreading quickly, and I shall be unable to restrain the people—' Here Augustus Frederick coughed, as though *he* would like to add something, when Mr La Trobe quizzically remarked, 'The Bill is incomplete until it has the Royal Sign Manual.' Nevertheless, he gave the required permission to celebrate that night, and the mayor scuttled off to light his private bonfire which is to be the signal for general jubilation.

16 November—A day full of surprises and excitement. At 6 a.m. the saxhorn band began to play a reveillée outside 'The Châlet': a performance which had been kept secret even from Mr La Trobe himself, who now appeared in a flowered dressing gown, straining his eyes at the window. He held my sleeve while some of the gentlemen put down their horns to sing 'Hark, Hark the Lark!' in a key that was too high for them; yet it sounded better than the French *aubade* which immediately followed. After this they recovered their instruments and gave us stirring polka tunes, although poor Madame, who had one of her neuralgic headaches, would gladly have forgone that part of the programme. Mr La Trobe then walked out onto the veranda to put an end to the music, but with the opposite effect, for, no sooner did the performers behold him, than they joined, some with voices, some with saxhorns, in a tremendous rendition of the national anthem. His Honour bowed, and they would have gone through it again had I not led him into the house...So they marched away, still playing polkas.

Upset by the saxhorn band, and fearful of any cannonading, Mrs La Trobe appointed me her deputy at the opening of the bridge, an arrangement hardly completed, when Mr Edward Bell blew a bugle to announce his arrival in a carriage and pair.

Behold me now, equipped in Madame's black satin polonaise

jacket, trimmed with Australian swansdown (a present from Mr Cowper, of Sydney) and my own grey silk bonnet! The Superintendent, having first of all handed me into the carriage, entered it himself followed by Agnes, Nellie, Cecile, Charlie and Mademoiselle Beguine. Adolphe de Meuron sat on the box, beside Mr Bell, and thus snugly packed together, we came to the Treasury, where Mr Bell changed places with His Honour who drove us, more slowly than his predecessor, to the corner of Swanston and Collins streets, and thence, after a view of the procession, to our proper stand—beside the Bishop's barouche—in front of the Prince of Wales Hotel. From this point of vantage, we had a clear sight of the hill, with its tent and a few field-pieces, opposite, while constantly moving banners, very small in the distance, glittered and went out again, according as the phalanxes changed places in the sun. Horsemen had hard work to keep onlookers from trespassing on the field, and we witnessed many rushes, but none of which broke the line. For want of control, the cheering was ragged, and, no doubt, if the two lots of instrumentalists that followed the saxhorn band had been more *d'accord*, the music would have been better.

At 12 a.m. Mademoiselle Beguine, who had been observing the hill through her *lunette d'approche**, exclaimed that she saw smoke, and, on the instant, there arose a prodigious noise of guns, the signal for us to set out for the bridge. Mr La Trobe gathered up the reins and we proceeded at a majestic pace until we reached the middle of the arch, seventy-five feet from either bank. Here His Honour stopped, and merely saying 'I declare Prince's Bridge open', drove to the opposite side. During our progress thither, we were passed by a procession of Freemasons, and each man, as he went forward, ducked his head to 'Madame', whose double in the black satin jacket replied with the most gracious salaams.

* Telescope.

At the summit of the hill, Mr La Trobe alighted, and, standing by the flap of the tent, spoke a few words suitable to the occasion. Mayor Nicholson said something supplementary, after which the Superintendent proposed the Queen's health, this being drunk off in small ale drawn from a barrel under a cart where it had been placed to keep cool.

His Honour then returned to us, and we accompanied him (walking) to the Botanic Gardens, where two thousand buns were distributed to children of all denominations; deduct from these, two begged by Mr Eyre Williams for his little boy, and one each to Charlie, Cecile and Nellie La Trobe.

Mademoiselle and myself were so hungry, we felt we could have eaten the whole two thousand between us!

The Superintendent drove us back to Jolimont, Charlie beside him, carrying the ceremonial sword. On the journey, a few spots of rain made me anxious on account of Madame's best jacket which had already been stickied by Nellie's saved-up bun. Then, when we arrived at 'The Châlet', the wind blew through the house, throwing the doors open, and the children made so much noise shutting them again that poor Mrs La Trobe retired to her bed. The servants were still absent, but the gardener's old helping-man, who had stayed at home, brought in a round of beef with vegetables, and on these we dined *en famille*, most heartily.

EDMUND FINN

The Origin of 'Larrikin'

About 1850, there was in the city police force, a Sergeant John (or as he was commonly called, 'Jack') Staunton, a medium-sized, bull-headed Irishman, with a darkish face, slightly asthmatic, and thick lips, through which, when giving evidence in the police court, he slightly 'slavered', and thereby acquired a habit of frequent application of his coat-cuff to his mouth.

Staunton, though somewhat dull, was a plodding and highly useful officer, and in his day did good service in ridding the community of some of the wicked excrescences which have existed in every state and every age. Little Bourke Street, with its purlieus, was then as now the main nursery of city crime, and Staunton was not only a power but a terror to the thieving and night-birding fraternity.

Staunton's education was on a rather limited scale, and in his vocabulary he was wont to include as 'larkers' everyone engaged in nocturnal illegalities about town, especially disturbances originating in public houses, or indulged in by persons during the enjoyment of late hours. Upon such offenders 'Old Jack' had what is known as a terrible 'down', and frequently appeared as police prosecutor in such cases. There was something wrong about the tip of his tongue, rather too big for its place, I thought, which imparted a lisp and stammer to the enunciation of some of his words, especially those where double consonants interposed, and one especially, 'larking', he could never distinctly master. The 'r' and the 'k' conjoined seemed too much for him, though separately he could manage them well. But when both united against him the guttural and palatal requiring for their amalgamation, a quivering motion of the tongue, with its pressure against the roof of the mouth, and a depression of the under jaw, was a mouthful quite beyond his capacity. Therefore, when a magistrate would ask Sergeant Staunton what his charge was against a particular prisoner, he would give his lips a wipe and a screw, and try to answer 'He was a lar —' the 'k' caused him to stammer and draw breath, and his plunging towards the far end of the word, he floundered between the 'r' and the 'k', and to enable him to reach the terminus, the 'r' was duplicated and backed by an 'i', a third syllable being so formed, which Staunton employed as a stepping-stone, and jumped across. The response therefore, took this form, 'He was a lar-ri-kin, your Worship', and so was coined a word now of common use, which will yet be incorporated in the English language, like other slang expressions seemingly so necessary that one wonders how they could ever have been done without...

The larkers in old Melbourne would as soon think of cutting their own throats as robbing a man, and I have found no authenticated instance of their having offered insults to any woman passed in the streets in their intoxicated raids.

The old skylarkers were drawn from the cream instead of the scum of society, the scions of families of good blood and reputation, who came to Australia in search of fortunes—gay sparks, some with light and few with heavy purses, the contents of which were sent flying in every direction. Many of them took up land in various parts of Port Phillip, commencing on the Plenty, and trending northwards along the rivers in the interior on the way to the Murray. From this aggregation stood out prominently what was known as the 'Goulburn Mob', dashing, gentlemanly, intellectual and good-looking fellows, who led a monotonous, industrious life in the bush; but the moment they got a chance to flock to Melbourne, went the pace there in a manner conducive to the health of neither body nor pocket, enjoyed life while they could, then returned to the drudgery of station work, and so came and went until the 'wild oats' were not only sown, but the crop reaped with a vengeance. Some of them, at the turn of the tide, settled down quietly and amassed fortunes, afterwards enjoyed both in the colony and at home; but death made sad havoc with many, for the best and the brightest and the gayest of the frolicsome scapegraces went down before its remorseless scythe.

WILLIAM STRUTT

Black Thursday

William Strutt arrived in Melbourne on 5 July 1850.
Seven months later he was witness to the vast bushfires
that blazed their way through Victoria on 6 February
1851, an event which became known as Black Thursday.
Strutt was an artist, and his painting depicting this event
is widely regarded as his most dramatic work.

It was on a Thursday morning, 6 February 1851, that the sun
rose lurid and red and the wind increased with stifling heat,
producing such a deadly languor that it must be felt to be realised.
The unextinguished little fire spread in the dry grass, and soon got
too fierce to beat out in the usual way with green boughs and
altogether beyond control. Thus it spread and coursed down the
ranges into the more level country, the burning patch widening
with the furious wind, till eventually it became one mighty, irresistible wave of flames about fifty miles broad, sweeping on! on!
on!! It leaped over the creeks, burnt fences, huts, stations; seemed
to spring into the trees, and with two or three whirls blazed up
and enveloped the whole mass of foliage, which roared and crack-
led till consumed: then sped on to another tree to serve it in like
manner. The flocks of sheep were burnt up by thousands, also
the cattle and the horses.

The terrified squatters and settlers hastily made their escape,
leaving everything. The sick, put into drays, were hurried off: it
was now a stampede for life, as represented in my picture of Black
Thursday. Kangaroos and other animals, immense flocks of birds
of all kinds, mingled in mid air, amidst the flying sparks, and in
the stifling smoke making for the south. Numbers dropped dead

from terror and exhaustion; even flying out far to sea and settling on the vessels. Several shepherds were burnt to death, whilst some had to plunge into creeks and just hold their heads out of the water to save themselves. In the town of Kilmore the inhabitants thought the end of the world had come, and clinging to one another bade each other, as they supposed, a last farewell.

The groans of the unfortunate horses and bullocks, half roasted, in the creeks where they had taken refuge, as one passed where they were after the fire had done its work was quite heart-rending. A company of travelling actors and an actress, *en route* for Sydney, having a cart filled with the necessary paraphernalia of their avocation, which they had intended following at the various towns upon the journey, became enveloped in the flames on the Big Hill, and the whole of their wardrobe and effects were destroyed, the only article snatched from the burning being a cornopean and a violin. The fire careered along at the speed of a racehorse. A traveller who reached Melbourne from the Pyrenees stated that for fifty miles of his route a chain of fire ran along each side of him, even to the margin of the road the grass and scrub was blazing—a fiery ride indeed!

Thus the devouring element continued its course of destruction till, after burning through the Cape Otway forest, it was arrested by the sea.

I can never forget the morning of that scorching Thursday, ever memorable in the annals of the colony as 'Black Thursday'. The heat had become so terrific quite early in the day that one felt almost unable to move. At the breakfast table the butter in the butter dish was melted to oil, and bread when just cut turned to rusk. The meat on the table became nearly black, as if burnt before the fire, a few minutes after being cut. Everything felt hot to the touch, even the window panes in the shade. Cold water you could not get, and the dust raised in clouds by the fierce wind was sand which penetrated everywhere. Layer after layer did I brush off from my lithographic stone whilst etching thereon a design for the Anti-Transportation League, at Messrs Ham's in Collins Street.

Before Black Thursday the flies swarmed everywhere and settled on the black coats of the pedestrians in the streets in the hundreds, and walking in the grass outside the town the grasshoppers sprang up in front of you as you walked in scores. But the fire settled them all on that day.

The sun looked red all day, almost as blood, and the sky the colour of mahogany. We felt in town that something terrible (with the immense volumes of smoke) must be going on up country and sure enough messenger after messenger came flocking in with tales of distress and horror. Our unfortunate man, severely burnt, tried in vain to rescue his wife and children, and just managed to escape with his own life.

For years afterwards the traces of this storm were still visible in the Colony, and the charred skeletons of many venerable monarchs of the forest stood gaunt and black against the sky, testifying to their baptism of fire.

CARL TRAUGOTT HOEHNE

This Is Not Arabia

Carl Hoehne was trained as a shoemaker but throughout his two-year stay in Australia never once practised his trade. Instead it seems he fell into a deep depression prompted by his profound dislike for the place. It was too Godless for the pious Saxon, but doubtless his lack of English did not help matters.

27 March 1851—…We left from Hamburg on 23 August 1849, and reached Brazil on 27 October, landing at Rio de Janeiro. We left from there on 2 December and after several storms saw the Australian coast on 2 February 1850, and landed at Melbourne on 8 February. On the whole journey fourteen people died. In addition to other difficulties, we had to suffer a good deal from fleas, lice, and bed-bugs. The emperor Napoleon erred when he went to Russia; we erred when we decided to go to Australia. Our Saviour says: In the world you have anxiety. See, this is not Arabia ('Arabia the blest'), but rather is there much misery.

Here in Australia everyone sees to it that he enriches himself at the expense of his neighbour. How greedy the people are here! It is boundless…

Dear brothers, here in Melbourne there is no Lutheran School and no Lutheran church. There are however various religious persuasions here. In the local Catholic Church I have found the first evidence of our Saviour, otherwise nowhere. There is little longing for school or church, but all the more concern for business and physical wellbeing. 'I have bought so and so much land and so many oxen'—that is the talk one hears daily. Thus God and His holy Word are forgotten and no one thinks of the wellbeing of his neighbour. How many souls are lost in this way: Therefore, dear brothers, consider what a heavy responsibility before God those will have who mislead people into coming to such a godless land with their deception…

21 June 1851—…Dear brother-in-law, I received your letter on 16 May. I took the letter to a rise outside the town and read it there. I cried and let my tears flow remembering the lovely church services at home which I have to do without entirely here, the beautiful spring water, the fine songs of the birds and the colourful flowers of the old fatherland, all of which are missing here. In Germany Australia is called a promised land. Here, however, it is called the English Siberia, which is true, because all the great robbers, thieves and other

criminals, who have really earned the death penalty are sent out or deported to Australia from England. There are now more than 80,000 such ne'er-do-wells spread over the whole of Australia. Here they are the greatest speculators and the most prominent gentlemen. They are masters at lying and deceiving. Those who do not know the English language are like the deaf and dumb, and cannot write or read anything. Even if they were the smartest persons, without knowledge of the English language they have to be servants of these ne'er-do-wells and acknowledge them as their masters...

I said at that time, if only half of what is written about Australia is true, it must be lovely there; but all these reports are lies and deception. My advice is: stay at home and provide for yourself in an honourable way.

Here there are no holidays apart from Sunday and Christmas.

Stealing, robbery and drinking are a daily occurrence here. People are attacked on the streets and left half-dead, and hardly anyone seems concerned. What terrible people there are here, it is shocking.

It is seldom that you meet someone who knows German and English. If ever you need such a person to tell you the right street, you have to pay 25 new silver Groschen. Thus a person who comes from Germany has the last Groschen drawn from his pockets until finally he cannot be given any other advice than taking a stick in his hands and a mantle over his shoulders and going 200 to 260 English miles into the unsettled heathland. There he finds some sort of old shed made from the bark of trees, and that is his house. The bed on which he lies is also of bark. If he takes more things with him, they are bound to be stolen. As for food, flour, tea, sugar and meat will be sent to him. The flour is then pressed into the bark, a loaf is made out of it, and it is somehow baked in the fire. Now you have bread, meat and tea one day; the next day you have tea, meat and bread; and for variety you again have bread, meat and tea and so on.

The Lonsdale Rush

Argus, 13 August 1851—Gold in Melbourne Streets

Yesterday forenoon, between eleven and twelve o'clock, two little girls, children of Mr William Henry Williams, a currier, residing in a lane off Lonsdale Street, between Stephen and Spring streets, were playing on a plot of vacant land adjoining Lonsdale Street, in the above locality, and making holes to play at marbles, one of them dug up a bit of china. In digging deeper to remove the obstacle, they came across what they called 'a pretty thing', and so delighted were they with their discovery, that they immediately ran off to show their mother the prize they had got. Mrs Williams, of course, had no knowledge of gold, but there being so much talk of the precious metal, and the suspicious discovery feeling very heavy in proportion to its size, a suspicion struck her that it might be gold. In order to solve her doubts, she took it to Mr Crate, jeweller, of Swanston Street, who immediately, from its appearance, pronounced it to be gold; but, in order to make quite certain he applied the ordinary tests, and declared it to be quite pure. It was then put into the scales, and found to weigh half an ounce and ten grains.

We had the pleasure of viewing the sample, which Mrs Williams very kindly brought down to our office. We found it to be an irregularly formed sample, rather long than broad, and somewhat flattened, having all the appearance of been run by the notion of intense heat, and resembling in this respect pieces of lead that have been thrown accidentally from the melting pot. It also seems at some time to have been walked upon, for both the upper and lower surfaces are much scratched and flattened, as if innumerable boots had been operating on it. To one of the sides of the nugget a piece of milk quartz still adheres; and in the opposite side a portion of quartz is embedded, mingled with a small piece of other matter.

Several persons, since the discovery was made, have been digging in the immediate locality, and have come, at the distance of fifteen or eighteen inches from the surface, upon a bed of dark quartz, which, it is expected, may be found to be productive of gold.

This discovery of gold in the very heart of Melbourne has very naturally tended to create considerable excitement.

*

Melbourne Morning Herald, October 1851 — Gold in Melbourne

Startling as was our announcement yesterday, that four men in a fortnight had accumulated 93lbs weight of gold at Ballarat, and had brought the same into town, we question if it took our readers more by surprise than the following fact took us — the actual discovery of gold in large nuggets at the top of Lonsdale Street, in the immediate vicinity, and situate exactly between, the Treasury and the new building used as the Government offices. The circumstances attending the discovery (into which we have made particular inquiries), are these. Yesterday a man named Payne, who had forwarded from Ballarat by the escort a parcel of gold of his own digging, went to the Treasury office, accompanied by Messrs Heffernan and Ryan; on his way thither he chanced to look at that part of the hill which is cut down some three feet on the northern side, and surveying it more minutely, intimated to his companions that it was out of similar clay he had obtained the gold for which he was then going to the Treasury. More out of curiosity than anything else his companions broke off some lumps of the clay, and on examining it minutely observed several particles of a yellow shining metal, which on being tested by Mr Walsh the watchmaker, were discovered and certified to be pure gold.

Hearing of the circumstance we repaired to the spot and found several parties picking out of the side of the excavation large pieces of clay, and in one instance we personally witnessed a man extract from a piece about three inches square a gold nugget the size of a large pea. Several other smaller specimens were found, and there is no doubt whatever that there is gold there and in large abundance. The clay is blue and very greasy stuff. Application was made to the colonial secretary for licences to dig, but they met with a refusal.

★

Melbourne Morning Herald, 24 October 1851 — A Hoax

Yesterday Mr George Say amused himself in cooking up a cock and bull story about gold being found in the gutter at the corner of Lonsdale and Swanston streets, and very near his late public house, the 'St George and Dragon'. He had the impudence to bring a specimen of it (as he called it) to our office, and told all manner of lies to induce us to perpetrate the hoax on the public. It appears that he procured a piece of quartz from some place or another, and over this he had sprinkled some gold-beaten leaf, and had rubbed some of the leaf into the crevices of the 'sample' to form the delusion. If Mr Say gets his window smashed in some fine night for carrying on such vagaries, we will not pity him one bit.

CHARLES JOSEPH LA TROBE

Gold

La Trobe's governorship found itself under increasing pressure as a result of the gold rush. In a dispatch to the colonial secretary Lord Grey, the struggling governor describes the early effects of gold on Melbourne and Geelong.

10 October 1851—...Within the last three weeks the towns of Melbourne and Geelong and their large suburbs have been in appearance almost emptied of many classes of their male inhabitants; the streets which for a week or ten days were crowded by drays loading with the outfit for the workings are now seemingly deserted. Not only have the idlers to be found in every community, and day labourers in town and the adjacent country, shopmen, artisans and mechanics of every description, thrown up their employment, and in most cases, leaving their employers and their wives and families to take care of themselves, run off to the workings, but responsible tradesmen, farmers, clerks of every grade, and not a few of the superior classes have followed; some, unable to withstand the mania and force of the stream, or because they were really disposed to venture time and money on the chance—but others, because they were, as employers of labour, left in the lurch and had no other alternative.

Cottages are deserted, houses to let, business is at a standstill, and even schools are closed. In some of the suburbs not a man is left, and the women are known for self-protection to forget neighbours jars, and to group together to keep house. The ships in the harbour are, in a great measure, deserted; and we hear of instances where not only farmers and respectable agriculturists have found that the only way, as those employed by them deserted, was to leave their farms, join them, and form a band, and go shares, but even masters of vessels, foreseeing the impossibility of maintaining any control over their men otherwise, have made up parties among them to do the same.

Fortunate the family, whatever its position, which retains its

servants at any sacrifice, and can further secure the wanted
supplies for their households from the few tradesmen who
remain, and retain the means of supplying their customers at any
augmentation of price. Drained of its labouring population, the
price of provisions in the towns is naturally on the increase, for
although there may be an abundant supply within reach, there
are not sufficient hands to turn it to account.

Curtis Candler

Matters of Honour

> Dr Curtis Candler landed in Melbourne in 1850, and
> served as the city's coroner for over forty years. It was a
> position that brought to his attention duels and duelling,
> which were very popular in the 1850s. His diary, which
> includes the retelling of many amusing anecdotes, was
> given to the State Library of Victoria by his descendents
> in 1973. These two entries, made some years apart, recall
> the lawlessness of frontier colonial life—a society with
> more than its fair share of hot-headed, thin-skinned and
> thirsty young men.

6 September 1852—…In Lett (28 Aug.) I noted a conversation with
Fitzgerald. I made a rough memo of it at the time. McMahon, then
chief commissioner of police, suggested to Fitzgerald and the
colonial secretary (Foster), that poor O'Hara Burke (the explorer)
was unfitted for the particular position he occupied in the police
force at that time; and that he was so good a fellow, that he would
recommend his promotion to a higher grade, where he would not be

called upon to perform the peculiar duties that he was then expected to do. F. coincided with M. and Burke received his promotion.

Not long after this Burke called on Fitzgerald and said that he had been informed of the reasons which had led to his being advanced to the position he then held, and that he considered them so insulting to him, he had called to ascertain if they were the actual reasons. Upon F. telling him that there were some grounds for what he had heard, Burke flew into a violent rage, denounced McMahon, said it was a studied insult to him as a gentleman, and ended by informing F. that he should at once demand satisfaction.

The idea of calling a man out for promoting him was so ludicrous that F., at first, was highly amused; but Burke was in earnest and he soon found it was impossible to dissuade him from his purpose. After trying every argument he could think of, in vain, he at last said, 'Well Burke, if you are determined to shoot McMahon on the ground you have put, you must first come out with me.'

'With you? Why that's absurd.'

'I know it's absurd that you should have shot at me for having promoted you, but if any person is to blame for that, I am.'

'No no—McMahon suggested it.'

'Yes and I carried it out. Therefore you must first meet me before you can treat with McMahon. You can go out with him afterwards if you like, but you must not forget that I come before him. You have spoken of the feelings of an Irish gentleman, and I appeal to you whether I have not a prior claim to McMahon, as the head of his department and as the one who actually gave you the promotion for which you intend on revenging yourself on him?'

'Oh! this is too ridiculous, Mr Foster.'

'I grant it; ridiculous, but I am an Irish gentleman too, remember, and do you suppose I can allow another man to be shot at for what I myself have done—at least before I have been out myself? No, Burke—if you have any private cause of quarrel with

McMahon, I can have, as a private gentleman, nothing to say to it; but I cannot permit this matter to be made the pretext for a challenge. I am responsible for it in the first instance, and I now tell you that I shall expect you as a gentleman—to take no steps until you have settled with me.'

'Well really—this is not at all what I contemplated,' pleaded poor Burke, who began to see his chance melting away. 'Gad! it's too absurd.'

'Yes it is—it's very ridiculous for two men who have no ill will to go out—but you have placed me in a dilemma and I see no honourable way out of it, but for you to meet me before calling out McMahon.'

Fitzgerald told me that Burke was completely sold. He had set his heart upon having McMahon before him for the fancied affront he had passed on him; but the new turn affairs had taken puzzled him mightily. He walked up and down and argued that, inasmuch as the sting of the whole thing lay in the original suggestion of McMahon, that he was not fit for the post he occupied, surely he was the man to be revenged on.

Fitzgerald said, 'Oh! Certainly he might be—but as a point of honour, you know, I have the priority. You needn't do more than wing me, you see, and then you can do as you like with McMahon.'

Burke laughed and left and gave it up. But he never forgave McMahon.

11 February 1868—…Not long after poor Snodgrass's death Farie, Bell, Zeal and some old colonists were discussing his fondness for duelling in his youth, and several stories were told of the early days. It appears he called out Sir Redmond, then Mr Barry. I forget whether they fought. He sent a message to E. Bell, who requested Farie to act for him. Farie mentioned that he would neither allow Bell to go out nor to apologise. Then Snodgrass

wanted to have him out, and wrote a most extraordinary letter that could scarcely be deciphered. Snodgrass was so screwed he could only just manage to hold a pen, and begged to be excused for the writing as he was *suffering from ophthalmia*! The subject of duels led to mention being made of one that occurred between Dana and Walsh. They were travelling together and came to a place where there was only one bed, about which they quarrelled. They had both been drinking heavily and as neither would give way, they determined to fight at once. It was so dark however they couldn't see beyond a few feet. In this dilemma, Dana suggested they should toss who should hold a lighted candle while the other fired; and, in the event of missing, they should have alternate shots until one or the other fell—the *survivor to take the bed*! This happy thought was at once acted on and they blazed away at each other without effect. They were so drunk they could hardly stand. It ended by their going in for a further supply of liquor, which they drank amicably during the armistice and by which they were so overcome that they fell asleep and dropped on the floor; where they remained till long after daylight, when they mounted their horses and rode off firmer friends than ever.

This started another *duel in the bush by candlelight* between two men also very drunk. In this instance the combatants had the advantage of being attended by seconds. Finding that their principals could neither of them stand, they hit upon a very ingenious device. They picked out two gum trees about the correct distance from each other and tied their friends to them—leaving the arms free. Then they placed a table handy to each gentleman and on it placed a candle, some powder and balls, and an empty pistol. When all these arrangements were completed, the adversaries were informed they could go to work as soon as they liked and fire away as fast as they could load. The seconds then left them to their sport and retired.

ANTOINE FAUCHERY

John Bull in the Antipodes

Antoine Fauchery arrived in Melbourne on 22 October 1852. This letter, from his collection *Lettres d'un mineur*, records the first impressions the city had on his continental mind. In 1854 Fauchery established the *Café-Estaminet Français* in Little Bourke Street. Café society was short-lived, however, and this talented and restless man moved on, working with considerable success as a playwright and then as a photographer. Still dissatisfied with his life, he sailed from Melbourne to Asia and died suddenly in April 1861, in Yokohama, aged in his mid-thirties.

The enormous number of newcomers to this little capital makes it an impossible place to stay in. Neither gold nor silver would get you a room there. A chair, a table, a bench, cost more than they would at the most splendid fireworks display, and barely half of this floating population that the English merchant marine casts on to the shore every day succeeds in obtaining any kind of shelter for a few days. Consequently, the other half sleeps in the open!

That still wouldn't matter: it is mid-October, when spring is beginning in Australia. But there is also the question of *bushrangers*, who infest town and country for thirty miles around. The bushranger, according to the portrait of him that is painted for us, is nothing less than a well-nigh fabulous being, a red-bearded ruffian with sharp pointed teeth and no end of pistols, who plunders everybody indiscriminately. These details make the ladies shudder, and even more so their husbands, who do not seem at all prone to familiarise themselves with the idea of an encounter with brigands. John Bull does not like armed conflict; his stiffness and his natural awkwardness make him keep away from it. He is a heavy bull of a man, swollen with beer, who can crush you with his weight, but is uneasy if a cap goes off. He has not, like us, been brought up with the sound of fusilades and gunfire; he knows practically nothing about the use of firearms, hardly ever goes hunting, and cannot fight at more than arm's length to save his life. Thus duels are rare in England. On the other hand, people there admire boxers who have killed four or five of their friends with their fists. That makes up for it.

I, who have but little to lose, have no fears, and I can give myself up to contemplation of the land, following the curves that the river makes through reeds and young thickets from which swarms of teal and wild duck fly off. The land...Alas, it is very dismal, the part that runs to the right and left of the Yara-Yara! It consists of vast plains slightly undulating, on which grows grass that is neither green nor yellow, and on which here and there a few thin oxen are grazing. Plains, and then more plains stretching out *ad infinitum*, like the boredom that comes over you at the sight of them. Everything seems to be null and void in nature here. It lacks the power to surprise or move you, and does not even have in its favour the heartbreak that there is in sterility. Oh, where are you, green shores, purple corals, mysterious forests, flowers and butterflies with the colours of the sun and the moon, as in those little green books? Oh, half-virgin nature, where one can still listen, in cool shades, to the murmuring of that sweet melody that the leaves sing to the branches, where are you? Further on perhaps? — No.

Further on, the ground becomes hilly without being any more attractive for that. We veer slightly to the left, and to the left still, the town, built on a hill-slope, appears to us in its entirety. We pass close to wooden huts spaced out along the two banks, and said to be boiling-down works — a piece of information whose exactness our sense of smell does not allow us to doubt. We creep through about thirty brigs, schooners and three-masters—barks that cannot be more than two hundred and fifty tons register, and we finally tie up at a stone landing stage, behind which are the customs' warehouses. In a few minutes I counted fourteen buildings dominating the town, all fourteen of them churches, they tell me. It would be a sorry state of affairs if, in a country where the good Lord has so many dwellings, some of His creatures had to sleep in the street.

However that may be, on disembarking, the chances of finding a place to live in seem to be still slighter. No more here than in the bay does Fortune, disguised as a gentleman, go looking for newcomers. There are numbers of people going and coming with a pen behind their ear and looking very busy, but they take no notice of us and pay only little attention to our bundles, thrown rather than carried on to the wharf, amid a pile of bales and all sorts of goods.

I would be ready to believe that after a trip of a few hours we are leaving the Saint-Cloud streamer at the end of the Pont Royal, were it not that the absence of the brook in the Rue du Banc and the payment of an entrance-tax for the town, levied on the luggage, brought me back to a sense of reality. I pay out eight or ten shillings and am free to go where I please. They even make this easier for me by sending me for the time being to the toll-office door. At this door two rows of carts are drawn up, which their owners put at the disposal of the newcomers for carrying their baggage. The place is bustling; prices are argued about, offers of service assail you; I fall into the arms of some thirty carriers—the English equivalent of our porters—from whom I try to keep the gear that I am dragging behind me for fear of seeing it *bushranged*. My plight is all the worse in that I am not only far from speaking the pure language of Shakespeare or even that of the roughest Durham herdsman, but can hardly make myself understood, and for my own part, do not understand anything at all.

Fortunately, one of the porters who is battling for my custom, calling me captain or governor, speaks French...just about as well as I mutilate English. From a gibberish that I listen to for ten minutes I gather that my man knows an Irishwoman who has a son installed as a cabin-boy on ship from Le Hâvre, and a room to let in Melbourne. That decides me, and, seeing that it is late, I hand over half of my baggage and am led away. We go up a very straight and very long street and arrive at the lady's place, She is drunk, and tells me a fine story in her native patois, crosses herself, and installs me in a loft, along with five people stretched out on the floor on palliasses. All this for three pounds a week (75 francs). 'It's given away,' says my guide as he takes six francs for his run.

Only on the following day could I see the town and there witness, when I woke up, a none too entertaining spectacle. Behind the wall of the prison built at the top of the hill, on the corner opposite the one where I am living, they were hanging a gentleman guilty of murdering his workmate on the road to the mines. The crowd was dense round the gallows, erected on a plat-form about twenty feet high, and ladies were handing each other, turn about, binoculars and field glasses, so as to miss nothing as they watched the victim's face. This poor wretch, clad in a grey costume and wearing a white cotton bonnet, arrived on the platform following the executioner, who led him under the cross-beam set horizontally across two uprights, with the rope dangling from the middle of it; then he tied the fatal knot round his neck, tightening it violently, and pulled his bonnet down to his chin. Next the minister, who was standing at the top of the ladder, opened a book and read a last prayer. This reading lasted for a good three minutes at least, during which time the condemned man, with his hands tied behind his back, stood firm and motion-less, with no shaking at the knees. Only his fingers were shaking convulsively, and under the tight-drawn tissue of the cotton bonnet, of a cruel, dead white colour, one could follow all the grimaces and anxieties of that face! Imagine, on human shoulders, a plaster head, alive and suffering! plaster temples beating, a plaster forehead all wrinkled, a plaster mouth twitching!!! It is horrible!...As the clergyman's final word was uttered a trap-door opened, the man disappeared suddenly behind the wall, and after that one could see nothing but the rope swinging in space.

The English scaffold is like ours. Whatever shape they assume, all scaffolds are the same everywhere. Hideous rather than terrible, they teach criminals how to die, never how to mend their ways. I had all the difficulty in the world forcing my way through the anxious populace, among which, no doubt, many were getting their first lesson.

Having got away from the hanged man, and his audience, I set out to go around the town. I confess that in this excursion also my disillusionment grew greater at every step, doubtless because nothing in the whole or in its parts turned out to justify the idea that I had formed of Melbourne. Whereas I had expected to find wooden houses, huts even, hastily erected and scattered among trees, I found houses of one or two storeys, solidly built, aligned as straight as a die, forming streets a kilometre long, very straight, very wide, perfectly macadamised, and in these streets black coats, collars, silk dresses, heeled boots, everything just as in Europe, everything including even barrel-organs.

The city, though essentially English as far as its habits, inhabitants and buildings are concerned, is laid out in Yankee fashion. It is a chessboard with an area of about three square miles. From north to south, six great roads run down at right angles to the river, and are crossed at right angles by six other arteries running east and west. The site, from the heights of which one can look down over the country and the sea, would be a most happily chosen one, if a fold in the ground about midway along the slope, a fairly deep indentation, did not to some extent place the centre of the town at the bottom of a valley. During the winter, which is marked by torrential rains, the water, rushing from three sides at once into this funnel, inundates the heart of the place, and not only interrupts traffic, invades shops and cellars, but even kills people, as is proved by the following notice, which says with laconic simplicity: *Another child drowned in the streets of Melbourne.*

The houses, hopelessly small, are adorned with sash-windows and front doors set above two stone steps, kept clean by a man-servant who scrupulously spends part of the day rubbing them with pumice-stone, so that the outside looks very well, at the expense of the inside, which is somewhat neglected, just as in London. The shops are already well cluttered up with wares, and the proprietor, standing soberly behind his counter, whistles softly in his customers' faces just like the first dealer or shopkeeper in Cornhill or Fleet Street; the Thames fogs are advantageously replaced by whirligigs of dust full of minute organisms, which the winds from the coast blow into our face for eight months of the year, and exactly as in London, again, are the public buildings, the private dwellings, the hotels and even the street names. It's a little pastiche on too restricted a scale, that produces much the same effect as a twopenny-ha'penny establishment in comparison with the stock of a serious firm. Fuel alone is lacking to complete the illusion. Only wood is burnt here, and wood by no means gives out that thick coal-smoke that wraps in such an imposing mantle of mourning the largest city in the world. *The largest city in the world!* That leaves a gap that irritates Melbourne people somewhat, but they console themselves for it by swearing by St George, drinking gin and becoming millionaires.

'Becoming a millionaire, there's nothing easier,' said in a melancholy way in bad French by a thin gentleman who was smoking his pipe at the door of a tobacco-shop where I had just lit a cigarette; 'there's nothing easier when you're English and have a few pounds put away.'

Now the Melburnians who founded the town, the first brick of which was laid in 1837, had been living in the colony long before that date. Some, younger sons of good families, officers of the Indian army on half-pay, retired employees, had obtained from the metropolis immense concessions in Australia, whither they had come as farmers. Others, who received very special attention, had been sent out free of charge as convicts. Younger sons and convicts—the latter forming the great majority—after paying their toll to the law or to loneliness, gathered together on the new site intended by the government to become the capital of the district of Victoria, acquired land at a low price, built as best they could, and lived as best they could up to the day when, the existence of gold having been ascertained, they set out to harvest the gold fields. While the great news was making its way on a ship sailing for Europe and emigration was being organised, these city folk have already lined their purses and come back to their beloved little houses, where they resolutely await the emigrants. When the latter arrive, many of them with the intention of essaying a business or exploiting some industry or other, room is very scarce; there is, so to speak, none at all. Actually, every business has to have premises. The Melburnians have the houses. Buy or rent a piece of land and have it built on? The Melburnians possess the building sites and snap up the workmen on their own account. There remains the public thoroughfare! The colonial government has promulgated an edict prohibiting all street sales without a licence which the afore-said government issues for three months at a time, and still reserves the right, on futile pretexts, to refuse most licences, thanks to the cries of distress uttered by the inhabitants.

Is that free trade? Maybe, save that it is difficult or even impos-sible for any but a member of the elect, someone belonging to the league of big capital holders. It is the demon of monopoly laughing at the demon of competition. And upon my soul, comparing one demon with the other, the bold fighter who wants an open arena is still preferable to the sly vampire, the big oaf that closes the door to all enterprise and brings to naught all contrivances. The former had made San Francisco a centre of perpetual motion, a veritable magic lantern in which all phases of militant life appeared endlessly in which skill, activity, imagination and dollars were on an equal footing, running on, bumping into each other, jostling one another, sometimes even tripping each other up, but, for all that, remaining the best friends in the world and, at any rate, always smiling, always moving on! The other demon seems to have made Melbourne a melancholy town, with no colour, no surprises, no dash, where one always drinks the same thing out of the same glass and always sees the same sullen creatures pocketing one's money with a crabbed and crusty air.

The most phenomenal and rapid fortunes are made by the publicans (those who are authorised to keep a public house). In English countries, and particularly in the colonies, the public house is simultaneously a hotel, a restaurant, a cafe and a tavern. The fortunate proprietor of these four establishments rolled into one is dependent upon the municipal authorities, and has obtained his licence, permission to sell spirited and fermented liquors, by getting accepted and carried out the plan for a special house and by soliciting more people, weaving more webs of intrigue than would be needed anywhere else to become viceroy of a large province. But further, the number of licences in Australia being very restricted, possessing one is a sure fortune and is negotiated at the most crazy prices. None of these establishments is commended by its aristocratic bearing. It resembles at one and the same time the shops of our liquor vendors and certain houses of ill fame in the former Rue Pierre Lescot. You can imagine, after that, what the public house must be like in Melbourne, the sole resort of the nomadic population, three-quarters of which are made up of ship's deserters, ex-convicts and Irish beggars; all of them, for that matter, intrepid miners, who come to consume

This corroboree, depicted by the colony's most celebrated watercolourist Wilbraham Liardet, took place on Emerald Hill in 1840. Although painted from memory many years after the event, it resembles the extraordinary performance witnessed by Lady Jane Franklin in 1839, and may indeed refer to that occasion.

This perspective of Melbourne, perhaps informed by an ascent in a hot-air balloon, was created by the Flinders Lane engravers Henry de Gruchy and Stephen Leigh.

e is the bustling city as it was in 1866, a year after Batman's Hill had been levelled. The MCG is plainly visible and the distinctive grid of the city is all but filled.

Nascent Melbourne, judging from the greenery, in the winter or spring of 1839: John Adamson's lithograph shows the settlement from across the Yarra, a place as yet unspoiled by rampant developm

This watercolour of Melbourne was painted by senior surveyor Robert Hoddle in 1840. From his office the outlook is of the 'government block', contained within Spencer, Collins, King and Bourke streets. The large building on the right is the temporary gaol.

there, in two or three days, the product of two or three months' work.

Drunkenness and fisticuffs being perpetual to these places, people with peaceful habits avoid them. As everyone cannot aspire to a windfall similar to that which I am enjoying, and which consists of being treated as a friend rather than a tenant, and paying only twelve francs a night for one sixth of a garret, the majority are forced to leave the inhospitable town, some going straight to the mines, others taking shelter in a plain between the river and the bay. With regard to this point, the municipal authorities have allowed migrants without means to form a temporary encampment. Thus any family that has at its disposal a few yards of canvas has the right to install itself as it likes, either in the north or the south; providing, none the less, that it pays in advance a fee of five shillings a week levied by the very paternal government of the colony for a tent-site in CANVAS TOWN.

Canvas Town! a floating city devoured by the sun, inundated by the rain and swept away by the wind when the latter is in one of its bad moods! You remember what the preparations are like for a national festival in the Champs Elysées, when a whole population of small traders makes for itself a pocket-handkerchief roof before bringing out its gingerbread and Punch and Judy shows? You feel sad, don't you, walking among those bare, grey tents? You pass through the dismal carcase of a festival in which the toy bells that should be there to bring it to life for an hour or so have not been hung. Well, it's just like that here; only, the gingerbread and Punch and Judy shows are missing, and you are always on the eve of a fireworks display which will never be set going. Amid the grass you bump into a strange medley of people and things, and breathe in the acrid perfumes of a bivouac though the smoke of which carefree children chase each other with shrill cries, while tall, stiff gentlemen remain impassive amidst this first collapsing of their golden dream, and the ladies, those incorrigible ladies, starched up to the neck, busy themselves with their household cares in their everlasting flimsy dresses, always with three flounces!

On the opposite bank of the Yara-Yara hangs, as a pendant to this rustic landscape so strangely and sadly framed with verdure and ultramarine blue, another picture which is in no respect inferior to the preceding one. On the Melbourne quay (the wharf), from the exit door of the customs house to the end of the bridge that has to be crossed to reach Canvas Town — a stone bridge comprising a single arch, recently built, the pride of the town and costing millions of francs — is installed a kind of bazaar where merchandise and vendors change every day. There, newly arrived emigrants, with little money and compelled to make some at any price, are allowed to put up their own spoils for sale. For a distance of about half a mile you pass between a double row of trunks and disembowelled cases whose contents, of more or less value, are spread out on the ground. Beside each little lot stands the vendor, with beseeching eyes on the stroller, who, already blasé with regard to this too often repeated kind of exhibition, and well stocked from yesterday or the day before, casts his eye absentmindedly over all the serious articles, such as underwear, footwear, clothes, and, if he does choose, only fixes his choice, as a rule, on an insignificant-looking object: a battered old piece of jewellery, a portrait in faded colours, a medallion, a bagatelle, a mere nothing. But to this bagatelle, this mere nothing that has no importance for most people, a memory is sometimes attached: it is the magic talisman with the aid of which the exile, picking up some crumbs of the past, can still sit at the family fireside and inhale the mists of his missing homeland. No matter: the capricious purchaser is responsive neither to the lustre of a coat of Lincoln cloth, nor to the finish of a pair of French boots; he remains cold even at the sight of a beautiful new umbrella. What he wants is the knick-knack, a little knick-knack that lies lifeless in his hands and which he will throw into a corner an hour after the owner has let him have it for a pound. Only the rigours of the situation justify the ingratitude that ensues after the conclusion of such bargains. The emigrants cannot think twice about it. The Melburnians' fancies are just bits of good luck, for here the coats of Lincoln cloth, the French-fashion boots, and even the new umbrellas can rarely be sold for fifty per cent of their real value, and one simply has to make up for this on something else...

I go up Collins Street. Of all the streets it is perhaps the one where you find the greatest display of shops, which, as I said earlier, are miniature rivals of the shops in English cities where you find the most fantasmagoric window displays; but the gold-brokers' show-windows are those that give your eyes the greatest delight. The metal is on view with no touching up and no coquettishness, just as it is, rivalling the sun, in paltry wooden bowls or heaped up on a little shelf fixed behind the glass; gold-dust sparkling particles, one-ounce pieces, pieces weighing one pound, ten pounds. It would have made me forget the vexations of the voyage, the bad impressions left by my visit to Canvas Town, it would have made me love the paltry wooden bowls, the Melbourne garrets, the inhabitants, if a most violent bump had not come to snap me out of my contemplation. It was one of those same inhabitants, going straight ahead like a wild boar, who would walk over you rather than step a foot out of his way.

Whichever way you turn, alas, only people like that go by. To the left, to the right, everywhere are the same cold faces, the same stiff, starched gaits, the same black coats, like those of undertakers' men. On the blond hair of the thoroughbred gentlemen as on that of the mason plastering his wall you find the same little British-style silk hat, with flat brim, high crown and short nap, which is as tightly attached to the skull as the hand is to the arm, and is part of the individual. Now, if you expect a smile from those pale lips, if you look for a gleam in those icy, lack-lustre blue eyes, it will be like asking the head to separate itself from the hat or the hat to separate itself from the head...

While I was giving myself over to the most bitter reflections on my present uncomfortable situation, I arrived at my Irishwoman's place. The savoury smell of a roast joint was perfuming the house, and in the kitchen I found the hostess setting the table while my room-mates looked after the cooking of an immense piece of beef. I had completely forgotten that according to the terms of our tenancy we enjoyed all the prerogatives that go with the garrisoned soldier's billeting slip: use of the fire, water and salt. This measure, generally adopted by private persons who sublet to newcomers, enables the latter to avoid going the rounds of dining-rooms and eating-rooms where the food prices are not always proportionate to the customers' resources...My garret-mates invited me to share their feast. Upon my soul, the offer was so cordial, and I had breakfasted in the morning on such a dry piece of bread as I went round the town, that I accepted without being too ceremonious about it, and reproaching myself little for the ill that I had been thinking, a few minutes before, of the nation to which my hosts belong.

There are five of them, coming from different English countries, all five are workmen and have a very cold, trustworthy, honest look. Though they arrived scarcely two days ago you would think, from what they say, that they have been living in the colony for two centuries, so well do they already know the advantages that it can offer them. One is a shoemaker, and will work for an employer at the rate of 20 fr. a day. Two others are printers and will receive 175 fr. each per week. It is impossible for me to find out what the fourth will do: he will have his work over by six o'clock every evening and will get 25 fr. As for the fifth, a bricklayer—the best wages are in store for him. For anyone coming from the old countries, nothing is more astonishing, more incredible, than the current rate of pay for those classed as building workers. Stone-cutters and masons earn 50 and 60 fr. a day;

painters, 25 fr.; labourers, hod-carriers, barrowmen, mortar-mixers 15 to 18 fr. It's fantastic! all those callings that are so poorly paid in France—the hammer-swingers, as our porters say with a tone of deepest disdain—queen it out here; the whole academic body put together would be less successful than a good tiler, and many people would readily exchange the eloquence of a Sorbonne professor for an axe—and for knowing how to use it.

O for a calling! knowing how to use your arms without being afraid of breaking or damaging them! that's what is really useful. That has been said before, I think, by all the old men—the good old chaps;—but if I repeat it, it is because I have never appreciated it as much as I now do. If only I could cook! Instead of bringing Rabelais and Montaigne with me, if I had simply brought *The Country House* or *The Middle-class Housewife*, I could, at this moment, turn out stews, gravies and sauces at the Black Bull hotel, where they are offering 500 francs a week for a French cook! There are also, more or less anywhere, in public houses, 12 fr. a day to be earned for peeling vegetables or washing dishes— at your choice. But besides not knowing enough English to aspire to one of these modest posts, there are the mines, which have to take precedence over these little dead-end jobs, to which access is limited to the unemployed and the needy. I have not as yet reached any humiliating limits; I have a good pair of legs and 150 fr. in my pocket, that is to say, about the price of two dozen oysters, a chicken, an omelet and a tip for the waiter.

I noticed, incidentally, at the table, that I was the only one to show signs of lively emotion, and that the demonstration of a state of affairs at once so real and yet seeming so fabulous aston- ished and amazed me alone. Newcomers and old ones alike, the workers, the men with arms, seem to accept the benefits offered to them by a town with a future but only just awakening, only as a next-best affair, and have at the back of their mind a thought that is distressing them. The mine! that is the one centre of attraction, the goal of all hopes, the dreamland where the sun rises! They disdain the gold stamped with the emblem of the State to dream of winning the gold that bears no effigy. It's the gold-fever; the fever for pure gold, virgin gold, gold hidden in the bowels of the earth;—a fever that is cold and held in check, but which is none the less active, driving all those who are stricken with it to throw up suddenly the most lucrative positions to run away and look for the uncertain.

Only being chained to Melbourne by a really imperious material impossibility can stop one from going up to the mines to *try one's luck*. If this impossibility stems from a lack of money, one very soon makes enough to pay travelling expenses, leaves the workshop and sets out. It is these continual desertions that force contractors to make wages so excessive. They are, I am told, talking of a further increase, hoping thereby to keep men on a little longer. Will they succeed? Not, at any rate, as far as my companions are concerned: all five of them swear that they will not work in town for more than a week.

As for me, I shall leave tomorrow...

Well, no, I shan't leave tomorrow. I shall stay one day longer in Melbourne, or at any rate in its neighbourhood. An Irishman who came to see my Irishwoman, or rather his, I believe, gave me the name and address of a French priest living in a small village eight miles from the city. I should not like to throw myself into a life of adventure in the woods without shaking hands with a compatriot. Who knows if I shall ever see any others?

R. H. HORNE

Dead Monkeys

At the time of his visit to Melbourne in September 1852, R. H. 'Orion' Horne was reputedly the most distinguished poet ever to grace Australia's shores. The short, balding man who wore his remaining hair in ringlets was dumped unceremoniously on the Melbourne dockside. He clearly did not appreciate the reception he received in the chaotic city.

September 1852—By the introduction and recommendation of my friend the Major, I was permitted, as a favour, to enjoy the little backroom of a two-roomed hovel, in which a woman and her daughter resided. About eighteen pence a week would have been paid in an English country town for such a place on the outskirts; but here, at this time, my rent was thirty shillings a week. My 'look-out' was upon a narrow patch of yard all bestrewn with shattered things: loose firewood, fragments of old furniture, boxes, trunks, and rags of clothes and bedding, with a mad conglomerate on one side emitting typhoid odours. Broken palings pretended to divide this yard from the yards on each side—one of these was all mud and cesspool, the other all wretchedness and squalor; the only conspicuous objects being heaps of broken ginger-beer bottles and a dead monkey. The backyards of Melbourne at this period defy description in any such space as I can afford. This represented domestic civilisation returning to chaos!

The two women were most insolent. Perceiving that their society was distasteful to me, they used to set the door between the two rooms ajar, and talk at me in subtle tropes and allegories with colonial finesse. Some people wanted to set themselves up as a sort of superfine over other people, who knew how the cat leaps as well as they; but all such people would soon be brought to humble pie with all their seven senses in this kolny, and be d——to them. 'You must do this—(must we?—ah!)—but the like of such chaps'll soon find out that here there's no must or ought. Jack's as good as his master.

ALEXANDRE DUMAS

Madame Giovanni

First published in 1855, Alexandre Dumas' *The Journal of Madame Giovanni* is something of an enigma. The famous and prolific novelist claimed it to be the true story of a Parisian lass who accompanied her Italian merchant husband on a ten-year journey round the world. She kept no journal of her travels, but instead told her tale to Dumas, who was her amanuensis. The true identity of Madame Giovanni remains a mystery and some doubt that she ever existed, instead crediting Dumas with fabricating the entire work. The narrative, however, is rich in detail and is most likely based on real travels.

I was beginning, as I have already said, to be bored with Hobart Town and to desire a change. So at the end of two months Mr Giovanni told me that, in view of my entreaties, we would leave for Launceston and from there for Port Phillips. I confess that this news was extremely agreeable to me and the day for departure, left to my choice, was set for the following one. I was already beginning to have that zest for travel which has since made me, if not the most agreeable, at least the most adaptable travelling companion in the world...

Port Phillip is situated on the far side of Banks Strait[*] directly opposite Launceston in Australia. Large steamers, however, remain at Port Williams[**]. Some strange caprice accounts for the development of Port Phillip where only small boats can land. To reach it, the banks of a river are followed—forgive my ignorance which, notwithstanding, I hope may prove one of the charms of the book—for I do not recall the name of this river. But what I do know is that these banks are merely a long series of slaughter-houses where sheep are killed; tanneries where their hides are prepared; and factories where their fat is prepared for the market. Here and there appear white mountains twenty-five, thirty, and forty feet high; these are the bones. These slaughterhouses, tanneries, fat, or rather tallow factories, these bones forming pyramids along the banks, give forth a pestilential odour that made me regard Port Phillip with horror even before arriving.

The commercial activity of England in fine wools, sheepskins and Australian tallow is well known. I have never seen herds like those that clip, as Virgil says, the hills and plains of Port Phillip. These immense solitary plains seem like vast seas where each sheep forms a wave. The various herds are in charge of free emigrants—Scotch, English and Irish. At the time of our visit the port was only a mass of houses, but this mass was increasing daily. Out of it a city appeared to be rising. Wealth, abundance, future luxury, all could be sensed in the affluence that was apparent on every hand.

But since this was only mildly interesting to us, we might have remained only twenty-four hours at Port Phillip had we not been detained by curiosity aroused by a certain event that had just occurred. A few days before our arrival one of the keepers of

[*] Bass Strait.
[**] Williamstown.

these vast herds just indicated had appeared at the shop of Mr B——, one of the leading goldsmiths of the city. The merchant knew at a glance that the man who had just entered his shop did not have the aspect of a purchaser. 'What do you wish?' he asked.

The Irishman (it was an Irishman) drew from his pocket a shabby, ragged handkerchief, unrolled the handkerchief, and from its folds extracted a brilliant object the size of a loaf of bread.

'Look, Mr Jeweller,' he said, 'I want to know what this is.'

B—— looked at the nugget encrusted with stones, turning it over and over.

'Where did you find this?' he asked.

'Down below, while watching my sheep. I saw something sparkling in the sun and I said to myself: "The first time I go to the city, I must show this to some jeweller." I came to the city, your address was given me, and here I am. Has this any value whatsoever?'

The jeweller touched the nugget. It was pure gold.

'Well?' asked the shepherd.

'This has some value, indeed,' replied the jeweller, 'but not so great as you think.'

'But at least it is worth something?'

'Yes.'

'What is it worth?'

'How much do you expect?'

'How do you expect me to know? It is for you to say what you can conscientiously pay me for it.'

'Well,' said the jeweller, 'here are four pounds sterling.'

'But you should certainly add some money to buy shoes, hose, and one or two old shirts.'

'No, provided I give you what is actually the value of your nugget. But wait. After all I will give you what you ask.'

And calling his wife he told her to prepare a package from his own wearing apparel of the things the shepherd required and to give it to him. Then, while his wife was wrapping shoes, stockings, and shirts in a napkin, he inquired: 'Are there many stones of this type in the place where the sheep graze?'

'I do not know,' replied the shepherd. 'I stumbled on this, picked it up, and brought it in to you. That is all.'

'Well, if you find more, bring them in, too.'

'I am certain to find them.'

'And you will bring them to me?'

'Certainly, I will give you first choice.'

Mrs B—— entered with the package. The Irishman thanked the jeweller and left, convinced that he had been duped. He was not mistaken; the nugget contained four pounds of pure gold, exclusive of the stones, and being virgin gold it was of the highest quality.

By the evening of the day the incident occurred, all Port Phillip knew the story. Almost immediately the demon of speculation spread its wings over the city. The shepherd was found and sequestered; a joint stock company was organised to exploit the gold at Port Phillip. Finally, the directors of the society sought an interview with the Irishman. An effort was made to persuade the shepherd to lead the speculators to the place where the gold nugget had been found. At first the shepherd shook his head and stubbornly refused. But after a series of promises and threats his resistance was overcome. 'Well, then,' he said, 'I will take you there.'

Until time to depart the shepherd was placed in a room, well fed and well cared for, but out of sight. An expedition was organised with shovels, pickaxes, carts, horses, mills for sifting the dirt, etc. Finally the expedition led by the shepherd departed. The party consisted of all the shareholders who wished to assist personally in the first work and of almost the entire village population, who, more or less inadequately equipped for the trip, attached themselves to the procession. Some even left without provisions, relying on what they could find. This indeed was a universal fever, under a sun that roasted all. We watched the caravan pass. It consisted of two thousand persons.

'As a matter of fact,' said my husband, 'I am tempted to follow them and see, not the mine they will find, but what they will do if the shepherd is a liar.'

'Do go,' I replied.

And my husband departed. As the trip held no interest for a woman, I let him depart alone. At the end of only four days I received news of the party from the advance guard of disappointed men. For two days the shepherd had led the caravan under a sun of thirty-five degrees; then, having reached a mountain wholly composed of rock, he had stamped on the ground, hands in his pockets, whistling, and saying: 'Here is where I found it.'

Soon everyone began to dig, spade and pick, uttering a cry of joy at each hope, a sigh of grief at each disappointment. The following day a search was made for the shepherd to ask him again whether this was the place the nugget that caused all this disturbance had been found. But the shepherd had disappeared. The shepherd had been carried off by a speculator.

A capitalist had said to him: 'You are unwise to content yourself with one-tenth of the dividends of the company. Come with me to Sydney; we will purchase whatever is needed for our work, hire two or three men to whom we shall pay good wages; we can return by way of the interior; from Sydney to Port Phillip by land is six hundred miles. No one will recognise us; we shall both work as miners and divide everything in half. In that way you will not be disturbed.'

The proposal was accepted. Thus the disappearance of the shepherd was accounted for. No one knew anything about this arrangement. I alone was taken into the secret, the speculator being a friend of my husband. Let us briefly complete the history of the shepherd. The speculator hid him in the bottom of the hold of the *Shamrock* and paid the captain eight guineas to waive the usual formalities for receiving passengers on board.

Having reached Sydney, the speculator fulfilled his promise, feeding, looking after, and humouring his Hen with the Golden Eggs. There the necessary tools were purchased, including a wagon, a cart, all working implements, guns, to the amount of fifteen hundred pounds sterling. Four men were hired and promised, in addition to two crowns daily, an equal amount in dividends. The itinerary that was to be followed in the interior of the country was traced and the day of the departure arranged. But when the time came to leave, the shepherd could not be found. The speculator called him, searched for him, sent others to search for him, but in vain; he was never seen again. His disappearance remains a mystery to this day.

But interest had been aroused; engineers were sent out to conduct experiments at points comparatively remote from one another and ultimately, after three or four years, gold mines were discovered. Today they are being actively exploited. I might say, in passing, that the speculator who brought the shepherd to Sydney, half laughing at the adventure and half serious at the thought of the results, happened to be my husband.

William Kelly

The Bunghole
of a Brandy-butt

William Kelly's two-volume *Life in Victoria* is a forgotten classic memoir of Australian life. The Irish lawyer and inveterate traveller informs us in his introduction, 'In the year 1850, crippled from the effects of my excursion across the Rocky Mountains and the great Sierra Nevada, and suffering from land scurvy after a severe winter's exposure in the northern diggings of California, I was advised to try a sojourn in those emerald gems of the Pacific…where fruits, vegetables and goat's milk over-abound.' He arrived in Melbourne in May 1853, and attended, if his account is to be believed, one of the most extraordinary performances of *Hamlet* ever witnessed.

When I stepped on its rickety pier, which rocked enough to make an inlander sea-sick, the only symptoms of a town I could discover were some large weatherboard arks anchored in the mud; one or two occupied as butchers' shops to supply the shipping, one or two licensed to stupefy their customers with adulterated alcohol, a leviathan eating-house, superscribed with the notification 'Dinners always ready from morning till night', and the postscript, 'Hot soups always on hand'. There was a large grey calico smithy alongside, emitting showers of sparks, which, curiously enough, flew upwards without igniting the inflammable roof, and close by a shipwright's yard, with an office and dry workshop, covered in by a long-boat inverted and elevated on piles. There was a straggling suburb of ships' galleys and hurri-cane-houses, with here and there a few buoys, as if to indicate the line of safe thoroughfares, while the shore, up to high-water mark, was covered with a debris of drift spars, broken oars, ship-blocks, dead-eyes, used-up passengers' beds and pillows, dilapidated hen-coops, empty brandy cases, broken bottles, and kegs with a ballast of salt water…

Although the current of the Yarra-Yarra is sluggish, it took nearly two hours to breast—not cleave—that tortuous river. For seven miles above its junction with the Saltwater River, its south-ern bank was thickly and deeply fringed with a tea-tree scrub, which would be impenetrable but for its suppleness…

The north bank of the Yarra, at that time, from the falls down to the slaughterhouses, was a slough of dark mud in a state of liquidity, only a very few degrees removed from that of the river, and along it the entire distance was a line of lighters and inter-colonial vessels, four deep, discharging promiscuously into the mire bales of soft goods, delicate boxes of dry goods, cases of brandy, barrels of flour, packages of Glenfield's patent starch, 'warranted used in the royal laundry', mixed pickles, real Havan-nahs, Cossepore sugar, Mocha coffee, Bass's pale ale, Barclay's brown stout, double-rose Cork butter, Scotch oatmeal, and a hundred and one other and sundry articles, piled up in moun-tains in the muck, of which the 'dry goods' not unfrequently constituted the lower stratum or foundation...

Endeavouring to kill two birds with one stone by combining business with amusement, we turned our steps towards Canvas Town, on the south side of the Yarra, with the intention of select-ing a site for a temporary habitation, for, judging from my Californian experience that lodgings would be our earliest and most urgent difficulty, I came provided with an excellent tent and camp apparatus.

On going along Swanston Street, gazing at everything internal as well as out of doors, I missed my friend H. from my side, and observing him glancing furtively into a ham and sandwich refectory, I returned a few steps to take a peep at the curiosity, which proved to be a waiter, with an unclean towel astride his arm, hurrying to and fro amongst a mob of clamorous customers. I looked again without being able to detect anything particularly strange, and while I kept looking, my friend kept shaking his head, half in doubt, half in abstraction. At length he informed me that the ministering angel inside was an old acquaintance of his, of excellent family, with whom he parted in Paris the previous October, 'being then, as he said, on his way to winter in Rome or Naples, bored to death with London fogs and English society'.

This was rather a strong dose for a person like H., roughing it himself for the first time in his life.

We then jogged along silently across Princess Bridge, absorbed in reverie, until we entered the precincts of the once celebrated but now defunct Canvas Town. Here we were considerably surprised at finding something approaching to regularity in the disposition of the gossamer tenements, for, overlooking it from the high ground on the opposite side of the river, it appeared to be a confused swarm of tents, pitched at random on a hillside, like a flock of pigeons after a long flight. On the contrary, however, there was a series of streets, not, to be sure, laid out in straight lines, or running parallel to each other, or intersecting at right angles, but yet streets to all intents and purposes, with central thoroughfares, and stores, and habitations on each side…The chief peculiarity in this novel aggregation of human dwellings was that all were devoted to business of one kind or another, some mechanical, some professional, and some menial; and the signs or notifications over the various booths were regular curiosities of literature in their way, both as regards spelling and composition. One occupant was a 'sale (sail) maker'; another intimated that 'boots were sold (soled) here'; a general merchant supplied 'coffee, reading, and refreshment'; while the person over the way confined himself to 'coffee threepence the half pint, bread-and-butter to shuit'. An aspirant in the hotel line 'had beds to let'; but directed inquirers 'to the back of the premises'; while a chef de cuisine professed his anxiety to 'take in joints for baking'. 'A lady, in her leisure hours,' would make dresses, French fashion, or instruct youth; and Mr Scott, hairdresser, in a discharged ship galley, 'set razors, drew teeth, and bled.—N.B. Mrs S. made up medicines in his absence'. In addition to which, barbers' poles bristled at every salient point; butchers' shops abounded; and if there were no licensed publics in this Rag Fair, the hecatombs of bottles, flasks, and gin jars strewed about, proved to a demonstration that there was a most unlimited, unlicensed consumption of ardent

Noyce created this lithograph of Collins Street as it was in 1840. The topography in the foreground
~newhat exaggerated in this idealised view. With the Yarra on the left the outlook is to the west of the
city, towards the notorious Lamb Inn, near the corner of William and Collins streets.

The punt on the Yarra that gave Punt Road its name was an idyllic spot, judging by this 1850s pho
Here, looking south-east, the rise of the road is unmistakable, but the gardens, fields and bush ha
since given way to a jumble of buildings.

By the 1890s Melbourne was a modern city, complete with street lighting, trams and power poles. Only horseless carriages and a few skyscrapers are needed to bring this image of Collins Street into the twentieth century.

spirits. A presumption otherwise materially strengthened by strong-flavoured personal indications, of which I had unmistakable proof in a masculine countrywoman in the dishabille of a sailor's pea-jacket, who waded across the street to inquire 'if it's washin' we wanted'.

'No, mam,' I replied, 'we must first find a lodging.'

'Oh, bedad,' says she, 'if that's what yer affter, I can fit your knuckle to a T. Look,' she continued, pointing to a barrel raised upon sods, 'at that fine chimbly; well thuther side o' that I've a stretcher 'll house yes both at three shillins a night.'

I managed to decline the proposed accommodation in as gracious a manner as I could put on; but, determined on business of some description, she fell back upon the washing.

'Ah, thin, surely,' says she, 'daycent gentlemen likes yes must have a deal o' washin' affter the voyage, and can't yes give it to an industris woman like me, who only charges ten shillins the dozen?'

'Or about four shillings above the usual price,' I remarked, in an audible soliloquy.

Upon which, putting her hands in the jacket pockets, approaching the attitude to which all voluble women incline in energetic declamation, she apostrophised us in the following vernacular terms: 'Sweet bad luck to the pair of yes, ye lousy lime-juicers. It's dirty linen that's too good for the likes of yes. I wouldn't give you a squeeze o' me blue bag for the money. Maybe yes think I wash for divarshun, and that me wood is laid down to me for thankee, or that I git me wathur for the whistlin'. May the devil purshoe yes out o' the daycent colony, you spalpeens ye.'

The dulcet tones in which she addressed us evidently penetrated throughout the neighbourhood, for an audience was converging towards us in different directions clad in a hybrid mongrel attire, which suggested the idea that the antipodes, amongst its other natural curiosities, contained human hermaphrodites; but they all proved to be of the gentler sex, the men being out at work for the day. The first on the field was a gaunt lady, standing five feet ten inches, in a pair of big broken Napoleon boots, and crowned with a towering greasy wideawake, which gave her quite the air of a disgraced bandit. 'Mrs Molony, dear,' she affectionately exclaimed, 'what are these saucy scamps a doin'' of, aggervatin' of you in this ways? Who sent for the mean hounds,' she promiscuously inquired, 'to insult decent women, an their husbans away an earnin' of their livin'? for three stars I would treat each on 'em to a mug of hot water.'

'And sarve 'em bloody well right,' exclaimed a livid-looking dame, who wore a porous shawl mantilla-wise, to screen a pair of eyes, which, if not boasting dark pupils, moved in the blackest of spheres...

Our retreat was the signal for an outburst of yells and screams that would have done credit to a Crow Indian warwhoop, and though there was no pursuit, a cloud of old boots, bottles, stones and bottomless tin cans was discharged after us, but fell short of the mark. We charged straight across the swamp to the rising ground beyond it, and only ventured to glance round when we placed the morass betwixt us and the Amazons, who were still concentrated in a formidable group, regarding their lost prey.

This rising ground was none other than Emerald Hill, christened from the rich verdure with which it is perpetually clothed. At that time it was very sparsely sprinkled with tents, with only one house on its eastern slope. This was a public house called the Emerald Hotel, fronted with a deep verandah, under which a row of men, in digging costume, were taking their after-dinner smoke. I found, on inquiry, that it was principally resorted by the more respectable and quietly disposed class of diggers who, instead of spending their vacation amidst the scenes of riotous, drunken debauchery of Melbourne, came over to board in this quiet, cleanly suburb. I ascertained, moreover, that close by there was a little street of weatherboard houses—the first erected there—and that probably they were not all let, as they were not all thoroughly finished...These houses, greedily snapped up at a rent equivalent to 208*l*. per annum, were wretched hovels, roofed with rough shingles, which, although they led off the rain, allowed the wind and light to stream in through their interstices. The same description will suit the sides, on which the boards only overlapped enough to carry down the drip, though it frequently bubbled up in high winds, finding its way into the interior. The partitions were simply constructed of sized long-cloth, which admitted the convenience of conversing with your neighbour without the trouble of leaving your own apartment. The arrangement, however, admitted of this delicate drawback, that if your candle at bedtime happened to be extinguished first, you might probably be startled by the shadowing phantom of Mrs or Miss A B C, next door, in her nightdress, preparing for the stretcher. The floors, whether intentionally or not I can't say, were laid somewhat on the hencoop principle, so that all garbage or offal might fall through. I know that some of our knives, forks, and I think a blacking-brush, disappeared through these slender slits, which also admitted such copious currents of wind, that a long-six stearine* rarely saw out our evening's repast...

It was now getting duskish, and the day's work gave us a good appetite, which we went to appease in an eating-house in Great Collins Street East, a little below the level of the street. I thought I heard my friend—who was a member of the Wyndham—heave a gentle sigh as, in surveying the rough-and-ready dinner apartment, he endeavoured to sidle into a seat opposite me, where we were obliged to dovetail as in an omnibus, the table betwixt us being barely broad enough to sustain the pair of half-wiped plates. We ordered steak and potatoes as the safest dish, and, while waiting for it—as we were not allowed any bread to pick at—we

* Candle.

endeavoured to derive edification from the general conversation. One good-natured, communicative man in a jumper, who saw that our attention was directed to his box—moreover perhaps moved by the destitute appearance of our table, which was simply decorated with a single salt and an eggcup of mustard—jumped up with a bottle and glass, and insisted on our joining him in nobblers. As there might have been danger in declining the intuitive hospitality, we made a virtue of necessity, and swallowed the potions in so clean, off-hand a manner, as to charm the heart of our unknown entertainer, who smiled affectionately, shook our hands vehemently, exclaiming, in guttural ecstasy, 'X-cuse me, gemmen—you're town folk—I don't make me money like as you do; I makes mine by fair bloody diggin'.' Saying which, he gave the bottle a flourish over his head that sent a shower of brandy about the room...

I found, during dinner, that several of the parties present intended going to the theatre, so I waited for the most respectable convoy that was formed, and went to see how the Royal Dane was represented in the antipodes. The evening was very dark and dank, and the streets apparently deserted; but there were murmurs of voices in the direction of Queen Street, and a lurid halo in the sky, which denoted by a murky irradiation where the magnet of the night was situated. Cabs and carriages too rattled towards that point, so that there was no mistaking the way. On making the turn out of Bourke Street, one would have supposed it was to have been an outdoor representation, in the Champs Elysées fashion, from the crowd and the glare of light which was blown about from a number of cans of fat and rags, which did duty as gas-lamps; but these I found to be indispensable, to enable the patrons of the drama to distinguish the lines of boards and stepping-stones which led from the hard street through the mud to the doorways of the temple of Thespis. A great many votaries, however, despising these imitations of gentility, showed their contempt of them by wading deliberately through the slush; others, in a less discerning state, using them alternately. The carriage folk had a special plank, which was altogether insufficient, for the vehicles, like so many Trojan horses, each contained a host, reminding me too of the hats from which conjurors keep pulling out an unlimited succession of cocks and cabbages; and when you would be ready to make oath that the last person had emerged, a compressed digger would come out of a corner with a bundle of rumpled satin in his arms, and failing to 'walk the plank', would carry it in triumph through the knee-deep mire to the dress circle entrance, while some of the more distinguées dames, with the right or privilege of 'private entrée', conducted their admirers through the bar of the adjoining tap, where, as a matter of course, there was sure to be 'a champagne shout' for the company.

I made my way to the pit as the place from which I could have the most comprehensive survey of the house and stage, paying 5s. into an aperture which smelled like the bunghole of an empty brandy-butt, and getting in return a disfigured penny piece as a pass, which I handed to a corrugated Amazon smoking a black pipe, who looked contemptuously at my over-decent appearance. As I got into the body of the house, I found the chandelier overcast by a dark cloud of tobacco-smoke, and I fancied I could, at intervals, detect the tones of a cracked flageolet, a screaming violin, and a flabby drum through the tumult of voices above and around me. The pit was apparently filled with pert gents, fast tradesmen, and mechanics, some few with their colonial wives, but no children. The dress circle was crammed beyond sitting posture with florid-looking women in too-low satin dresses, some in their smeared hair, with their pinned bonnets dangling in front of the boxes; others crowned with tiaras like rose bushes in full bearing, and all hung round with chains, watches, collars and bracelets of the most ponderous manufacture. Their lords-in-waiting were habited either in tartan jumpers or red worsted shirts, smoking short pipes, and indulging in indelicate attentions, which frequently 'brought down the house' before the rising of the curtain. I saw several pendant samples of the style of dress-boot in fashion as Eagle Hawk swells got astride the leaning cushions, and heard several cordial recognitions, such as, 'Damn your bloody eyes, Bill, is that you?' or, 'Poll, may me beer-can, how's your coppers?' shouted from side to side. The upper tier, as well as I could judge, held more of a medley audience. The shriek-ing Bedouins of the streets mustering strongly, often in the capacity of bear leaders to stockriders from the interior, and cicerones to a heavy class of digger, who gaped and stared in hiccuping admiration at nothing in particular, damning by turns every portion of his internal anatomy, from the liver all round, 'if ever he seed nothin' like it never afore'. There were also groups of sailors with their Dulcineas, who, judging from external appear-ance, were the *femmes de chambre* of the ladies beneath them, sporting their cast-off satins, which retained the grease stains much better than the original dyes in the washing; and if they were not over-encumbered with jewellery, they could boast instead a species of facial ornamentation not usually put on with a brush. There was a tumultuous uproar all the time without any lull whatever, made up of all sorts of discordant yells, noises and exclamations, original and imitative together, with a stamping and thumping which caused the chandelier to quiver. But in the midst of the hurricane a man in the pit was seen to stand up on his seat with his back to the orchestra, and gesticulate earnestly, as if to obtain a hearing. At first his object was misunderstood, and he was variously suggested as a 'target for an empty bottle', or a 'subject for cowhiding', or an 'ambassador to the infernal regions'; but there was a certain pertinacious suavity about him which at length induced a still silence, and extracted from him a profound bow. He then said: 'Ladies and gemmen, I thank you for your kindness—I am, in fact, obliged to you. (Loud cheers.) I suppose you all recollect me; if not, I beg to inform you I am Tim Jones, who kept the shavin'-shop in Flinders Lane. (Applause.) I'm just come from the famous Eagle Hawk, where I dug up one hundred and fifty ounces; and I'll be damned for the future if ever I'll shave another b—— of the lot of ye.' (Thunders of applause.) ('Bravo, Tim! What'll you take?') And a tempest of other tender inquiries followed, in the midst of which the curtain rose, but Bernardo, Marcellus and Horatio failed to divide attention with Tim Jones until the Ghost made his appearance in an outré rig, almost as comical as Wright's in 'Paul Pry'; then, indeed, there was a roar of laughter, accompanied by shouts of 'Well, I'm blowed!' 'Holy Moses!' 'Does your mother know you're out?' enough to try the gravity of a real dead ghost nineteen centuries old.

Marcellus first, then Horatio, and finally the Ghost came to the footlights with great obsequiousness, but poor Tom Steele himself, the Head Pacificator of Ould Ireland, could not allay the uproar; so the scene and the act proceeded in dumb show amidst immense applause.

The first interval was enlivened by renewed pleasantries, explosions of champagne, and demands for nobblers, which were ministered with wonderful assiduity, to the total exclusion of oranges and soda water. Toasts were given in the pit, and warmly responded to from the gallery, and healths were interchanged in regular digger vernacular across the house. The second act commenced without its being apparently noticed until the entrance of Ophelia, which was the signal for a tempest of clapping and savoury compliments, that admitted of no intermission until the King and Queen with their train stalked in, when they were greeted with ironical applause and the Victorian *doubles ententes*, provoking bursts of general laughter, which an enthusiastic god was so impressed with the jolly-good-fellowness of the King, that he sent him down a bottle of brandy by the thong of a stockwhip from the gallery. So that the second act of the Stratford *chef d'œuvre* was wound up by an exchange of hob-nobbing between the house and the stage. The third act was transformed into a most amusing colloquy between the Danish gravedigger and the gold-diggers from Eagle Hawk, made up of mutual inquiries about the depth of the sinking, and the return to the tub, which so tickled Hamlet that he gave up the soliloquy and joined in the joking.

After this there was a fierce row caused by the accidental falling of a brandy bottle from the gallery into the pit, but which was resented as an intentional occurrence. There was at first an attempt made to go round and attack the gods in the rear, and then an escalade was essayed, in which two sailors succeeded in climbing up the pillars which sustain the boxes, but instead of a display of bloody hostilities, a festive scene ensued, which soon spread into a regular epidemic, during which brandy bottles were let down and others hoisted up by ropes made of handkerchiefs, amidst a tempest of toasts, sentiments and hip, hip, hurrahs.

The manager at length came forward to invoke a hearing, but nobody seemed aware of his presence. Then poor Ophelia, with straws in her hair, endeavoured to bring the lunatics to reason, and after a world of curtseying, she induced a pause, but as she was about uttering the first word of remonstrance, a riotous sailor roared out, 'Come, give us "Black-eyed Susan", old gal!' which produced such an unconquerable relapse, there was no alternative but to cut down the remainder of the performance to the last scene, where the poisonings and sword practice brought the performance to an agreeable conclusion. But Hamlet, Ophelia, and the Ghost, in undress, were obliged to appear before the footlights to bear a pelting shower of nuggets—a substitute for bouquets—many over half an ounce, and several of which fell short of the mark into the orchestra.

WILLIAM HOWITT

The New Hairystocracy

William Howitt was a professional author who sailed
for Australia in 1852 accompanied by two sons. The trio
spent two years at the diggings, with little success, but
the publication of William's reminiscences under the title
Land, Labour and Gold was widely acclaimed. His
observations on Melbourne's 'hairystocracy' and the age
of 'diggerdom' are some of the most acute available of
the city in the throes of gold fever.

You know that I expected to see a fine collection of the scum
of the earth here, including Sydney and Van Diemen's Land
convicts, and Californian adventurers; but I did not, and do not
apprehend any danger from them. There is no denying that crime
has already reached a height which is awful. The vast mass of
rude fellows who flock here from all quarters of the world, and
then get extraordinary sums of money, such as they hitherto have
had no conception of, makes this no wonder. Here, too, they
mingle with the worst escaped convicts, and receive a *finish* to
their education in all depravity which they could not obtain elsewhere. The number of drunken fellows which you see about the
streets is something fearful; and their language is still more so.
Successful diggers! (that is the phrase) are everywhere; either
galloping along, rude figures as they are, on rude horses, or standing about the doors of public houses.

Everybody gallops here, or at least goes at a canter—which
they call the Australian *lope*. Boys who take horses to water go at
a headlong rate over steep gullies, torn out by the rains, and amid
everywhere-standing stumps. I often wonder that they are not

dashed to pieces; but I suppose the young rascals are reserved for another fate. I see them go right into the river at this pace, and never stop till the animal stoops its head to drink. The streets here, spite of the fine weather drawing off immense numbers daily to the diggings, are crowded with rude-looking diggers and hosts of immigrants, with their wives, their bundles, and their dogs. All down, near the wharves, it is a scene of dust, drays and carts hurrying to and fro, and heaps of boxes, trunks, bundles and digging tools. Here you see ships unloading all kinds of goods, and scores of drays fetching them away, making it almost impossible to pass among them without being crushed; and the fellows are not at all mindful of you. It is every man's business to take care of himself here. They are just as independent in their speech as in their actions. It is a wonderful place to take the conceit out of men who expect much deference. The Governor was yesterday riding along among this crew, attended by one soldier; but not the slightest notice was taken of him, not even by a touch of the hat.

They are just as free in helping themselves to your property. All seem bent on fleecing their neighbours to the utmost in their power. Shopkeepers, innkeepers, boatmen, draymen, wharfingers, all get all they can out of the unfortunate gold-adventurers. My effects will cost me more in getting them up to the town from the ship then they did in bringing them hither from London; and to do this a fortnight has been consumed—thus detaining the whole ship's passengers in the town at a terrific cost, and away from the goldfields, where they might be reimbursing themselves. Surely never had the colony made less preparation for what it must have foreseen twelve months ago.

Everybody ought to calculate that the fortnight he will probably be detained here will cost him as much as the whole voyage, and make his arrangements accordingly; besides which, without the strictest watchfulness on his part, his luggage will be plundered; for the thieves proper are a very active class of gentry here. One of our fellow-passengers has had his boxes regularly gutted; and we ourselves have had our mining boots and other boots and shoes stolen. The mining boots are indispensable to us, and cannot be replaced here at less than 9*l.* per pair, of their quality...

But the one great principle of the colony is the Dutchman's maxim: 'Get honestly, if you can; but at all events, get!' People avow the principle. They come here, in fact, as they go to India, to make fortunes, and then—'go home'. That is the phrase. Everybody talks of England as home. They are all going home some day. This and that person are selling their property, and going home. Others are going home for a visit; but in any case it is towards home that their thoughts tend. Hence so little is done for the colony, this splendid colony! Everyone thinks of himself, there is no patriotism, because no man looks upon this country as his home. All are in a sort of temporary exile—the servants of mammon, that they may spend 'golden earnings at home'...

Kind as our friends here are, we shall be glad to be out of this Melbourne. While I am writing, the wind has shifted to the north, and brings along with it the most astonishing dust-storm conceivable, as it invariably does. The accounts I have read, speak of this nuisance occurring about twenty times in the year. It occurs about every third day, so far as our present experience goes. Whenever the wind is in the north, there it is! You hear this wind the moment it commences. It howls about the doors and windows like a winter's wind at home, and the air is immediately darkened with one vast, driving volume of dust. Sometimes in summer it is so thick that you cannot see your hand before you. Even now it blows through the sash and covers me and everything in the room. I dare say this paper will be gritty with dust when it reaches you. In the streets you cannot walk without a veil over your face, or your eyes and mouth are speedily filled. So far as I have seen, it is the worst thing they have and a terrible drawback to the climate

it is. That of itself would drive me out of town; for up the country
they say there is little or nothing of it; but near the roads which
are neither macadamised nor scraped, it is a perfect pestilence. It
would drive your English ladies mad to see their houses, and all
their beds, sofas, and beautiful furniture every few days literally
buried in fine dust. But it is admirable with what patience the
ladies here get to endure the inevitable evil. How coolly they wait
till the storm is over, and then set about to have all cleaned up,
shook out, and put in order again.

So a hasty good-bye for awhile to this odd, but extravagant
Melbourne, which every day becomes more droll—actually that is
the only phrase for it—droll in its extravagance of all sorts. My
brother amused us this morning by reading some of the contents
of a 'little bill' from his wheelwright. 'To greasing his cartwheels
twice 1*l*. 0*s*. 6*d*.,' or 10*s*. 3*d*. each time. 'To putting a nut on one of
the cart screws, 15*s*.' a really sixpenny job! And the diggers actually, in their folly, encourage these harpies in this style of charge.
One of them the other day asked the fare of a cab for the day.
'Perhaps more than you'd like,' said the jarvie, for the digger was
a very common-looking fellow. 'What is it?' asked the digger.
'Seven pounds for the day.' 'There is ten,' said the fellow; 'you can
light your pipe with the difference.'

A gentleman, high in government, told me the other day that he
was about to take one of these carriages for some distance; but
the man said, 'We don't drive the likes o' you now-a-days.' 'Well,
but what is the fare? My money is as good as another's, I suppose.'
'Oh!' replied the fellow, hesitating, 'I don't know—in fact we
don't drive the likes o' you now!' And that was all he could get out
of him. The diggers are styled 'The New Aristocracy'; and the
shopkeepers flatter them with the title in their advertisements.
Here is one: 'To the New Aristocracy. If you want the best
article of any description to be had in the city, you can be supplied
by De Carle and Co., Gold Diggers' General Provision Stores,

Little Bourke Street.' Whilst this new aristocracy, or more properly *hairystocracy*—for hairy enough they are in all conscience—thus encourage their own plundering in the town, the bushrangers are practising it at its very gates. Four fellows, last Saturday, armed with guns and pistols, stopped successively twenty people, and tied them under a tree on the most frequented highway to the very next village, St Kilda, and that in the broad day, at half-past three o'clock in the afternoon. This game they kept up till half-past five, or two full hours. Numbers of wealthy merchants go out that way about that time of day, and some of them were caught. There is a report that the Governor himself was on that road very nearly at that time. The fellows having finished their work, then went off towards the Dandenong ranges, 'sticking up', or 'bailing up' in the colonial phrase, that is, stopping and robbing everyone that they met. Government has offered a reward of 2000*l.* for their apprehension.

As for ourselves, we had a little alarm the other night, which, upon the whole, however, was rather amusing. I had sat up writing. It was one o'clock. I had thrown down my pen and jumped into bed, but was not asleep, when Dick, a little funny black and tan terrier, who sleeps on the rug by the door in the hall, began to bark furiously, and became every moment more and more angry. There had been some daring burglaries just lately in that immediate neighbourhood. I got up, and the Doctor came out of his chamber. We went downstairs, I armed with a double-barrelled gun. We heard somebody treading about in the portico, but could get no answer to our demands of who was there. Still there was a great trampling attended with the vilest smell of a barnyard I ever smelt. It poured through the door into the house like a pestilent steam. Dick grew more and more violent. At length we got to learn that it was a drunken tanner, who very freely said he wanted a bed, and should pay 5*s.* for it. It was useless telling him that he could have no bed here. He was too drunk to reason with; and if he stayed there Dick would not let anybody sleep. So Alfred got his revolver, and he and the Doctor set out on the dubious adventure of discovering a policeman. They sallied forth by another door through the garden, and traversed the streets in vain for half an hour; for the police here are just as discerning fellows as yours at home, and greatly prefer warm beds, or warm pot-house firesides, to rambling about cold streets at midnight. Their last hope was in the central police station; and there they found two officers, who, however, held a long colloquy in the Dogberry style, as to whether the house lay in their beat. When at length they were put in motion, they had many discussions whether they should go up this street, and whether they should avoid that, which one asserted was *dangerous*.

At length they arrived, and, by the aid of a bull's-eye, discovered the scamp, a most filthy villain, dead drunk, and lying almost naked in a bed of prickly-pears. Apparently he had fancied that he had got a bed, and had undressed himself, as far as his muddled brain allowed him. If he had one spine of the prickly-pears in him, he must have had thousands; and anyone who has been punctured by them well knows how painful they are. But the wretch appeared totally insensible of them, though he had crushed the whole bed down. The policemen had enough to do to raise him, shake him, try to make him walk, and finally haul him away with his shoes off. One of the policemen was actually sick with the fellow's stench. He was an Irishman, and had all the look of a debauched digger, tanner as he was, and smelling worse than the vilest tar-pit in Christendom.

Céleste de Chabrillan

The Governor Is Going to Give a Ball!

The wife of the French consul, Céleste was devastated by Governor La Trobe failing to invite her to his ball, but revenge would be sweet. Her account of Lola Montez's performance was kinder than most—Melbourne's newspapers excoriated the actress, and it was widely rumoured that Montez appeared on stage in a state of considerable intoxication. The actress' spider dance, nonetheless, was the talk of the town.

We are surrounded by people who are probably very honest but who look like veritable bandits. All are armed. Is it to attack or defend? Time will tell. They have begun to macadamise the road in front of our house. This consists of throwing broken stone into the deepest ruts in the road. The men employed for this type of work wear a uniform of grey cloth with their number written across the chest. Those who guard them are armed with muskets. The men have chains on their feet and are shackled like horses in a field, none of which prevents them from appearing reasonably happy with their lot. These are the thieves and murderers who are put to work rather than being fed to do nothing but while away their time in prison. But I think to myself as I watch them from behind the curtains: 'Heavens! I only hope their chains are strong!'

It seems that we live in an area which, because of its isolation, is a favoured haunt of criminals. Of an evening, people in the area fire their rifles or pistols to let the criminals know that they are armed. Our front windows opens onto the street, there are no shutters. Simply by lifting the frame, anyone could enter our house at any time of the day or night...

The month of May begins with a wind that lashes our faces and torrential rain that comes in everywhere. Lionel puts his papers in the so-called living room which he uses as an office; they are drenched and he is forced to place an umbrella above the table to do his correspondence. The wind makes our hut shake, and I have the feeling that it is going to take off like a balloon. To top it all off, it's very cold, and wood costs seventy-five francs a small cartload. However, when we have some it lasts a long time: it's red, hard as stone, it turns as black as coal and doesn't burn.

Thefts and crime are increasing. Last night, a poor Irishman was killed for his tools. It happened just 100 yards from our place. I had only been sleeping a little, now I don't sleep at all.

We have just found a small four-roomed brick house. It's barely finished, but here you don't even give the walls time to dry. This house is situated on Victoria heights. From the first-floor windows one can see, on the right, the town of Melbourne; in the distance, on the left, the harbour filled with ships; opposite, a hill where the Chinese emigrants have permission to set up their tents for the first few days after their arrival. At the foot of this hill, the Yarra-Yarra; on the left, in a valley, a huge village called Richemont*...

The whole town and countryside are in a state of wild excitement: the governor is going to give a ball!...Seven hundred invitations have been issued. Lionel has received one, but it's for him alone. As far as I am concerned, it is an affront which would be of no great concern, were it not for friends, especially women friends, who constantly arrive to talk to me about the ball, which should be a splendid affair. They ask me what I intend to wear and how I plan to get there, as the governor lives several miles from

* Richmond.

Melbourne. Carriages will cost no less than 250 or 300 francs for the evening, so people want to share the hiring expenses. My reply to them all is that I have not been invited. This gives rise to an endless series of sympathetic protests and recriminations...

The Governor's Ball was held yesterday. More than 700 people set out to attend it in foul weather. The rain fell in torrents. All available carriages, even miners' carts, had been pressed into service at exorbitant prices, but nevertheless everyone was looking forward to a wonderful time!...They were very soon disappointed. The Toorak rooms were twenty times too small to accommodate the crowd. Many people could not even get in, and had to wait outside or in their carriages. The ladies' outfits were completely ruined. Some protested; others sulked. All the men could think about was the lavish supper to which they intended doing full justice. The much-awaited hour arrived. They did not push; they rushed forward in a crush; they trampled each other underfoot. But what a disappointment was in store for them too! On the sideboard were a few cold meats entirely surrounded by nothing but hams, and the only drink available—a keg of colonial beer! The newspapers have printed scathing articles criticising the governor. They are of one voice in their complaints, which border on impertinence. If it's true that he is very sensitive to criticism, he must be most unhappy, and bitterly regret holding what they call 'the beer ball'...

17 July—On the twelfth of this month, the riflemans held a subscription ball in aid of the wounded in the Crimea. The riflemans are voluntary national guardsmen. No one here would be rich enough to hold a ball at his own expense. The exhibition building is therefore hired out to all those who want to organise such entertainment.

The town notables must always figure at the top of the subscription list. They cannot refuse to pay their dues for fear of being ridiculed. That is why we sometimes go to a ball. There one meets the elite of Melbourne society, tradesmen, miners and others. It's a strange mixture of people indeed.

Lionel had the idea of also organising a subscription ball for our wounded. He named me Grand Master of Ceremonies. I was allotted the Crystal Palace Room for the 16th, which should be quite a new attraction for the ball. I decided to hold a tombola for the ladies. As I am not wealthy enough to buy the prizes, I shall donate some dresses cut out but not made up, which I brought from Paris, two fans, two little gold bracelets, laces and ribbons, music albums, a writing set and a needle-work set. There will be twenty-five winning numbers. I am delighted to donate these things, for I know they will tempt the ladies, who only pay ten shillings, but don't come unaccompanied, and the gentlemen pay two pounds. I would be so happy if we could send several thousand francs to France.

They are fighting to get our ball tickets. They even come down to St Kilda to get them. Oh! *ma belle France*, how easy it is, and how good it feels, to be able to do something for you!

It's an ill wind that blows no one any good. For some time now, everyone seems to want to make me forget the mean, spiteful way the governor treated me on the day of his *beer ball*. They are still talking about it. Epigrams and caricatures are still appearing morning and evening.

On the occasion of the Emperor's name day, my husband was obliged to give a lavish dinner for the town dignitaries. It goes without saying that there were no women present. They never go to these celebrations, which are usually held in a restaurant.

They drank to the health of all the crowned heads of Europe, to France, to our wounded in the Crimea. Then they passed around some small pieces of paper and wrote on them in pencil the names of people who were absent, but who should be toasted. It was requested, as a matter of deference, that Mr Justice Williams's paper should be read out first. He handed it on to be passed around the table until it reached the governor, who read my name aloud. This was greeted with three rousing cheers. Lionel was so delighted that he came home drunk as a lord...

Our ball took place on the 16th. The people of Melbourne had never seen anything so fine. My tombola was all the rage. The ladies found my husband the most gallant of men...for it goes without saying that my name was never mentioned in connection with the little gifts supplied by me from my cabin trunks; that would have made them lose all their appeal. In spite of our success, my joy was mixed with a good deal of sadness. I spent the night fighting back tears. They played all our national songs, then these words: France, the French, repeated a hundred times over disturbed me deeply. There is no getting away from it, I'm a Parisian to the core!

Our subscription ball raised about 30,000 francs, which we will send off through the bank. It caused me a good deal of heartache and fatigue, but fatigue is nothing when compared to such a wonderful result.

Today I can laugh about it, but yesterday I had the kind of fright one never forgets. We had an earthquake that stopped the clock and rattled the glasses in the cupboard. In these circumstances it's better to have a wooden house that one made of stone. The unexpected movement did not frighten me at the time, because I did not know what caused it, but it made me feel something akin to seasickness.

Lola Montez arrived here a while ago with her troupe. She is putting on shows at the theatre. She was so frightened last night that she went out into the street in very flimsy night attire...She still has the same lovely face and eccentric character...

She has written, or has had someone write for her, a play in five acts entitled *My History*. The first act is called 'The First Era'. When the curtain goes up, some working-class men are talking about Lola in terms like these: she is a goddess, divine, an angel of purity turned dancer because she has a philanthropic task to accomplish on earth. She gave her ring to one person; she paid ransom for another. The King of Bavaria comes to hear of her, as they say she is very good at diplomacy. He has her kidnapped.

In the second act she is in the king's palace. She deliberates matters of state with him, constantly proving that he has no idea what he is talking about. The Jesuits fear Lola's clear-sightedness and want to poison her. During the performance she falls ill on stage, but this does not stop her giving everyone a piece of her mind, shouting at the top of her voice.

In the third act, there has been a popular uprising. Lola is accused of being the old king's mistress, of having spent a lot of money belonging to the state, and is ordered to leave the town immediately. She is furious, she protests and fights with her rifle. Her house is set alight and she escapes, letting out blood-curdling screams all the while.

In the fourth act she is a wandering outlaw. Attempts are made on her life, for even from afar she is the light, the soul and the spirit of the king. All her possessions are stolen. In the end, she has only one thing left, or rather two: her conscience and her virtue. 'Let people malign me if they wish,' she says, 'they maligned Joan of Arc, didn't they!'

In the fifth act she also makes a speech to the audience. She asks for their support, for their protection. They can prove their goodwill by coming to her plays every day. She blows kisses to everyone.

'Reduce the price of the seats,' shouts an Irishman, lording it in the stalls. Lola answers him and they argue back and forth for half an hour. Others call out to her; she replies with remarkable presence of mind. She speaks English very well. They clap and whistle. There is an infernal din.

The play is followed by a ballet composed and danced by Lola! It consists of moving about a lot while frantically shaking the folds of an extremely short gauze skirt. There is a spider hidden between the folds; it's called the spider dance. I don't know why, but all the women walked out before the end of the ballet, although there is nothing improper about it. However, the police have banned a second performance.

Lola says that all the nations are rising up against her: they fear her influence, politically speaking, that is. People say she's mad, but she is simply very excitable. She came to see me. I don't really remember what she said to me. She speaks very quickly and her ideas have no logic to them. She was leaving that evening to perform on the goldfields. She promised to come and see me on her return. She's counting on making a fortune here. I hope she does but I don't think it will happen.

The inhabitants of Melbourne have an insatiable need for entertainment. Miners are encouraged to come to town and to leave as much money here as possible. Bars, cafés, concerts and dances are increasing in number. Everyone requests *the honour of your company* at the same time. That is the way invitations are worded. Because of people's eagerness to attend our ball, we are obliged to subscribe to theirs. We have not a moment to ourselves…

14 November—…As neither of us was feeling very cheerful, Lionel and I decided to have dinner in Melbourne, so that we could go to the theatre in the evening to see *Richelieu* played by an English actor called Brook, of whom we had heard a good deal. When we entered the theatre, the scene was set in the Orangery at Versailles with Louis XIII moving about in front of the footlights. He wore a wig *à la malcontent* and a moustache. The seams of his stockings were twisted like a corkscrew from his heels to his knees. Brook himself is really remarkable, but the rest of the cast take away from his performance. I can speak reasonable English, but I have difficulty understanding the actors. Like our artists, they have a particular kind of diction, and at times all I can hear is strident shouting.

No matter how good an English actor is, I prefer to see him in comic roles, so I was waiting impatiently for the second play which featured Copping. Copping is a fat man, with a belly like a Chinese figurine. He sometimes slaps his stomach as if he were playing a bass drum, which makes the audience roar with laughter. He jumps, turns somersaults, throws punches, gets kicked. The audience adores him and they applaud with all their might. In the intervals he goes down to the bar (in the pub). He's the owner. He keeps his stage costume on while serving his customers. He's director, artist, wine merchant and waiter all in one.

He parodies everyone. He does a caricature of Brook as his main subject, and has just composed a ballet based on Lola Montez—the spider dance. He is dressed as Cupid, only his gauze skirt sits bunched up on his hips like a baker's smock. On his head is a garland of white roses. He blows kisses to the audience, then after much prancing about that makes them die laughing, he throws a stuffed rat on the ground and jumps on it with both feet.

He mops his brow, comes forward to make a speech, simpering and imitating Lola's voice exactly. They throw wreaths of hay decorated with vegetables at him; Lola was thrown lots of flowers. He pirouettes while he picks them up and exits, walking into one of the uprights. They call him back, he comes back on stage looking serious and says: 'I'm a poor fugitive. I have enemies everywhere, but I have right on my side and my bar on the ground floor. God protect me! I know who my true friends are when they come and drink with me.'

They shout: 'Encore!'

He blows more kisses and adds, puffing like a grampus: 'I'm too weak to do the dance again, but till tomorrow, if you'll give me the honour of your company.'

He exits not to cries of 'bravo!', but to boos and catcalls. They say that Lola had wanted to horsewhip Copping, but that she had changed her mind once she laid eyes on this colossus who was preparing to receive her with a birch.

As we left the theatre, we heard the alarm bell ringing. Every-one was shouting as they ran: fire! fire! fire! In the distance you could see a great red patch outlined against the sky. The village of Richmond fell prey to the flames. The wooden houses collapsed so quickly that people scarcely had time to get out, and with nothing but the clothes they were wearing.

Good Lord, what a country! I constantly feel the world is coming to an end.

ANONYMOUS

Revolution

This description of a meeting held in early December 1854, on the eve of the Eureka uprising, appeared in *Social Life and Manners in Australia* in 1861. The rebel diggers were protesting against licence fees and as many as thirty were killed by government troops. This piece conveys a sense of the precarious grip that the govern-ment had during these restless times.

Five hundred diggers, it was said, were on the road to Melbourne, well armed, and hoping to meet the troops before they arrived at Ballarat. There was a narrow pass on the road, which, if properly defended, was almost impregnable, and there they were to fall upon the soldiers, trusting that, fatigued by long and rapid marches, they would be easily overcome. This accom-plished, they were to march upon Melbourne, where they expected to be joined by the dregs of the population; and finally they intended to take the Treasury and the banks, and pillage the city! In this state of anxiety we remained until the 99th Regiment came over from Tasmania, to protect us.

Howqua

A Chinese Interrogation

Howqua was a Cantonese who had lived for nine years in England before coming to Melbourne. What follows are excerpts from an interview undertaken in 1855 by Victoria's Select Committee of the Legislative Council on the subject of Chinese immigration. The committee, chaired by John Fawkner, was deeply disturbed by the thought that up to 40,000 Chinese were in Australia.

'Have you been long in this colony?'
  'Eleven months. I came here from England.'
'Have you been in California?'
'I have not been in California.'
'Have you been digging here?'
'I have been to the different diggings.'
'Where?'
'Ballarat, Bendigo, Castlemaine, Mopoke and Forest Creek, and Simson's.'
'Did you find many of your countrymen at the diggings?'
'A great many.'
'How many do you think there are of your countrymen altogether in this colony?'
'I think there will be 10,000 altogether.'
'What part of China do they principally come from?'

'They come from 4 District. My countrymen are from 5 District, Canton.'

'Are they mostly Tartars here?'

'Mostly.'

'Not many Chinamen?'

'No.'

'The Tartars come from 4 District, and the Chinamen from 5 District?'

'Yes.'

'Have they a good feeling amongst themselves?'

'The Tartars are fond of gambling, and the Chinamen do not like it. Chinamen like digging, and a Chinaman makes more money and keeps it. A Chinaman will accommodate himself to the English habits, the Tartars do not. The Chinamen like to stay here, the Tartars like to go home.'

'What is the difference between a Tartar and a Chinamen in the face; do you know them when you see them?'

'They are greatly different; the Chinamen are rather fair; the Chinese Tartars are rather darker.'

'Do they both live in the same way and cultivate the ground for rice?'

'Yes.'

'Have they the same laws and customs?'

'Yes.'

'When did you leave China?'

'I left China in 1846.'

'Have you been there since?'

'No.'

'Do you hold communication with your friends in China, by letter?'

'Yes.'

'Do the Chinese here, as a body, communicate with their friends back in China?'

'Yes, they write letters and put them in the post, and they are sent to Jardine, Matheson & Co.'

'Do the Chinese hear of these letters in China, and see them?'

'Yes.'

'And these letters bring them down here?'

'Yes; bring them to the diggings.'

'Has any letter of yours been printed, do you think?'

'Yes, in China.'

'In the Chinese language?'

'Yes.'

'Does it get much circulation?'

'In China, people are not so clever as the English gentlemen; my countrymen are rather stupid.'

'But by printing in the sheet they circulate some news among the people, do they not?'

'Yes; news just like a newspaper.'

'Do you think many of your countrymen will come here?'

'Yes, more coming every year. In Hong Kong, some Chinamen go home and give good accounts, and say, it is no use going to Sydney, but they come out, and come across here, and go up to the diggings.'

'The Chinamen take away the water at the diggings, and make the diggers angry?'

'Yes; that is what I have been speaking about.'

'Do the Chinese understand now the injury they are doing by taking such a large quantity of water?'

'Yes, they understand it. In the winter time you go and take plenty of water, in the summer time you cannot take a drop of water.'

'Are the government of China favourable to the people coming away?'

'They were not before, but the present government is.'

'They see them bringing back gold; do the Mandarins get the

gold from them when they go back?'

'No, they keep it themselves, and buy land and build houses.'

'Can you buy land in China so as to have it to yourselves for ever?'

'Yes, you can buy a piece of land and pay so much.'

'Can you get land pretty cheap?'

'Yes, and make a house very cheap.'

'What position would £500 place a Chinaman in in China?'

'Very rich, plenty rice.'

'Is there any law to prohibit Chinawomen from coming here?'

'I never knew any come, except two from San Francisco.'

'Is there any law in China to prevent their coming with the men?'

'No.'

'Why do they not accompany the men?'

'There are not a great many of my countrymen so rich as to bring them; they cannot afford it.'

'Do the Chinese like remaining in California?'

'Yes.'

'Do they carry on their religious observances there?'

'Yes.'

'Are they carrying them on here? Have you got any joss houses here?'

'No, no joss houses, but some like the Wesleyan Society—a great many like the Roman Catholic Society—just like in my country there is a joss house, but a great many will not go.'

'The Chinamen here belong to different religions?'

'Yes.'

'Have you one religion all over China?'

'No; different images—different gods. In England, they say, "One God, one Spirit, one Jesus Christ." So in my country they have different images. They take a piece of wood, and make an image; and they take a large stone, and make another to put up; and so on.'

'There is a new religion, is there not, since this rebellion in China?'

'Yes, they have burned up the idols altogether, and put them into the river. The Chinese now are all Freemasons, and form one brotherhood. The old emperor and his son are Chinese Tartars, and the new emperor intends [to] carry out all one brotherhood—Chinamen, and Americans, and Englishmen—and open the country to all.'

'What number of Chinamen do you expect to come here within this year?'

'I do not know; I heard of 500 coming on the day before yesterday. A man had come from Hong Kong, and he said some more Chinese were coming.'

'Do you think 500,000 are likely to come here within the next twelve months?'

'Plenty of Chinamen go home, and plenty of Chinamen come out.'

'Would the Chinese buy land and settle down here; are they fond of cultivation?'

'Yes.'

'Would they be able to grow wheat and vegetables?'

'Yes.'

'Would they rather do that than dig for gold?'

'All Chinamen like farming.'

'Do the Chinese complain about anything or grumble about anything here?'

'No, there is not much complaint, except that they are short of water just now.'

'Do the Chinese keep up a communication amongst themselves, so as to be ready to assemble at one time when wanted?'

'Yes.'

'You could assemble them all in a month, could you not?'

'Yes.'

'Are there not a large body of them under one man?'

'Not under him; he listens to what is to be done, and takes their orders.'

'Has he the power of compelling them to go home?'

'A great number tell him they want to go home, and they give him the money and go home.'

'Is there not one person who has the control of two or three hundred of them?'

'Yes.'

'What advantage does he get from them; do they support him or does he work; is he a chief amongst them or governor?'

'No; no governor.'

'Does he make any laws for them?'

'No, nothing.'

'They do not introduce the Chinese laws amongst them here?'

'No; not at all.'

'Will those Chinese who go home return here again?'

'They go home and buy goods and come again.'

'Will the government take any money from you when you go back?'

'No.'

'Any percentage at all?'

'No percentage at all. If I go home with so much money, I can buy so much land and a house, and buy so many wives, four or five wives, or ten or a dozen. All the merchants have four, five, or six wives.'

KINAHAN CORNWALLIS

Oh, Melbourne, Where Are Thy Charms?

Kinahan Cornwallis spent time in Melbourne as a public servant and seemed obsessed with the possibilities of swindlers and assault. His 'seven senses' evidently worked in odd ways—and perhaps he needed every one to survive in the dangerous and unpredictable city. He left the country in 1855.

This was Melbourne. This was the El Dorado. The fact of there being no gold to be found here was of little consequence. There were few people to be seen moving, and the only sign of commerce was a solitary bullock team, waiting in front of one of the before-mentioned wooden stores.

At the top of this street a more promising scene met our view. The cathedral stood at one corner, and the market, forming a square, and by-the-bye, the only one in the city, at the other, while Collins Street, the Regent Street of Melbourne, divided them. The bank of New South Wales fronted the religious edifice, and several brick and plaster hotels, and a few modern shanties, and an iron house, faced the marketplace.

The latter consisted of a confused assemblage of tents, Jews, slop goods, and fruits. With one of these hotels worthy of St Giles's, several of us proceeded to make acquaintance. It was our first venture, and we were very uncertain as to the amount of capital necessary to be invested in the cause of a bottle of ale.

'We'll have wine,' said one of my companions, a rash red-haired young man of sanguine temperament; 'I'd like to see what their colonial wine's like.'

'Just so,' I remarked, and awaited with some curiosity the result.

'A bottle of wine,' demanded the rash young man.

He appeared to entertain the idea that colonial wine was all alike, and that no other was to be had.

'Sherry?' asked the barman.

'Isn't it colonial wine you have?' asked the other.

The barman smiled, half in pity, half in pleasure.

'I haven't seen any yet,' said he, 'new chums come here with all sorts of queer things in their head.'

'I beg your pardon?' said I.

'Notions, I mean,' promptly retorted the man, favouring me, at the same, with a knowing wink; 'there was one of 'em digging up Collins Street yesterday, and trying to wash the mud clean.'

'Let's try the sherry?' said the aspirant for colonial wine.

'Eighteen shillings,' said the man, and he drew the cork.

A low, but expressive whistle followed this announcement.

'Rather high,' remarked one of our party.

'Ah, you don't know yet,' replied the liquor dealer.

'Well, there's one thing we know, and that is, it takes a colonial to pay colonial prices.'

'To be sure it does,' continued the man, 'what's the use of English money?'

This was a new argument, which, however, was speedily concluded, by the comment, that its use was a matter beyond question, but that its quantity evidently required to be considerable, if Melbourne prices were to be met; and with this reflection we paid our money, and drank our wine, the worst I had ever tasted…

I resolved to merely look about me on this first day of my arrival. Everything looked very cheerless. The sky was dark and threatening, and beyond the moving about of the new arrivals there seemed to be but little life stirring in the city. We had hardly

reached Collins Street when it began to rain, and with a violence
which I had never before experienced. I made a dart into a Jew
gold-buyer's office, in the window of which there were exhibited various small parcels of dust and nuggets, to each of which a
ticket was affixed, bearing the name of the gold field from which
it had been taken. In the centre of this collection, and occupying
a very prominent position, lay a Colt's revolver, ready loaded and
capped. The shower lasted about twenty minutes, after which we
set out in search of lodgings for the night, having resolved not to
return to the steamer before the afternoon following.

Continuing on our way to the bottom of Elizabeth Street, we
reached Flinders Street, separated from the banks of the Yarra
Yarra river by a strip of waste land stretching the entire length of
the street, at the end of which the river curved off a little to the
south. Here the mud became deeper, and the ground was intersected with numerous gullies and lagoons, through which we
found it a difficult matter to navigate. Several times our progress
was arrested by our boots being either held fast or pulled off
our feet by the mud. We had proceeded only a few yards through
this mire, in the endeavour to reach one of two houses standing
alone in this street, and to which we had been directed for
accommodation, when we arrived in front of the desired habitation; it was one of the old houses of the colony, and characterised
chiefly by the numerous panes of broken glass patched over with
brown paper and pieces of old newspapers, which abounded in
its windows, and by the general dinginess of its colour and
broken exterior; for the houses were of brick, covered over with
plaster, and coloured in imitation of stone, and as large pieces of
the plaster had crumbled and fallen away, their entire aspect was
damp and wretched.

At the door of the first of these two houses we knocked. In
answer to our inquiries, to our joy we were informed that we
could have beds there for the night, and moreover, would be

charged only five shillings a head for the accommodation… Feeling somewhat more satisfied at having at least secured a roof for ourselves in the colony, we strolled back into Collins Street…At about eight o'clock we emerged from the restaurant into the dark and silent streets. No lamps; no pavement; no shining moon; no illuminated shops were there to cheer us on the way to Flinders Street and our lodgings. All was mud and darkness.

Over slippery streets, abounding in gullies and lagoons, on this the last day of April, did we wend our noisy way, laughing at our mishaps and defying garrotters, for it was then such a common occurrence for strollers by night to be 'stuck up'; not in the ordinary English sense of *stuck up* people, be it observed, but stuck up with a vengeance; that is, brought to a dead halt at the revolver's mouth, or with a blow of a heavy life annihilator, commonly known as a 'life preserver', or at the point of a bowie knife. It was either 'your money or your life', or both, and woe unto the unarmed. We were not afraid of such assassination; we had each either a knife, or a swordstick, or a revolver, and there were four of us, and very courageous indeed we professed to be, and very mirthful under the colonial ordeal we were. We arrived at the house after sliding, stumbling, and sticking in the mud as we advanced to the door. Truly, Melbourne at that time was as much a ditch in winter as it was represented to be a dustbin in summer…

'Oh, Melbourne, where are thy charms?' said somebody; but I was too eager, too impetuous, too excited, to care about his words. There was no time for inquiries. Men had to accept the evidence of their seven senses, and rest content with such. Everybody was looking out for number one; there was no time for anyone to follow anyone to his grave had he died; nobody cared for his neighbour; everybody cared for himself. Such was the prominent feature of the new tide of population and society at Melbourne.

Yet all this clamour and anxiety seemed to subside or hide itself with the approach of night. Then everyone sought out his lair, and remained there till morning. I speak of the majority; of course some went to the circus and the theatre, and on their way home were more or less liable to be knocked down and robbed.

Australian Rules

Australian Rules football is one of the most notable productions of colonial Victoria. Melbourne's newspapers documented the game in great detail, from its first match in 1858 onwards. Thomas Wentworth Wills, mentioned here as the captain of Melbourne, was instrumental in the development of footy as we know it.

Morning Herald, 9 August 1858—Richmond Park was unusually lively on Saturday. Under the auspices of a fine day and their respective magistrates, the juvenile presbytery and episcopacy came out uncommonly strong. Both masters and boys appeared to reach the acme of enjoyment, and most jubilant were the cheers that rang among the gum trees and the she-oaks of the park when the Scotch College obtained a goal. This event occupied nearly three hours in its accomplishment. The compliment was shortly reciprocated by the opposition, who made a grand effort to do the deed. Evening's anxious shades cut short an amusement which, to judge by the evenly balanced scale of results, and the apparently inexhaustible physique of the combatants, must otherwise have been interminable.

*

Argus, 16 August 1858—...Football seems to be coming into fashion in Melbourne, and as it is a most manly and amusing game we hope that it may continue to grow in favour until it becomes as popular as cricket. To lookers-on a well-contested football match is as interesting a sight as can be conceived, the chances, changes, and ludicrous *contretemps* are so frequent, and the whole affair so animated and inspiring.

★

Argus, 14 May 1860—...Under the humane legislation of the Melbourne Football Club tripping has been tabooed, and 'hacking' renders a member liable to excommunication. The rare old 'bullies', so famous, at one time at least at Winchester, Eton and Harrow have no place in Victoria, and in vain do we in these degenerate days anticipate the spectacle of a dozen players rolling on the ground together. But if sore shins and aching a shoulders are less common, and the excitement be less intense, we make up in some measure by increased good humour and the absence of severe accidents...'Pushing' is now the destructive element remaining in the game, which in other respects might without impropriety or danger, be part of the calisthenic course of a young ladies' seminary—that is, if they played entirely among themselves. So much for the ethics of football, as it is both in Melbourne and at the Pivot; for the Geelongese, too, have a club or clubs of their own, and last year adopted the metropolitan rules. This season let us hope they will venture on a trial of strength with the Melbourne or Richmond club, and not let their modesty stand in the way, as it did before.

And now for the match of Saturday between the last-mentioned clubs, which had for some weeks been looked forward to with considerable interest. The Melbourne players have been slightly the favourites, it being considered on the one hand that all who would be chosen on that side were adept at the sport, while the other ranks must be supplemented by recruits of more or less rawness. Such as affected Richmond, on the contrary, argued that, with Wills as captain (a host in himself), and such powerful auxiliaries as Harrison, Bruce, Wardell, and others, their favourite team would make a capital fight of it, even if it did not prove victorious…

The numerous vicissitudes of the game we cannot undertake to chronicle, nor yet relate and who made the best 'drop-kicks', who was the boldest and most successful in 'charging', how often the ball was out of bounds, or how frequently the rules were infringed. That the ball was so much out of bounds may be accounted for partially by the sloping character of the ground, but not altogether. A little knot, consisting of some half-dozen players, seemed to take a special delight in obstructing the game in this way, thereby earning for themselves the unenviable title of 'The Corner'. Another drawback to an otherwise almost perfect afternoon's enjoyment was the objectionable shape of the ball, which was oval, and is said to have gained the prize at the Great Exhibition, besides being of the kind now in use at rugby school. This class of ball may fly further than a round one, but assuredly, in nine cases out of ten, does not fulfil the expectations of the propeller, more particularly if there be any wind. Considerable dissatisfaction was expressed when the game began at the Richmond captain's maintaining his right to the choice of ball, and a great deal more after the play was over. Next year we may expect to have patent octagonal or parallelopipedal cricket balls, or some geometrical monstrosity equally inapplicable to the required purposes. There can be no objection to a man playing football in thigh boots or in pumps, if he has a weakness in that way, for no one else suffers; but the ball is, as it were, common property, and any abnormal condition in it affects all alike.

The two goals made on Saturday were kicked, for Melbourne

by Mr Baker, and for Richmond by Mr Nicholls. It were almost invidious to single out any players for special mention, when nearly all exerted themselves to the utmost. No one, however, can feel slighted if we bestow a passing word of praise upon the consummate dexterity displayed by Mr Wills, who alternately 'raged, in the van', and defended his post against all comers with almost unvarying success.

HORACE WILLIAM WHEELWRIGHT
Melbourne's Magpie-geese

Horace Wheelwright's anonymously published *Bush Wanderings of a Naturalist* is a classic of Australian natural history writing. A passionate field sportsman, Wheelwright came to Melbourne around 1852 and became a professional shooter, working within a seventy-kilometre radius of the city to supply the meat market with game. Somewhat surprisingly, he was a keen advocate of hunting laws and the preservation of wildlife. Had his ethic prevailed Melbourne may have retained its skeins of magpie-geese.

I do not believe that any country in the world is better adapted as a home for waterfowl than Australia. Dreary swamps miles in extent, lagoons of immense size, where the bulrush and reed vegetate in rank luxuriance; creeks and waterholes, completely hidden from view by dense masses of tea-tree scrub, afford unmolested shelter and breeding places for the birds; and a few years ago, when the sounds of a gun was rarely heard in the solitude of morasses and fens, the country around Melbourne must have literally swarmed with wild fowl. When I first came into the country, the palmy days of the duck shooter were in their zenith; the fowls and buyers plentiful, the shooters scarce. The year previous there was not a float or big gun in this part of the colony, and the first punt that ever floated on Melbourne Swamp was built in Melbourne Street, where the market now stands, in the morning, launched in the afternoon, fitted up with an old musket, and the birds shot and sold in Melbourne before night. In this winter, £1000 was cleared off Melbourne Swamp and its neighbourhood by the two men who launched this punt. The diggings were then in full swing, money was like dirt, and the birds sold at any price. The buyers were not particular. Many a brace of seagull have been sold for 5s. and once I knew a pair of old shags with their beaks trimmed up, sold for 15s. as 'rock duck'. But this did not last long. The duck shooters of that day, like the diggers, never heeded the morrow, and not one laid up for a rainy day. As the birds became scarcer, the shooters increased, and prices fell, till at the present day duck shooting is not worth following within fifteen miles of Melbourne. What a change has six years made in the appearance of this country. The swamps and lagoons near Sandridge are all drained or built on, and a railroad now passes over ground on which, at that day, four of five couple of ducks might be killed with ease in a night's flight-shooting.

Eight species of wild duck are more or less common in this district, and I believe these are nearly all the ducks indigenous to Victoria: the mountain duck, the black duck, the wood duck, the pochard or China-eye, the whistle-wing or pink-eye, the shovel-bill, the teal, and the musk duck. I have seen one other species in Melbourne, said to have been shot in the neighbourhood, as large as a black duck, but more resembling the British gadwall in plumage. This I believe to be only a rare and occasional visitant to these parts, although I have heard that it is common in some parts further inland.

The black swan is common throughout the winter after the young birds can fly, on all the large swamps and lagoons; sometimes in good-sized flocks, but generally in small companies, which I took to be the old birds and birds of the year. Early in summer they retire to their breeding-haunts, and we saw very little of them again until the swamps and waterholes filled. They appear to breed in August and September. The nest is a large heap of rushes, and the female lays five to seven dirty-white eggs, not so large as those of the swan at home. They breed a good deal on some of the large islands in Westernport Bay, and I attribute the decrease of swans in this neighbourhood to the quantity of eggs that are yearly taken by the fishermen in this bay. Swan-ponds near the Heads, is also a great place for them; in fact, they are by no means rare in this district, and an odd pair or so breed on most of the large swamps. The black swan is not nearly so shy as the European hooper, and they are by no means difficult to come up to with a punt-gun. They are a heavy-flying bird, and don't care to rise on the wing, if they can save themselves swimming...

The swan is hardly worth shooting here for the market, as they only fetch 5s. each, and they are a heavy bird to carry about. The flesh of the young swan is excellent, and one roasted in a camp oven generally with us formed the duck shooter's Sunday dinner, whenever we could get one during the season. I wonder the skins are not more highly prized for the down, which is very thick. This is the only species of swan indigenous to Australia; but I once saw the real *rara avis* out here, or white swan, flying up the bay about a quarter of a mile out to sea. Nobody believed me when I mentioned it, but I pointed it out to a friend who was with me. I can't pretend to say where it came from. One would naturally think it had escaped from some aviary; but nobody at the time kept tame swans in this neighbourhood that I know of, although a pair may now be seen in the Cremorne Gardens[*].

Two species of wild geese are met with here—the magpie, or tree-goose, and the Cape Barren goose.

The magpie, or tree-goose (ongak[**]), is the common wild goose in this district, and, as far as I could learn, is the only common wild goose peculiar to Port Phillip. Although met with here only in small flocks, generally I think families, there are lakes in the interior where they swarm. I think they remained in our district throughout the year, although we used only to see them at uncertain periods, and never for long together. As the name denotes, colour of the magpie-goose is pied, dull black and white: it is about as large as the British brent goose, and the tail is very square. It is a singular bird: the beak is higher in shape, and not so broad, as in the common goose, has a palish rough cere, and the upper mandible is long, and has a powerful curve or hook. It has a large warty cere, extending over the front of the head, which is in shape like that of a game-cock, cut out helmet-combed. The feet are semi-palmated, and formed for perching; the claws long and sharp. I rarely saw them either on the ground or on the water, never, certainly, in open water, although I have raised them out of the thick reeds and grass that choke up many of the creeks and lagoons here. They are generally perched high up in the tea-tree scrub, where they will sit for hours; and a curious sight it is to see them sitting upright, with their long necks stretched out on the watch. They have a very loud, hoarse call-note when alarmed, nothing like that of the common wild goose. The greatest curiosity of this singular bird, however, is the windpipe, which has three folds, like that of the European hooper; but, instead of being folded within the breastbone, it lies on the left hand, outside, bedded in the flesh. They breed sparingly with us, for I have found the nest in a thick tea-tree scrub; and I fancy the small flocks that we see in the

[*] In Richmond.
[**] Aboriginal name.

autumn are families, which had been bred in the neighbourhood, and that they do not pack and make distinct migrations like the wild geese at home. Although a shy bird in the open, they are by no means difficult to creep up to in the thick tea-tree scrub, and many a pair have I killed right and left. They are capital eating, and will fetch from 12s. to 15s. per couple in the market.

The Cape Barren goose, the New Holland *cereopsis* of naturalists, looks like a cross between a goose and a turkey, and is only a rare and occasional visitant to our parts. It is rather larger and heavier than the magpie-goose, of a light grey colour, spotted and chequered all over with black; and the beak and feet in shape resemble those of that bird. I never saw them here but twice—once in a small flock, and once when two pitched with the tame geese at Mordialloc (this, I believe, they are fond of doing), and which were caught alive. They soon became tame, and used to stalk about the paddock; but they were very pugnacious with the other geese: their call-note was a deep trumpet-like sound. They very little resemble a goose when walking, but put me more in mind of the Canada goose in shape than any I know. These are the only two species met with here, and neither of them appear to be true geese...

None of the Australian ducks, except the black duck and the teal, appeared to fly in large flocks; and all the male birds had that particular excrescence in the windpipe peculiar to the British wild ducks. I fancy most of the ducks out here breed in trees. The common wild duck of this country is the black duck, and whether for its flavour at the table, its wild, gamy appearance, or the sport it affords the shooter, is certainly equal to any duck in the world...

The shoveller, or 'spoony' of the duck shooters, is something like the shoveller at home in size, shape and general appearance, but the plumage is not so handsome. They are chiefly found in creeks by themselves, but occasionally joined by a mob of black duck on the plains. It is rather a pretty duck, next in size to the black duck, and, except the teal and black duck, the commonest of all the ducks in this district. The plumage of the male is bright chestnut mottled with black, the breast dark, the scapulars long, the speculum on the wing pale blue, and the bill broad. They seemed to be partial to particular localities, and I knew one creek, called the Skeleton Creek, above Williamstown, in which I could always find a flock. The best shot I ever made at ducks in my life was in this creek. I was beating for snipe on the banks, with a small single gun and one ounce of No. 7 shot. I fired into a mob of spoonies which were going up the creek about fifteen yards from me. I bagged eight.

CLARA ASPINALL

The Gayest Place in the World

Clara Aspinall was clearly taken with the Melbourne social scene as it was around 1860. And indeed the picnics held at beauty spots around the bay were significant events and appear to have been delightful. The sister of barrister, journalist and politician Cole Butler Aspinall, she was in a position to enjoy the best that Melbourne society had to offer.

Melbourne is one of the gayest places in the world, and the ladies and gentlemen (those in the gay circles) are the most indefatigable, and I believe the most accomplished, dancers in the world. Dancing is the accomplishment which is the most cultivated in the colony, and it is therefore the one which is brought to the highest state of perfection. There have been lately in Melbourne professional walkers at the circus—men who undertook for a wager to walk a certain number of miles round and round in a certain number of hours. Now, I feel pretty sure that any practised lady dancer in this gay metropolis (if the band only struck up her favourite galop), with the assistance of an equally accomplished partner, could *dance* the same number of miles in half the time, without, like the professional pedestrians, requiring medical treatment before or after for the feet. For the gay, then, there are balls and small dances on the *tapis* continually; for the more quiet and conversational, dinner-parties; and for the musical, there are most agreeable *soirées musicales*.

Picnics too are greatly the fashion in summer, and very enjoyable to those who are vigorous, and can go through the exertion which they entail. Sometimes these gatherings happen on a hot-wind day, when a blast like that from a furnace is blowing; but this does not appear in the least to damp the ardour of the picnic devotees, who generally conclude the day's entertainment by dancing; indeed some of them assured me that the only relief, on a hot-wind day, was to dance without ceasing, as, if they remained in repose, they found the heat unbearable.

I only had the courage and enterprise to go to two of these Melbourne picnics, and they were a fair sample, for my friends told me that they were two of the best in point of arrangement, &c. that had ever been given. The first was to a favourite spot called Picnic Point, at Brighton—a pretty little promontory jutting out towards the sea, where there was a most appropriate circle of grass, like a fairy-ring, snugly enclosed by the tea-tree 'scrub'. No expense was spared in this picnic. A delightful brass band played continually, and a large marquee was erected, in which was spread out one of the most *recherché* of cold collations I had seen in the colony. There was dancing on the greensward; the gentlemanly and lively officers of HMS——

contributed greatly towards the animation of the scene; some, however, preferred the *dolce far niente* to hard labour, and sat in groups under the tea-trees; whilst others wandered about the beach, looking for seaweed, or watching the tumbling surf,

> 'The fair breeze blew,
> And the white foam flew,'

'and all,' as the saying is, 'went merry as a marriage-bell.'...

The other picnic to which I went is also well engraven on my memory. It began charmingly. Several boats were hired, and we were rowed up the pretty winding Yarra; the gentlemen, being allowed the privilege of rowing the ladies, exerted themselves, out of gratitude, most strenuously both physically and mentally; they vied with each other in entertaining the ladies and in feathering their oars; and of course, under these happy circumstances, they did not feel the heat at all. But, alas! all our enjoyment was suddenly nipped in the bud by—a snake in the grass! One of the ladies, in getting out of her boat, stepped upon this deadly creature, but happily escaped being bitten, and it was killed instantaneously. The poor lady's nerves were, as may be imagined, terribly shaken, and she could not be persuaded to leave the boat.

Archer by a Country Mile

In November 1861, Flemington racecourse was host to the first running of the Melbourne Cup. The race, run over 3200 metres, proved so popular that by 1879 the first Tuesday of November was declared a public holiday for Victorians and soon became a national, then an international, event.

Argus, 8 November 1861 — ...The attractions of Flemington Course appeared yesterday to have lost none of their powers of fascination, for the attendance on the part of the general public was much larger than we remember to have seen on the ground on any day for the two years last past, with the single exception of the occasion of the Two Thousand Guineas Stakes being run for.

The weather was especially favourable to the enjoyment of the visitors and the turf, being throughout in excellent order, was in the best form to ensure to horses of the best class the full measure of advantage due to their intrinsic superiority. There was a very fair show of fashionable company upon the grandstand. Early in the afternoon His Excellency Sir Henry Barkly arrived, attended by Capt. Bancroft, and the presence of the governor threw an increased animation into the scene. His Excellency visited the saddling paddock during the half-hour preceding the Cup race, and noticed, apparently with interest, the general character and condition of the competitors, as they passed up and down and stripped for saddling. The enclosure on the hill, open to the public on this occasion at a charge of one shilling for admission, was patronised to the extent of about 2000, the grandstand added some 600, and the elevated ground outside, with the crowds next the rails on the course, furnished about 1500 visitors to the course; so that the total number present may be estimated at about 4000 persons. The most perfect order prevailed throughout the day, and the police had little more to do than to enjoy a view of the racing.

On the ground were the usual racecourse amusements, and the ordinary minor speculative games of skill or chance that frequently tempt the unwary and the rash to diminish their stock of ready money by the unwise means they employ to add to it. The refreshment-booths drove a thriving trade throughout the day, and the refreshment rooms of the grandstand, where Messrs Spiers and Pond were the caterers, were also largely patronised, and the good things of their providing met with general approval...

Next came the great event of the day, the Melbourne Cup, for which seventeen of the twenty-two acceptances came to the post...The appearance of the principal favourites was carefully scanned as they afforded opportunities for the observation of the cognoscenti, and it appeared to be generally admitted that, whatever might be the difference between their relative merits, they had all been profited to the utmost of their capability by the care and attention bestowed upon them by their respective trainers. The condition of Archer, Mormon, Flatcatcher, Inheritor, and Despatch in particular were superb. The Sydney horses were admirably brought out, and the winner, Archer, looked the perfection of health and power, a fitting competitor for the Victorian champion, who looked pounds a better horse than on the Two Thousand Guineas Day.

About twenty-five minutes to four the flag fell, and a good start was effected, Flatcatcher, Medora and Mormon getting to the front in a few strides. As the horses rounded the turn, coming to the straight running, a terrible accident occurred, through Twilight, Medora and Despatch falling, with fatal results to the two last mentioned mares, and inflicting very severe injuries on their riders. This unhappy contretemps reduced the field to fourteen, and these came along at a tremendous pace past the stand, the front rank being composed of Mormon, Archer, Fireaway and Antonelli. At the river side the two Sydney horses were in front, but on nearing the old stand Inheritor beat a retreat, and Antonelli became the immediate follower of the Sydney crack.

From this point, however, Archer was never more closely approached, and the only changes took place in the order of precedence amongst his followers; for the New South Wales hero kept away from his horses, and came in comparatively an easy winner by several lengths.

The catastrophe that occurred in the race cast a general gloom over the face of the proceedings for the rest of the day; and on making inquiry as to the extent of the injuries sustained by both men and horses, we learned that Morrison, the rider of Despatch, had received a compound comminuted fracture of the left arm, and that the bone had come through the skin in two places. The sufferer was promptly attended by Mr F. T. W. Ford, and the bones were set, the materials for bandages and splints being furnished by Mr Pond, he tearing up one of his tablecloths, and knocking up a cigar-box, which expedients were successfully employed temporarily. Morrison was afterwards removed to the hospital. Haynes, who was riding Twilight, was also much shaken, and had his collarbone broken, but the mare got up and broke away uninjured, while both Despatch and Medora received injuries which must prove and probably have already resulted fatally, Medora having three of her legs broken, and Despatch having broken her back. The rider of Medora, John Henderson, was also much shaken, and rendered almost insensible. It appears to be extremely difficult to arrive at a correct solution of the causes of the melancholy accident, the riders themselves being utterly unable to give any reliable account of the affair. From what appeared to be most reasonable and best supported by evidence of parties near the spot, it would appear that Despatch got her forelegs entangled with the hind legs of some horse before her, and fell, Medora and Twilight then fell over her. Other accounts variously state Medora and Twilight to have been the first to fall; but, all agree that the unfortunate occurrence was only an accident, and that no person is blameable for the results, however they may be deplored.

JAMES SMITH

A Very Fine Skull

James Smith joined the staff of the *Age* in 1854, where he worked as a leader-writer and drama critic. In the year he wrote these diary entries, 1863, he travelled overseas to seek relief from his 'severe intellectual labours'. In 1870 he converted to spiritualism and three years later was predicting the imminent end of the world. He lost his fortune in the 1890s depression and died in Hawthorn in 1910. But before all this happened Smith meticulously recorded events in Melbourne, including the historic interment of Burke and Wills, after their bodies had been retrieved from Cooper Creek. The fate of Burke's purloined teeth remains obscure.

1 January—Last night the bones of Burke and Wills were deposited in their metallic coffins. The skull of Wills and the hands and feet of both had disappeared. Burke's skull a very fine one. In taking a cast of it some of the teeth dropped out which I procured. The woollen shirt of Wills still hung in tatters round his ribs. Mrs Dogherty (Burke's nurse) who had 'stretched' his father and mother, performed the last sad office for her darling, wrapping the cere-cloth round his bones and placing a little pillow beneath his skull. The room (the Royal Society's Hall) hung with black and dimly lit, with a catafalque and baldacchino in the centre, had a sombre and solemn effect. Wrote a species of requiem for performance at the Theatre Royal on the evening of the funeral. To the Exhibition of the Fine Arts...Alas for art in this colony! Guerard[*]—the ablest, most conscientious and most

[*] Eugene von Guerard arrived in Australia in 1852 and travelled as an artist on expeditions by Howitt and Neumayer. He is best known for his sweeping, romantic landscapes.

industrious of the painters told me that his whole earnings last year were only £120—less than the wages of any artisan.

21 January—Public funeral of Burke and Wills. All business suspended. The procession about a mile in length, started from the hall of the Royal Society, passing through Spring Street, Bourke Street and Elizabeth Street to the new cemetery. The footpaths lined with spectators, who also clustered on the housetops, on the awnings, at the windows, on cars, coaches, carriages and wagons, and wherever a view of the cortege could be obtained. From all the suburbs of Melbourne, and from the country districts people had been pouring in all the morning, and I should compute the number of persons who witnessed the imposing spectacle at not less than one hundred thousand. I rode in the same mourning coach with Burke's foster mother, Mrs Dogherty, and the survivor of the Expedition, John King...

5 February—...To Lyndhurst in the evening to dine with Barden. The other guests consisted of Messrs Sasse, Duigan, Teale and Labertouche. After dinner our conversation happened to turn upon the sensual extravagances of Martley (solicitor general in a former administration, who is married to a charming woman...) On one occasion Martley is said to have been found dancing, naked, in a brothel, surrounded by prostitutes. On another he gave the wretched inmate of one of those houses, situated in a right of way off Bourke Street, a cheque, which was dishonoured. The women of the house took away his clothes, and he was a prisoner for two or three days, until a brother barrister sent him a suit and released him. Someone observing that such a man ought to be castrated, Duigan said that he knew a lady (née Kate Featherstone) who, having detected her husband, a major in the army, in an act of infidelity, actually excised his penis with a razor, from which he nearly lost his life.

17 February—Aspinall tells me that the brothels of this city are under a police surveillance not altogether dissimilar to that

which is practised in Paris. They are classified and those in which
the visitors are liable to be robbed are carefully discriminated from
those which are conducted on 'respectable' principles. In some
cases the prostitutes are serviceable as thief-takers, giving information to the police when notorious bushrangers and others pay
them a visit. Captain Standish—my informant adds—is furnished
with a report every morning of the number and the names of those
who have spent the night in the better class of brothels. The record
must be a curious one and calculated to lift the veil from the secret
immoralities of many of the outwardly moral and respectable...

19 May—Festivities in honour of the marriage of the Prince of
Wales to the Princess Alexandra of Denmark. A steady rain until
2 p.m. when it cleared up until midnight. The city and suburbs
gay with garlands, triumphal arches, flags, banners and greenery.
At night a brilliant illumination, the streets thronged with
spectators, and the general effect impressive if not imposing.
Transparencies innumerable were exhibited, and tons of Chinese
crackers must have been exploded. In the Chinese quarter, in
Little Bourke Street, so incessant was the discharge that it resembled a sustained fire of musketry, and was accompanied by the
beating of gongs, tom-toms, and all sorts of discordant instruments. From the roof of the library, the *coup d'oeil* was
magnificent. All Melbourne and its belt of suburbs was visible.
Bonfires were kindled on Mount Macedon, the You Yangs, Plenty
Ranges, and at other points on the horizon, and showers of
rockets were sent up from the Botanical Reserve. Coloured fires
were burnt on the roof of the Melbourne Club, the Bank of
Australasia and other elevated sites; two huge A's flamed in front
of the university; a gigantic cross of light sparkled in front of
St Patrick's and St Francis's cathedrals; and a huge cresset blazed
at the unfinished tower of the former. Looking down Bourke
Street the sight was very animated. The yellow light gleamed upon
a dense mass of upturned faces, reaching from Spring Street to

Queen Street, and through the midst of the crowd slowly wound a serpentine line of carriages, each with its pair of lamps, and looking, in the mass, like a monstrous snake with luminous scales. In most of the suburbs, oxen were roasted whole, and barrels of beer set flowing; while the poor and the inmates of the charitable institutions were universally regaled.

28 May—Governor's Ball—Frazer MLA got very drunk and on the way home quarrelled with a cabman, who called in the police. He abused these as being either orangemen or papists, O'Shanassy's spies or Standish's pets. Eventually he was taken to the watchhouse, but was liberated on his own recognisances. About daybreak, accompanied by Dr Macadam, he knocked up the mayor (E. Cohen) and entreated him to take the charge off the charge sheet. Upon the mayor refusing to adopt such an illegal course, Frazer shed maudlin tears of penitence, wiped his greasy face with a skull cap (which he pulled out of his pocket instead of a handkerchief) and presented a most ludicrously woebegone appearance; being half sober, and wholly dirty and demoralised in appearance. What makes his escapade the more amusing is that he is chairman of a legislative committee, now sitting, to inquire into and report upon the organisation, discipline and management of the police force.

WILLIAM BARAK

My Words

William Barak was a prominent Woiwurrung leader. He dictated this memoir of his experiences in early Melbourne while at Coranderrk mission, near Healesville, sometime after 1863. In this piece Buckley's 'word' was for Barak to bring no harm to the new settlers. Captain Lancell is probably Captain Lacey of Fawkner's vessel *Enterprise*, Mr Focner is John Fawkner and Mr Lanon is George Langhorne. Barak's final sentence may convey his sad understanding that the wealth of the land had been appropriated by the Europeans.

I was born in the year 1813 at Brushy Creek, and was about eleven years old when Batman visited Port Phillip Bay. I never forgot it. I remember Buckley's word every time. Captain Cook landed at Western Port. Then Batman came in looking for the country. Looking around the sea he found a lot of blacks other side of Gealong, and found Buckley in the camp. Know trousers, all raggety; he wore opossum rugs, and he fetch him back to Batman's house. Batman sent some potatoes from Melbourne to the camp of the Yarra blacks.

Then the blacks travel to Idelburge[*]. All the blacks camp at Muddy Creek. Next morning they all went down to see Batman, old man and women and children, and they all went to Batman's house for rations, and killed some sheep by Batman's order. Buckley told the blacks to look at Batman's face. He looks very white. Any man that you see out in the bush not to touch him. When you see an empty hut not to touch the bread in it. Make a camp outside and wait till the man come home and finds everything safe in the house. They are good people. If you kill one white man white fellow will shoot you down like a kangeroo. A lot of white fellow come here by and by and clear the scrub all over the country.

Captain Lancell just coming in and Mr Focner, and Mr Latrobe came from England. At that time we heard our Minister Mr Lanon. We got a school room in the German garden, and the school masters name was Mr Smith. We was singing Hallalooler.

[*] Heidelberg.

Henry Barkly coming in when Mr Latrobe went home.

All the Protectors Mr Thomas protector to Melbourne blacks. Mr LeSouef belong to Loddon tribe, Mr Tuckfell Colac tribe. Buckley say bring the stone tomahawks and give them to Mr Batman. Then stone go to England all aboriginal.

CHARLES KEAN
A Walking Tragedy

Charles Kean was the son of Edmund Kean, the immortal tragedian whose performances were singularly suited to the sensibilities of the Victorian age. From this letter to his daughter Mary, it would seem fair to judge that Charles—also an actor—had difficulty confining tragedy and pathos to the stage.

22 April 1864—I shall be delighted to get away from these colonies for I neither like the climate or the people.

Patty, strange girl, says she would rather live in St Kilda than any place she has ever seen after Paris! Paris first, St Kilda next!! Why the very insects here are enough to disgust one. The swarms of flies are truly a plague, spiders crawl upon your pillow, some poisonous. The mosquitoes are counted by myriads. I have totally lost all appetite through these wretches.

At breakfast I am compelled to place my saucer over my cup making hasty snatches at my tea to prevent the flies falling into it. The weather is cooler now but yet these disgusting creatures do not diminish. This is town life, but in the country it is truly awful.

Snakes and everything horrible you can think of…

Patty has grown very thin. I think her family bother her, her brother John through our influence got a job in the government printing house the other day for a fortnight but was dismissed at the termination of the first week. Patty tells me because there was not sufficient type to supply all the hands. I hope for her sake and for his that may be the true version but I am afraid it is not so. What is to become of him and that fool Maria I do not know, both are out of employment now and nothing seems to offer.

They have one and all, Patty and Nancy excepted, behaved so badly to me that it has destroyed all ties of tenderness and care on my part towards them. Fancy during my illness at Sydney when the daily telegrams intimated I was dying, that girl Maria never wrote one line to her sister inquiring after me, not one word has she written to Uncle and Aunt since our arrival in the colony. Is it not, my dear child enough to harden the kindest heart?

I wish I were at home again safe and sound taking my farewell round of acting.

America will assist my retiring pension I expect by at least £2000 to £3000, perhaps more. The poor little doctor won't like this Yankee trip.

Did you ever hear of an insect somewhat resembling a grasshopper, called a mantis? Well, one of these gentlemen fell on my newspaper the other morning while reading in bed, in the act of devouring his breakfast which consisted of a good fat fly which he tightly held in his long arms. Such are the pleasures of Australian life. The wind is now howling in the most piteous manner although the sun is shining brightly.

John Thompson Mason

The Civil War Comes to Melbourne

When the Confederate raider *Shenandoah* docked at Port Melbourne in January 1865 seeking repair, 'revittaling' and recreation for her crew, Melbourne society was set alight by her dashing and gentlemanly officers. The vessel had been sent into the Pacific to destroy Yankee whalers which were busy supplying oils vital to the Union war machine, and in this they were spectacularly successful. The Lincoln government regarded the *Shenandoah* as nothing more than a pirate, and following the Union victory later that year the State of Victoria was compelled to pay substantial reparations. In this hitherto unpublished journal extract, we see the twenty-year-old midshipman John Mason enjoying Melbourne's reception.

29 January—The *Shenandoah* has been in port now for about three days and has created no small excitement in the harbour, we have been received with a great deal of kindness and hospitality (but I regret to say that some of the officers have behaved so badly that I fear we will not carry away the same reputation we brought with us; the fact of the matter is we have too many good for nothing fellows that we were compelled to make officers for want of others and the consequence is they go on shore in uniform, get drunk, raise a row and disgrace the ship, the uniform and of course the people are bound to judge by those they see the whole of us, so I am now almost ashamed to show my face on shore).

There is a great deal of work to be done, the propeller must come out and the vessel must go on the [slip]ways to be repaired.

The caulkers have been at work ever since we have been here and the decks are covered with pitch and dirt; in spite of this we have been flooded with visitors, two or three tugboats and any number of little sailboats have been plying all day, ladies, gentlemen, men, women and children of all sorts and description. It was enough to set anyone crazy I am sure, but we made ourselves as agreeable as possible showing all sorts of people around and talking the same monotonous nonsense all day long. I suppose that if I explained all the parts of the ship and the guns once I did it a thousand times.

I was on watch all day nearly and I never did see such a tremendous crowd. Indeed, we were obliged to send away two steamerloads of people, for our decks were crowded to suffocation, one could not turn around. This tremendous rush continued until sundown when we put a stop to it and the ship became quiet again.

2 February — I find it impossible to write up my journal regularly here in port; I thought I would have plenty of time to do that and write all my letters, but on the contrary, I find now that I have time to do nothing scarcely...

Tuesday I went on shore and spent the morning, coming off at six o'clock. Since being here we have been treated in the most hospitable manner by everyone, having received invitations from everywhere: the railway company immediately sent free tickets to all the officers to travel on the road as long as they might stay in the harbour, we were voted members of the cricket club and of the 'Melbourne Club'. All the wardroom officers were invited to a large dinner at the latter place, and a deputation came from Ballarat, one of the principal mining districts, to invite us to visit the place at their expense and we would be shown around the mines, after which a sumptuous dinner, and a ball in the evening to wind up with.

Tuesday night was that set aside for the dinner at the 'Melbourne Club'. Captain Waddell, Dr Lining, Mr Smith, Lt. Smith Lee, Lt. Scales and myself went to the dinner, the rest of the officers being on duty or unable to go. The dinner came off at seven o'clock and a remarkably fine one it was, being attended by sixty members of the club, which is the only thing of the sort in town and all the first people of the town, all the members of Parliament, the judges &c. &c. are amongst the members. The dining room was a most magnificent apartment and the dinner was excellent, all sorts of fine things, wines &c. I enjoyed myself very much but in a reasonable manner.

At the end of the dinner the vice-president of the club, who presided, proposed the first toast 'To the Queen' and a few minutes after 'To the *Shenandoah* and her officers' or something of that sort. Three hearty cheers were then given for the *Shenandoah* and two more to make them good, our captain was about to make some reply, but several members of the club requested him not to do so saying it was against the by-laws of the club to make any speeches of any sort and that if he broke through the rules it would lead to speech-making on all sides, so things remained as they were without more remarks on either side. After dinner we went into the smoking and billiard rooms and spent an hour or two knocking around in the different rooms talking with the gentlemen who were very jovial. About midnight we took our departure, but as it was too late to get back to Sandridge the captain gave us permission to stay all night in town which of course we were not sorry to do. I went around with the rest of the crowd on a 'bit of a lark' and then went and turned in at the Albion Hotel.

My two neighbours were jolly 'coves', one of them had been to Paris and spoke a little French, about as much and as badly as most Englishmen who have spent a few days or weeks in the French metropolis and made some slight improvements on his school-learnt [French]. The gentleman on my right was a Dr B., a jolly old fellow who was very kind and polite, invited me to go with him to visit the lunatic asylum in the suburbs of Melbourne. It seems that he is one of the inspectors or something of that sort and obliged to visit the institution once a week. Although it was not his regular day, he very kindly promised to drive me out on the morrow in his dog-cart and show me all the lions[*]. I accepted the offer most willingly for although such things are not unheard of in our country, it happened that I had never visited an institution of the sort in my life. I enjoyed myself very much at the table, although the conversation was not of a nature that I could take much part in. My friend on the right seemed to be entirely wrapt up in his profession and entertained me during the whole of the dinner with a dissertation about hanging—how the cord should be adjusted. He contended that instead of placing the knot behind the ear as is usually the custom, it should be put behind the neck immediately upon the neckbone, when the fall would snap the neck off and thus produce instantaneous death; whereas with the old custom of placing the knot behind the ear, always five and sometimes ten minutes was required to produce death.

Dr B. told me that he had been allowed, when last in England, to make experiments of this theory upon condemned criminals, and that he never 'had a death under five minutes' with the old system, but with his new plan instant death always ensued. So much for hanging—I listened very attentively to the doctor's conversation for politeness' sake and indeed I believe it was about as interesting as any other we could have hit upon, and the sum total of it all is that if ever I am to be hung, I shall beg the executioner to put the knot behind my neck...

2 March—At sea. My journal writing has made slow progress lately, for it is just two months since I commenced this book and I have not written half a dozen pages. I am getting disgusted with myself and *must* make an effort to do better.

Firstly, I must wind up my account of the Melbourne affairs.

I have already said that I had made this appointment to visit the insane asylum...Smith Lee went with me, we drove around to the

---

[*] Perhaps this word is being used facetiously as in 'social lion'.

doctor's house in a cab and being a little late (having waited for the captain) we found the family already at table. Mrs B. was a stout, healthy, good-natured-looking woman who was very hospitable to us and there were several other elderly people at the table. We sat for about an hour and answered numerous questions about our ship and how we liked Melbourne and all such hackneyed topics and finally arose to start for the asylum, which is about three miles out from town. The doctor had a very nice little horse and we had a very pleasant drive...

The institution instead of being one immense building as we generally see at home, consisted of little cottages built of stone, each ward being separated from the others by a nice little flower or vegetable garden, which the harmless patients were made to cultivate under the guidance of one of the attendants. In this manner the buildings occupied a very large space, some twenty acres I should think being this admirably well ventilated. They were as neat as a pin and supplied with every convenience and every modern improvement.

Smith Lee and myself were both very much pleased, as it was something entirely new to us both; we spent about four hours in going the rounds. There were 960 patients male and female and we visited them all both docile and refractory. Men and women and also a few children who were most them mere idiots. Some of the cases were very interesting, one in particular an old woman who imagined she was the Queen and sometimes the Empress of the colony. The day we were there she played the Empress, and when we arrived she received us most graciously, and although stark mad she seemed to know by our uniform that we were naval officers and spoke of the respect due her from us her subjects etc., etc. We amused ourselves for about five minutes listening to her.

Another case was an old man who seemed almost sane. He came up as we entered the ward and gave us a most polite reception, invited us into his room and showed a quantity of paintings that he had done himself while there, and all of them were passable. He then showed us his plants that he was growing out on the balcony and talked about them in a most rational manner. He also seemed to know exactly who and what Smith Lee and myself were. He said: 'I have been to your country a great many years ago. That is to the northern states, 'New York' and other places, but I have a great deal of sympathy for your cause and hope to see you successful.'

He told us when exhibiting his plants that he was making a collection and if ever we came to Melbourne again we must be sure to make him another visit and bring him some plants or seeds from our country — he would be so glad to have anything of the sort.

I noticed that when he talked there was a very curious noise of air escaping as if from a valve, and upon examining more closely I discovered a large cavity in his throat from which the air would escape when he spoke. As we were going out of the room, the doctor told me that about ten years ago he had cut his own throat most dreadfully in a fit of insanity and the healing of the wound was thought quite a medical feat…

This evening was the day appointed for us to go to the Theatre Royal by special invitation of the proprietor, so Smith Lee and myself went around to try and find some of the rest of the crowd, but not one could we 'skare up', so we went and dined together and afterwards went to the theatre where we met several of the other fellows. The performance was miserable I thought, but the theatre was crowded, in the *entre-acte* the band played 'Dixie' and the crowd commenced cheering and the opposition put in hisses and groans all of which was excessively annoying to ourselves, so I took the earliest opportunity of leaving the theatre and went down to Sandridge in the eleven o'clock train.

DAVID COLLER

They Even Know in Toorak!

Ferdinand von Mueller was a highly esteemed nineteenth-century botanist. For sixteen years he served as director of Melbourne's Royal Botanic Gardens, during which Germanic rigour and a classification-based system of plantings became his hallmarks. David Coller's letter to von Mueller concerning the goings-on of fellow employee William Smith was, by all accounts, the first von Mueller had heard of the incident.

10 March 1866—Dear Sir,

Will you excuse me for taking the liberty of trespassing on your valuable time, but I think it my duty to inform you of certain rumours in circulation concerning Mr William Smith and a certain female in consequence of their being surprised in an act which I can bring proofs to the fact in the tea-tree scrub enough to shock any person having even the slightest claims to morality as a married man.

It is not through any ill feeling that I inform you of this but I think it is but right for you to know that it is in everyone's mouth, not only in the immediate vicinity but even in so remote a locality as Toorak. I cannot go outside the door but people ask me if that is true about Smith and the girl in the gardens. I say of course that I know nothing about it. I do not know whether you have been informed of the facts before, but I sincerely believe you have not or else you would have had it thoroughly sifted ere now.

LUDOVIC DE BEAUVOIR

No Local Tone at All

The twenty-year-old Marquis de Beauvoir was a travelling companion of the Duc de Penthièvre and they
visited Melbourne in 1866. The city surprised de Beauvoir—not because of its distinctiveness, but because it
was such a faithful replica of England. He seemed to
detest the real Australia, making naive but disparaging
remarks about both eucalypts and Aborigines—
his comments on the latter are as noteworthy for their
contempt as Dampier's.

In a quarter of an hour we were at Melbourne, and jumping
into a cab drove to Scott's Hotel, which had been recommended as the best in town. We were immensely astonished at the
mixture of waiters buried in false collars and white ties, and little
Chinese servants trotting up and down the stairs.

They brought us our letters at once, and we devoured them
with unspeakable pleasure. What tender thoughts rose on opening
them! We all three crowded up to the light that we might read
them, and any little bit of good news was instantly read aloud.
They are two months old, and the first that we shall send will
arrive in Europe five months and a half after we left...

We enjoyed walking about the big streets of Melbourne
immensely that night, Collins Street and Bourke Street, which are
two fine thoroughfares, parallel to one another, very wide, with
flagged footways and lighted with gas; they are the Rue Vivienne
and Rue Richelieu of these parts. We sauntered along them,
looking at the well-furnished shops which fill them from one end
to the other, and whose contents would rouse the envy of any of
our second-rate towns in France. People had said so much about a

pair of boots costing a hundred francs here that I was much surprised to find that everything costs precisely the same as at home. Yes, there is no doubt that landing at Melbourne is very astonishing; there are cab stands like those in London, theatres, quantities of people walking about, handsome and luxurious houses many stories in height, policemen uncommonly well set up, open restaurants, and walking advertisements, well-lighted squares— everything, except the size of the streets, combines to produce the most striking likeness to England; and since I have landed it has struck me that the local tone of the country consists precisely in being no local tone at all, and that the colony, contrary to custom, resembles the mother country in a very unusual manner…

When we returned to the town we found it in a wonderful state of agitation; great red placards announce that the European mails have arrived in Adelaide (the capital of South Australia), and that the telegrams are going to be published. The mail only arrives once a month, and you must come here to understand why there is no longer our daily indifference for daily news- papers, but rather an excess of excitement, and a longing for news, which possesses all minds; ten minutes later, and there were the yellow placards, with their sensational advertisements:

GREAT WAR IN EUROPE!
GIGANTIC ARMAMENTS!
GIGANTIC PANIC IN THE MONEY MARKET!
NO MORE MONEY, NO MORE CREDIT!

This news put us into a great state of anxiety…Whilst standing greedy for news in the midst of this restless crowd, which was as excited as one in the streets of London, we suddenly saw a sight which contrasted strangely with any ideas of needle-guns, or the Derby, contained in the telegrams—a most offensive and horrible group of men and women passed along, with skins as black as a crocodile's, dirty woolly hair, and low and degraded countenances. They were Aborigines. Ragged old trowsers did not sufficiently hide their repulsive bodies; a miserable appearance of old boots at the end of a bare thigh and leg; rags of European dress, whose colours might formerly have been tartan, but were now as black as the skin which they barely covered; Gibus hats*, reduced to the consistency of a dried apple, or plumed hats, with which no doubt some Irishwoman had presented them, to save her blushes at their want of clothes. A collection of wretched rags on their mean little bodies, uglier than any monkey in the world—such is the aspect of the ancient possessors of this continent; such is the race with which, rightly or wrongly, we dispute the possession of this enormous extent of soil, thrusting them each day farther back into the bush.

Some of them, intoxicated with tobacco and strong drinks, both of which are no doubt new to them, stumble in walking against the walls of fine houses built in the European way, or against glass windows which exhibit the finest specimens of gold that have been found at the diggings—these unknown treasures which this black race, who are now beggars, so long trod under foot, and with which the white men build palaces and towns… Some among them have a mass of unkempt white hair, like a snowball, surmounting their body and limbs of ebony, but dirty ebony—and who knows but what these withered old men, whose limbs are like sticks, may not have been here thirty-four years ago, and seen the ground an uncultivated forest, which now supports a gas-lighted town containing 130,000 souls? Who can tell whether they may not have hunted the opossum in the hollow trees on the very spot where now streams of people wait in the flagged pavements to take tickets for the opera? In less than half a lifetime the whistles of steam engines have succeeded the shrill

* A soft hat which can be crushed flat.

and wild cry of the cockatoo; and instead of the line of fires lighted by cannibals, as a sign that there were some white men to be eaten, the lines of the telegraph cross cultivated ground, and announce to an excited town the winner of the Derby...

Today may barometer and chronometer rest in peace! I am off to a stag-hunt, for which Captain Standish has mounted me on a splendid horse. The meet was seven miles from Melbourne, and I could hardly believe from the appearance of the country that fifteen years ago this was wilderness; I fancied myself on my way to Epsom to a meet of the Surrey stag-hounds, when I saw the whole road filled with elegant phaetons and four-in-hands. We were more than a hundred and fifty horsemen at the start: red-coats, ladies in riding habits and a stag brought from England! Wherever Englishmen establish themselves, whether it be at Gibraltar, the Cape, or Australia, they always carry with them the customs and amusements of their native land. They have their cricket matches, as well as their stag and kangaroo hounds, and many an English hunt might envy them their well-chosen pack, fine horses, and excellent horsemen, who boast themselves, not without reason, to be the best steeplechase riders in the world.

Off at last, and we gallop at a terrific pace, across meadows, cornfields and marshes, intersected with deep ditches; the pace is killing. Fence follows fence with no breathing space between, there is no end to them, and some are really frightful...The master of the hounds was good enough to ask me to dine with the hunt at the club, where everything was served with the degree of luxury you can imagine amongst the fortunate inhabitants of this golden land. It was a good specimen of an English hunt dinner, full of life and animation. What endless subjects we discussed! ranging from Paris, its sights and charms, to sheep-walks, kangaroos, and the South Pole.

Amongst other things, I was given an account of a cricket match here two years ago. An Australian eleven entered the lists against an

English eleven, who took ship and travelled twelve thousand miles to play one game of cricket. It really was a little too much of a good thing. The game being won, the English eleven, after being most cordially entertained by the vanquished party, returned by way of Cape Horn, as if they had done the most ordinary thing in the world, merely taking a return ticket to the Antipodes.

HRH Prince Alfred

Age, 29 November 1867—Undoubtedly, the largest assemblage of people there has ever been in Victoria was at the Zoological Gardens yesterday, where there was to have been a free banquet for the million…the vast multitude of people assembled on the occasion was not only the largest that ever previously assembled in the colony, but it was also the most diversely composed, and included a greater number of representatives from the chief towns of the colony than has ever previously met together. And, unfortunately, it is under these circumstances that we have to report that the whole affair was a signal failure, that if there was anyone there who did not grumble, there was no one who had not occasion to do so, and that for one person who succeeded in getting anything to swallow more acceptable than dust, there were hundreds who could not get even sufficient water to wash that out of their mouths…

It was expected that the Prince would arrive at two o'clock, and for a considerable time previous to that hour there was a dense crowd of people ranged round the barrier protecting the dais from intrusion. The manner in which those close up to the barrier were pressed against it, and one against another, is almost indescribable. Each person in the dense throng must have been pressed within a compass half as small as he would in an unconfined state embody. Some who lifted their arms, hoping thereby to gain greater room for their bodies, could not by any means get them down again, and those before them on whom they rested their unimprisoned upper limbs, complained unavailingly that they were weighed down above as well as flattened below. At this time almost the only vocal sounds heard from the crowd were brief ejaculations of pain, or low and surly grumbling. But a little later, when they attributed their misfortunes to the non-arrival of the Prince, and to their being in consequence delayed from their dinners, their impatience became noisy and demonstrative; and there was some danger that they would force the barriers. It was estimated that there were then about 70,000 persons present, and yet for fully an hour afterwards streams of people continued to enter the ground from every gate, until at length it was not possible to walk three yards in any direction without being jostled by somebody...

At five minutes past three o'clock, Mr Smith caused the flag to be hoisted, and proclaimed the banquet open, whereupon the crown gave three lusty cheers. A few minutes afterwards he stated that Captain Standish had just arrived upon the ground, and intimated that his Royal Highness was unable to attend the feast. The truth of this announcement was, however, discredited by many, who seemed to think that the committee had circulated the rumour for the purpose of inducing the crowd to remove to some of the reserve less numerously occupied. They did not, however, do so, but whether from incredulity, or from a wish to remain in close contiguity to the wine, must remain a question open to slight doubt.

At the same time that one party, following their stronger propensity, rushed the wine butt, another made off pell-mell for the tables with all the eagerness and determination of a foraging party, but only to be disappointed, for the tables had been well watched by those who cared more for tongue and ham than even for the sight of a live prince. They had given up the chance of a good view of the Prince for the sake of securing a lion's share of the provisions, and when they saw the rush towards them from the dais they set to with great celerity, and made everything eatable disappear in an amazing short time.

The late arrivals who were unsuccessful in getting any of the provisions forced their way into the space behind the tables, with rails knocked in the heads of beer barrels, and smashed the bottles to get at their contents, and by these proceedings wasted very nearly as much liquor as they drank. Apparently to ward off danger, the bread was thrown out among the crowd in junks by those behind the tables, who hoped by that liberality to purchase their forbearance, and this bread, those who could by no possibility consume any more of it, they dipped into buckets of ale, and then pitched, in a playful spirit, into the faces of those near them.

In the course of a few minutes the tables were cleared, not only of their meats, but also of plates, knives, and of everything that had been laid upon them, and if the committee have no reserve fund, they are likely to experience some difficulty indemnifying those who have suffered from the general scrimmage or free scramble into which the free banquet was converted. The tents behind the tables were in many cases torn down, and in some, we regret to have to state, robbed of ladies' shawls and other wearing apparel.

MARCUS ANDREW HISLOP CLARKE

Bourke Street
at Midnight

The renowned writer Marcus Clarke arrived in
Melbourne in 1863, aged seventeen. By 1867 he had
begun contributing pieces to the *Argus*. This account of
Melbourne's nightlife appeared in the paper on 28 February 1868 and reveals a lively, gritty world after dark. His
novel *For the Term of His Natural Life* remains Clarke's
best-remembered work.

The rapid progress of Melbourne has long been proverbial,
and nothing shows it more strongly than the night life of
the city. The scenes in Melbourne streets after dark are of a very
different nature to those which took place some fifteen years
back. One no longer sees diggers, temporarily rich in some two
or three hundred pounds, reeling from tap to tap, or hears of
'a body' found with 'two knife-wounds in the breast, and the
pockets turned inside out'…The good old times are happily
over, but some curious sights are yet to be seen under the
gas-lamps.

Perhaps, for its size, Melbourne is as vicious a city as any in the
southern hemisphere, but the artificial impetus given to crime by
the outbreak of the gold mania is subsiding, the permanent settlement of a large number of industrious persons having in a great
measure absorbed the floating criminal population. The dens of
infamy and vice, which were for a long time the disgrace of the
city, and which were used as schools to train the young of either
sex for the gallows and the hulks, are rapidly being destroyed by
the demand made upon house-room by the respectable working

population. There is little open violence, and the criminal class prefer to keep to themselves, and as much as possible avoid thrusting their miseries before the public...

The large streets present no spectacles of extreme poverty or extreme vice. They are the haunt of the 'upper ten thousand' of Bohemia only, while, owing to the rapid rise of the city, and the natural tendency of a young population to centralise, the theatres and casinos are nearly all in Bourke Street, which thoroughfare is filled nightly to overflowing, while the other streets are almost deserted. Bourke Street at midnight is something very little better than the Haymarket (London) at two in the morning, and from 9 p.m. to 1 a.m. presents a scene of the most varied kind. There is not perhaps that excess of vicious brilliancy that an older city would show, but some of its features are peculiar to itself. Let us take the Portico bars for example, which at the time of our commencing our 'round' will be in the full heat of business.

Passing through the iron gates, we find ourselves in a large hall, open at one end to the street, and closed at the other by the pit and stall entrances to the theatre. The curtain has just fallen upon the piece of the evening, and the crowds from gallery, pit, and stalls are refreshing themselves before the farce. On each side are covered bars, where some twenty or thirty girls dispense, with lightning rapidity, the 'brandies hot', 'glass of ale', 'cold without', 'colonial wine', 'nobblers for five', 'whiskeys hot', 'sherry and bitters', 'two glasses claret', 'nobblers for two', 'dark brandy', &c., which expectorating crowds of men and boys call for on all sides.

White-coated waiters shoot like meteors through the mass, bearing coffee to some of the more quiet frequenters of the place. These sitting at little marble tables drink and smoke philosophically. At the furthest table from the door sits a knot of government clerks—young Piffins, of the Treasury, and Biffins, of the chief secretary's office; beside them reclines in drunken slumber Tom Bambury, of the customs. Some two more friends of the group coming up, and commencing to fight with sticks over the inebriate's head, he is at length roused to a sense of his position, and staggering up, passes into the little door where a woman in blue silk and white lace is standing. That door leads to the 'ladies' refreshment-room', but is known to its fast frequenters by another name. The women who assemble there are well dressed and orderly. They live for the most part in adjacent streets, paying a high rent for their houses, which are usually leased and kept in order by some old woman, who is too old to attract; and the less public of them frequent the theatres more for their own amusement than with other designs.

A notable feature of Bourke Street, from nine to eleven, is the number of sewing girls and milliners' apprentices that haunt its pavement. These girls, neatly and sometimes handsomely dressed, will pass and repass for hours, either for amusement or for the purpose of making assignations. There are nearly 2000 girls, from the ages of fifteen to twenty-five, employed in Melbourne, and in their manners and mode of life they are daily assimilating themselves more nearly to the Parisian *grisettes*.

Walking up the street, we meet a knot of station-men from the Murray with cattle. They have just put up their horses preparatory to 'goin' on the bust', and walk down the pavement four abreast, all booted, breeched and smoking violently. Reeling after them are some half-dozen sailors from a passenger ship now in harbour; these are evidently 'on pleasure bent', and with vehement addresses as to everybody's eyes, limbs and internal anatomy, lurch into a convenient bar for drinks round. A cab, loaded fore and aft with a still more drunken and melodious crew, goes flying over gutters and round corners, en route for Sandridge and the harbour. Presently we come upon a group of Celestials, pigtailed, blue-coated and mandarin-capped, chattering in their teeth-breaking lingo. 'Well, John, how goes it?' 'How-yeh! Yoh! Aaaah! G'night!'

and a burst of gutturals drowns the remainder of the greeting. These turn down Little Bourke Street into an opium house, and will probably spend the remainder of the night in gambling away their hard-earned gains. The pavement is crowded with people. Piffins and Biffins pass arm-in-arm up the street, the former peering under the bonnet of every woman that passes, in the hope that he may meet a girl with whom he has an assignation. Ha! — he has met her at last, and they cross the road to one of the numerous public houses, which, under cover of a 'bar trade', do a most lucrative business as receiving-houses and bagnios.

The pavement is crowded with persons, all strolling quietly on as though it was a public parade. What Collins Street is from three to six, so is Bourke Street from nine to twelve, with this difference, that respectability is at a discount in the latter. It is the seamy side of Collins Street and its 'humours' are all of the grosser sort. In the gutter a purple-faced man, with sodden eyes and unsteady gait, gasps forth the last notes of a ballad, and an itinerant 'seller of songs', a little higher up the street, is screeching in humorous conjunction the titles of some of the 'noo and fav'rite' melodies that float yard-long from his stick. The coffee vendors have already erected their stall, and are thinking about commencing their night's work, while the man with the telescope, who shows Saturn's rings for a penny and describes Jupiter's moons for a glass of gin, is putting up his machine, and preparing for home and bed.

At the corner of Bourke and Stephen* streets, a crowd is assembled round a 'street-preacher', who, with hat off, and his hand upraised, is giving out the first verse of a hymn. Numerous persons join in chorus; meanwhile, three little boys have been busily engaged picking pockets, and, before the strain is finished, sneak off with their booty into the convenient sanctuary of Little

* Renamed Exhibition Street in 1880 to commemorate the Melbourne Exhibition.

Bourke Street. Dirty and draggle-tailed women begin to appear at the ends of the right-of-ways, and the popular music-halls have just vomited forth a crew of drunken soldiers, prostitutes and thieves. There is a masquerade at one of the casinos, and the entrance is crowded with fast men and 'gay women'. The brass band at the window of the Waxworks Exhibition is vigorously playing 'The Last Rose of Summer', previous to going home for the evening. Cabs commence to draw up against the doors of the refreshment places, into which bevies of *lorettes* and their attendants are going for supper. The cabs are drawn up close against the kerb, awaiting orders of their hirers. Cabmen are frequently in league with prostitutes, and if an unsuspecting individual hires the vehicle the woman is taken up as passenger, and frequently succeeds in inveigling the pigeon into her house. On one line of road, indeed, this practice is notorious, many cabmen living as the 'fancy men' of the women of the town, and assisting them in robbing the sailors whom they have in tow.

Coming down the street are four young thieves. One of these, 'Nosey Samuels', is a Jew boy, and has already done four years' imprisonment, or, as he terms it, 'four stretch', for a robbery of jewellery. They are on the loose tonight, and will probably finish the evening in one of the numerous dens in Romeo Lane*. The theatres are closed by this time, and from the stage-doors the wearied supers and scene-shifters are issuing; but the casinos and dancing halls still give forth beams of light. Tobacconists still are ablaze with lamps, and anyone who took the trouble of watching the doors closely would see many persons enter and not come out again. A great many of these shops are 'blinds'. The real trade of the place is done upstairs. The upper rooms are fitted up as gambling saloons, and the arrangements for communication with the shop below are so

---

* In 1876 Romeo Lane was changed to Crossley Street.

perfect that on a stranger attempting to enter the *penetralia* the 'office' is at once given by means of a wire, and all signs of the occupation removed. Not long since a raid was made upon two of these places by the police, and nearly thirty persons captured; but the affair was a long time in arranging, a detective having been employed for some weeks in insinuating himself into the good graces of the proprietor, and obtaining admission to the upper rooms.

Turning round into Stephen Street we come upon a new phase of life. Pawnbrokers' shops abound, old furniture shops and old bookstalls are rife, while from out the villainous dens whose lighted windows shine only dimly at the bottom of the rights-of-way the sounds of a cracked fiddle and the discordant laughter of the miserable women who inhabit them fall upon our ears. At the door of one of the pawnshops stands an old man, with a face like a caricature of Ernest Griset's. He might pass for an ancient dealer in curiosities who sold Balzac the shagreen-skin. That is Jacob ——. He is a Dutchman, and still talks pathetically of Rotterdam and the Boomjees. He is the most knowing and artistic 'fence' in Melbourne. Like Shakespeare's apothecary, his shop shows but a beggarly account of empty boxes, but he has a store of wealth somewhere hidden. His shop has a back entry, where many a case of jewellery or watches has entered, never to return again. Old Jacob is 'friends', to a certain extent, with the police; and his old wife—a Tasmanian Jewess—professes much affection for the members of the D division.

Nightcabs, with gorgeous-hued dresses swelling over the footrails, rattle past. In 'shy' houses lights glimmer through the shutters, while in some of the doorways flaunting but shabbily dressed women peer forth, like spiders from their webs, on the lookout for prey. Most of these women are thieves as well as prostitutes; and in the fetid and dingy back premises lurk ill-looking ruffians, who are prepared to silence any opposition on the part of the not sufficiently stupefied victim.

Coming up the street with leisurely step is Detective Fox. A robbery of £30 from a sailor has been reported, and he is taking a stroll around the 'cribs'. The woman at the door inquires, 'Am I wanted, old son?' and being answered in the negative, gives herself a defiant shake, and requests a 'shout' instanter. A little further up the street Fox stops to speak to an orange woman. This personage is termed 'Dandy Sal', and is a sort of hanger-on of the police. She is much above the average of others of her class, and how she came to her present position is a mystery. She has travelled through the greater portion of the Continent, and speaks French and German fluently. Her son is the companion of young thieves, and often extracts much information, which his mother duly reports in proper quarters. There seems to be nothing particular to communicate this evening, for Fox, after a brief consultation, strolls leisurely on. At the corner of the street he comes plump into the middle of five men, who, recognising him, chaffingly ask after his well-being. These belong to a notable class of street-walkers. They are 'magsmen', and their occupation, as Fox tersely puts it, is 'kidding on the flats'. They will follow a man from up the country, and engage him in cards, drinking or betting, and end by fleecing him of his money. The big man, with the 'mouse mark' on his cheek, is Luke Isaacs, the Jew; and the one next to him, who wears a velvet waistcoat, and looks altogether not unlike our old friend Mo' Davis, is Cornstalk Charlie, who has just come from Randwick Races, and is on the lookout for a man who 'owes him a pot, s' help him!' The little one at the end is named 'Slipslop Joe', and has only come out of gaol a week back, where he was rusticating for three months for winning £19 from a sailor by the 'dog-collar touch'. They have got a 'flat' in their toils now, and are off with him to some friendly drinking house.

It is now half-past two o'clock, and the shops are all closed. The streets are tenanted only by a few wretched creatures, who still wander disconsolately up and down, on the look-out for some stray victim. A few 'bar loafers' are shudderingly creeping down into the back slums, and wondering if they can get another 'nobbler o' P.B.' shouted, before they finally turn in to their private gaspipe for a night's repose. The 'coffee stalls' are nearly deserted, and their owners are taking a snooze, preparatory to their 'early morning's business'. Two or three cabs still hover about, but the policeman reigns supreme, and even the itinerant trotter-seller is going home to his hovel. The shutters are up, and the lights in the newspaper office are the only signs of industry. Melbourne is asleep, and street life is over for one night.

JOHN CHRISTIE

The Long Arm of the Law

Detective Inspector John Christie's canny Scots family sent him to Melbourne in the hopes that his emigrant uncle, Hugh Reoch, might make him heir to a colonial fortune. In his early days in the colony young John—an accomplished pugilist and rider—travelled widely atop 'Wandering Willie', his trusty steed. When plans for his inheritance were frustrated Christie joined the Victoria police, where his fondness for disguise and his methodical information-seeking soon became legendary. Despite sporting a handsome moustache he was evidently seductive in female guise, and his impersonations of sailors and swagmen were impeccable. Here we meet him in the role of a drunken sailor as he foils an attempted storehouse robbery.

I was living at Seaforth House in Franklyn Street in June 1868. One evening as I was on my way to the detective office, and while passing the old Lamb Inn in Elizabeth Street, I observed an elderly man, whom I recognised as an old burglar named Briely, walking down the street carrying a ladder about fifteen feet long.

As it was just getting dark, I knew he was up to no good with the ladder at that time of the evening, so I determined to watch him.

As we proceeded down Elizabeth Street, I picked up a cab, the driver of which I knew. I engaged him and jumped in. The driver had a big heavy overcoat which I got him to lend me, also a red woollen muffler, and, changing my boxer hat for his old wide-awake, I donned them and my disguise was complete.

I now got up in front and, telling cabby to get out and follow at a distance on foot, I drove slowly after Briely. He turned down Flinders Lane West and I saw him turn up a right-of-way about 100 yards off; which I knew to be a blind right-of-way. As he was now out of sight, I went slowly down towards the place. On arriving at the entrance to the right-of-way I saw he had put the ladder down against Heymansons Store, which was one storey high, and as he came out I said to him with a broad Hibernian accent, 'Where is the Port Phillip Livery Stables?'

He replied, 'I don't know, I am a stranger here.'

He then walked away up Elizabeth Street in the same direction as he had come.

I now knew if he was on the job that night I had only to watch the ladder. So I called the cabby and told him to go to the detective office and get Detective Hannan and bring him down at once. He soon returned with him, when I showed him the ladder and told him to watch it from a distance till I returned.

I jumped into the cab and returned home. On the way I gave cabby his coat &c., and on arrival at home I put on an old fore-cabin stewards' rig-out, with plenty of bright buttons on it, and the cap. I then tied a handkerchief round my head over one eye, and put some spots of a red liquid which I had on my nose and mouth to resemble blood. I then put my ordinary clothes in a bag in the cab, and started back to Elizabeth Street, where I got out (gammoning to be very drunk) opposite the Duke of Rothsay Hotel. I staggered down Flinders Lane to where Detective Hannan was. Finding all right, I told him to keep me in sight at a distance. I then lay down in a store doorway commanding the entrance to the right-of-way where the ladder was laying.

I was pretending to be asleep when the constable on the beat came along, turned his bullseye* on me and shaking me said, 'What ship do you belong to?'

I stammered out, 'The steamer *Aldinga*.'

He said, 'Well you get out of here or I'll lock you up.'

I rolled down the street in front of him. When he got to Elizabeth Street, as his time was up, he went off up to meet the relief.

As soon as he was gone I went back pretending drunkenness (as Briely might be watching in the vicinity) and dropped down in the same doorway, and almost immediately Briely came along and seeing me came over to me and had a look at me. He caught hold of me and shook me saying, 'Hallo, mate. What's up?'

I replied in a drunken state, 'Is this the Modle Lodging House?' and dropping my head on my knees rolled over.

Briely knew the constable who was coming on the nightshift would soon be along so he walked over to the right-of-way, and although it was pretty dark I could see him put the ladder up to the wall and go up on to the roof of Heymansons warehouse.

I could see him then putting a rope through the top of the ladder which made me think he was going to have it up after him. But I soon saw different as he pushed the ladder away and, lowering it down with the rope, pulled the rope up after and disappeared across the roof.

* Lantern.

After a few minutes I got up and staggered down the lane to Elizabeth Street where I met the new constable just going into the lane. I called to him round the corner and told him who I was and told him to wait till I changed myself in my cab. I soon did it and giving a peculiar whistle Hannan joined up.

Briely had now been about half an hour on the roof, so we slipped slowly down to the warehouse and listened at the front door. We heard some noise inside and then I put the constable at the front door and Detective Hannan at the back, and, putting the ladder up, I got on the roof. I had the constable's dark lantern so I examined the roof (Briely must now have known he was discovered) in the far corner.

I found where the corrugated iron roof had been prised up, leaving a large hole, through which I crawled onto the ceiling of the store, which was of wood nailed onto the rafters. And as it was an inch deep in dust, I could easily track the direction Briely had gone in. I crawled along between the ceiling and the iron roof and I had not to go far when I came to a square hole he had cut in the half-inch lining boards of the ceiling.

The hole was about eighteen inches square, and the saw (keyhole) and brace and bit he had used to cut it with were lying alongside. And there was a rope tied to one of the rafters overhead and hanging down through the hole into the store—it was also knotted about every foot. I looked down through the hole and turned the bullseye on all over the store. It was full of merchandise silks &c. (I could now see that Briely was the inside man who went in overnight and packed up the goods ready for removal at five o'clock the following morning when the constables would be changing.)

I determined to go down the rope. So I let myself down into the store having first darkened the lantern. On getting to the floor I lay flat down to listen and just as I did so I heard something whiz past and strike the wall. (We afterwards found an alderman jimmy with the sharp end stuck in the boards which linked the partition.)

I now turned on the bullseye and commenced to explore. At the office down near the front door I caught sight of Briely and put down the lantern. He made a rush at me and we had a desperate fight for some minutes, which the police outside could hear but not assist. At last I got his head in chancery and throwing him over my hip, fell on him, knocking all the wind out of him. He then gave in and I handcuffed him. And as the doors were all very massive ones, and were locked and padlocked as well, I had no other alternative but to take him up through the hole in the roof again. So I called the constable and Detective Hannan to get up on the roof and come to the hole in the ceiling, which they did.

I then put a large packing case on the counter and got Briely on the top of it, and the constable got hold of the handcuffs, and between my lifting and their pulling we got Briely through the hole on the roof.

I then went through the store and close to where I had first seen him I found four beautiful skeleton keys. One opened the padlock and the largest one opened the main lock of the front door of the warehouse. These he would have passed out in some way to his mate in the morning to open the padlock...

We locked Briely up for storebreaking. He was committed for trial and at the criminal sittings of the Supreme Court he pleaded guilty and was sentenced to five years' hard labour.

Anthony Trollope
Don't Blow

By the time Anthony Trollope made his first visit to
Australia in 1871–72 he was one of the most famous
writers in the world. His output was prodigious, for he
penned 3000 words in the three hours before breakfast
each day. Trollope was no friend to Melbourne. I can
just imagine the middle-aged, plum-pudding-fed writer
staggering up and down the city's topography during
the height of summer, disliking what he saw from under
his sweat-stained brow. Nevertheless, Trollope does
make some grudging admissions, not least the place
Melbourne had made for itself

Melbourne has made its place for itself, and is the undoubted
capital, not only of Victoria but of all Australia. It contains,
together with her suburbs, 206,000 souls, and of these so-called
suburbs the most populous are as much a part of Melbourne as
Southwark is of London...

Though it stands on a river which has in itself many qualities of
prettiness in streams—a tortuous, rapid little river with varied
banks—the Yarra Yarra by name, it seems to have but little to do
with the city. It furnishes the means of rowing young men, and
waters the Botanical Gardens. But it is not 'a joy for ever' to the
Melbournites, as the Seine is to the people of Paris, or the Inn to the
people of Innsbruck. You might live in Melbourne all your life and
hardly know that the Yarra Yarra was running by your door. Nor
is Melbourne made graceful with neighbouring hills. It stands
indeed itself on two hills, and on the valley which separates them;
and these afford rising ground sufficient to cause considerable
delay to the obese and middle-aged pedestrian when the hot winds

are blowing—as hot winds do blow at summertime in Melbourne. But there are no hills to produce scenery, or scenic effect. Though you go up and down the streets, the country around is flat—and for the most part uninteresting. I know no great town in the neighbourhood of which there is less to see in the way of landscape beauty.

Nevertheless the internal appearance of the city is certainly magnificent...It is the width of the streets chiefly which gives to the city its appearance of magnificence—that, and the devotion of very large spaces within the city to public gardens. These gardens are not in themselves well kept. They are not lovely, as are those of Sydney in a super-excellent degree. Some of them are profusely ornamented with bad statues. None of them, whatever may be their botanical value, are good gardens. But they are large and numerous, and give an air of wholesomeness and space to the whole city. They afford green walks to the citizens, and bring much of the health and some of the pleasures of the country home to them all.

One cannot walk about Melbourne without being struck by all that has been done for the welfare of the people generally. There is no squalor to be seen—though there are quarters of the town in which the people no doubt are squalid. In every great congregation of men there will be a residuum of poverty and filth, let humanity do what she will to prevent it. In Melbourne there is an Irish quarter, and there is a Chinese quarter, as to both of which I was told that the visitor who visited them aright might see much of the worse side of life. But he who would see such misery in Melbourne must search for it specially. It will not meet his eye by chance as it does in London, in Paris, and now also in New York. The time will come no doubt when it will do so also in Melbourne, but at present the city, in all the pride of youthful power, looks as though she were boasting to herself hourly that she is not as are other cities.

And she certainly does utter many such boasts. Her population is not given to hide its light under a bushel. I do not think that I said a pleasant word about the town or any inhabitant of it during my sojourn there, driven into silence on the subject by the calls which were made upon me for praise.

I suppose that a young people falls naturally into the fault of self-adulation. I must say somewhere, and may as well say here as elsewhere, that the wonders performed in the way of riding, driving, fighting, walking, working, drinking, love-making, and speech-making, which men and women in Australia told me of themselves, would have been worth recording in a separate volume had they been related by any but the heroes and heroines themselves. But reaching one as they do always in the first person, these stories are soon received as works of a fine art much cultivated in the colonies, for which the colonial phrase of 'blowing' has been created. When a gentleman sounds his own trumpet he 'blows'. The art is perfectly understood and appreciated among the people who practise it. Such a gentleman or a lady was only 'blowing!' You hear it and hear of it every day. They blow a good deal in Queensland—a good deal in South Australia. They blow even in poor Tasmania. They blow loudly in New South Wales, and very loudly in New Zealand. But the blast of the trumpet as heard in Victoria is louder than all the blasts—and the Melbourne blast beats all the other blowing of that proud colony. My first, my constant, my parting advice to my Australian cousins is contained in two words—'Don't blow.'

JOHN CHRISTIE

The Chinaman Jack Robbery

In this adventure Detective Inspector John Christie exhibits remarkable talents as a banjo-playing minstrel— all part of his quest to catch a thief.

In March 1873 a contractor named John Pigdon was stuck up and robbed of a valuable gold watch with chain and seal attached. Also several sovereigns…amongst some silver there were two rupees, one of which had a small round hole in it.

As there had been several similar robberies about the time, I determined to disguise myself and have a look through the various drinking dens.

So I blacked up à la Christy minstrel [with] black skull cap, and when I got on my plantation clothes and old battered white belltopper, I looked the character. I got this rig-out in a present from George Arnott, an old nigger minstrel. I got my banjo, which was one of Frank Weston's worn-out instruments. This completed my make up.

I got a cab and on getting to the corner of Stephen and Little Bourke streets, I instructed my batman to go down [to] the Golden Fleece and wait for me.

I walked down Little Bourke Street and into the Morning Star Hotel. The bar was full of speelers, mapmen, thieves and prostitutes. They hailed me with 'Good then, Bones, give us a tune.'

I played and sang 'Ten Thousand Miles Away' to a rousing chorus of thieves—I was taking stock all the time.

After the song I made a collection which amounted to about 2/6. They insisted on another song so I gave them 'The Old Log Cabin in the Lane', after which I left and started down to the Star of the East, kept by an ex-sergeant of police named Andrews who had got very low in the world, and his house was the resort of notorious burglars and highway robbers.

There was only a few prostitutes in the bar with a drunken bushman, so I went round into the back parlour which was pretty full of thieves. They were having a barney about changing a coin. The barney was between the landlord and a desperate character named John Wallace, alias Chinaman Jack.

On seeing me, Jack said, 'I say, Darkie, can you change a florin?'

I replied yes.

He handed me what I saw at once was a rupee, but pretended not to notice it. I gave him 2/- and they all, including Jack, heartily laughed at me, thinking I had been gulled. I played them a tune and sang 'Ten Thousand Miles Away' and went round and collected somewhere about 1/6, after which I had a clue to Pigdon's robbery through the rupee.

I left the hotel and went quietly down to my cab and told him to drive me to the detective office where I picked up Detective Hartney and we called at my hotel close by, where in less than five minutes I was dressed in my ordinary clothes (and the black face turned white). Rejoining Hartney we proceeded to Little Bourke Street. On the way we examined the rupee and found it had a hole in it (stopped up with bread) and was no doubt the one Pigdon lost…

We strolled down Little Bourke Street and outside Mrs Morris boarding house we saw Wallace talking to some prostitutes. I went up to him and told him to get into the cab which was following us.

He cursed dreadful and fought like a demon, but Hartney and I got him in, and although he struggled violently all the way, we landed him in the detectives' office where we stripped and searched him. In his socks we found Pigdon's seal and some of the sovereigns, and in his pocket we found the other rupee.

I never let on to him that I had the other rupee, but he swore mortal vengeance against the nigger who he said has put him away because he had done him with changing a rupee.

I pretended not to know what he meant, but he swore he would get even on the nigger some day when he met him. At the same time he did not have the slightest idea that I was identical with the darkie.

I took him to the watchhouse and charged him with assault and robbery on John Pigdon, and next morning I was in waiting at the watchhouse to see if any of his pals would bring him some breakfast. I was right in my conjectures as a notorious character named Kate Laurence called at the watchhouse with some breakfast for him.

After she had departed I shadowed her home and on searching the house I found a quantity of stolen property including Pigdon's watch and chain, all of which was concealed in a hole under the hearthstone which I had to raise.

Both were tried and convicted for the robbery. Wallace got seven years and Laurence two years. And I got a £25 reward from Mr Pigdon.

John Gurner

A Chinese Oath

John Gurner, a grandson of Edward Curr, commenced practising law in Melbourne in 1877. By the time he became crown prosecutor in 1889 he had already seen a great deal of colonial life. Gurner wrote his 'reminiscences' in old age, but his recall of legal practice in a multicultural Melbourne while still a student is fabulous.

One of the cases tried was a charge of arson, a Chinaman being the defendant. This involved the examination of a number of Chinese witnesses, who were sworn, I remember, some by the breaking of a saucer, and one by the chopping off of a cock's head, due precautions having first been taken. In later days, the accepted method of swearing Chinese witnesses in Australia was the blowing out of a match. As translated for me by the official Chinese interpreter, Mr Hodges, who, I believe, was a Chinese mandarin, the oath was: 'You have come here into Court before the Judge to speak the truth. If you speak the truth, God and the whole body of discerning spirits will help and protect you; but if you speak false, they will punish you, probably by annihilation as by the extinguishing of this fire. Blow out the match!' But there was a story told of a civilised Chinaman, possibly of agnostic tendencies, who, being asked in what manner he chose to be sworn, answered: 'Me swear alle same anyway; clack 'im saucer, chop head off cock, blow out match, smell book—me no care.'

Beyond question, whatever the form of oath, perjury is rampant in all countries and in all courts of justice. Lord Darling once said: 'It is supposed that the Book is covered with microbes and that people get ill through kissing it. My experience is that a great many people commit perjury and get punished in no other way.'

Of course, Asiatics present a two-fold problem, the first of which is to devise a sufficiently practical and binding form of oath. In Victoria it is customary to swear a Hindu holding a glass of water in his hand. He is satisfied—why? It represents water from the sacred River Ganges. But why not on the same principle swear a Christian witness upon a copy of *Robinson Crusoe*? Surely the principles which allow a glass of water from the local town supply to pass muster as water from the Ganges, would allow *Robinson Crusoe* to masquerade as the Bible.

A Eurasian interpreter who acted for many years in Victoria assured me that the only form really binding on the Hindu is to get a calf into court, and cause the witness, whilst repeating the oath, to pass his hand down the calf's back, head to tail. The introduction of a frightened calf into court would inevitably be followed by unpleasant consequences, and it is to be remembered (Sir James Stephen, I think, points it out) that if a Hindu, having been sworn to tell the truth, inadvertently says something which may not be true, he is, in his belief, as hopelessly damned as if he had lied wilfully. And that therefore, however firmly he may be bound by his oath, still, recognising that a slip into inaccuracy is almost inevitable, he, whether from the weakness of human nature or life-long habit, lies as freely as if not speaking under the sanction of the most binding form of oath.

JOHN COWLEY COLES

Holy Roller

Wesleyan Methodists have been prominent in Melbourne life since the 1830s—George Langhorne, Joseph Orton and Francis Tuckfield are three from the early days. In 1865 John Coles was converted to the faith while working on the Talbot goldfields. Here the Reverend Coles takes us into the death-cells of early Melbourne with a most sympathetic eye. Coles' deep religious conviction and evangelism were probably laughed at by many, yet he played a vital role in caring for the helpless in a brutally capitalistic society.

On 1 December 1875, I arrived in Melbourne under an agreement with the Home Missionary Committee, to go to Wesley Church, Lonsdale Street, where I was to labour amongst the poor, the degraded, and the lost, in that terribly low neighbourhood...

On my first interview with my superintendent at Wesley Church, he told me that there was a man condemned to death in the Melbourne gaol, whose name was W——h. He said, 'When he was sentenced by the judge, he made a request that he might be attended by a Wesleyan minister. Of course this request was granted. He had been sentenced to death for an attempt to commit murder. He was reprieved from this, and his sentence was imprisonment for life. He then made an attempt to murder the late Mr Duncan, with a knife in his hand. The warder who sprang between Mr D. and this prisoner, and was the means of saving his life, in the struggle with the prisoner, seriously injured his spine. I visited this man frequently in the Melbourne hospital, where he died.

W——h was represented to me as a blood-thirsty murderous man, *only a grade removed from a wild beast.* I was informed that at Pentridge he had been put into a cage and fed through the bars. The Rev. J. G. Millard (my superintendent) said, 'Mr Burnett and I visited him yesterday; a warder was present. I prayed in the cell.' He remarked, 'We are told to "watch and pray", but I tell you, when I prayed with the man, if ever I watched as well as prayed, it was then.' He added, 'Now that you are come, I will hand him over to you. You will now have charge of him. We will go and see him.'

This was the first time I had ever entered a gaol in my life, and consequently the first time I had ever seen a heavily ironed criminal in a condemned cell. As we passed through the outer gates, the late Mr Castieau (the governor) said, 'Be careful what you are about; keep your eyes open. He is a dangerous fellow; we know him.'

Before entering the cell I had pictured to myself a great unintellectual-looking brute in the form of a man. (I saw a murderer once captured by the police, in the bush in South Australia, whose head was more like that of a 'baboon' than a human being. He had no forehead, and his hair came nearly to his eyebrows.) I had pictured W——h just such a man. I entered the cell first, and I saw a small man (but very wiry) sitting in the corner. He had rather a pleasing countenance if it had not been for the peculiar low cunning that is seen in the faces of all confirmed criminals until they are converted.

On seeing us he rose to his feet. I went right straight to him, and offered him my hand, which he took, and which he held in his. I said, 'My brother, I am so sorry to see you in such a position as this; if I could do you any good I would. I feel that I could almost die for you. However, that would do you no good, but I have come to tell you that Jesus Christ loves you, and that Jesus Christ died to save you.' While I was speaking, I felt the man commence to tremble. I could see the tears starting to his eyes. (I thought, thank God, there is a soft place in this man's heart yet.) With a broken voice he almost sobbed while saying, 'Gentlemen, will you sit down on my bed?' I believe it was a very long time since he had been spoken to in a loving and kindly way before. After talking and praying with him we left.

The next morning I visited him alone. At this time the late Mr Castieau said to me, 'Are you going in to see W——h alone?' I answered, 'Yes', to which he replied, 'I cannot hinder you from doing so, but it is my duty to warn you, that for the sake of having an opportunity of being again brought before the Judge to ventilate his grievances he would murder you.'

I remained with him for half an hour; he seemed truly penitent. On another visit he said to me, 'When I woke up this morning the thought came to my mind, if I go to hell, I will go trusting in Jesus.' Looking at me, he said, 'This, sir, I have made up my mind to. Do you think a person feeling like this, and trusting in Jesus, could ever perish?' I said, 'No, I do not; hold on to what you have; hold on to your present confidence.'

On one occasion I said to him, 'The people are standing outside the gaol waiting for the news that you have murdered me.' He answered, 'Murder you, sir; I would not hurt a hair of your head.' I was so drawn out in prayer for him in the cell, that for a time I could not cease praying. I afterwards called on him to pray. He commenced: 'O God, have mercy on me, a vile sinner; give me Thy Holy Spirit that I may have no unkind feeling towards anyone; save me from the power of the devil. O save me, for Jesus' sake!'

He told me the next day 'that on awaking in the morning, he did so weeping bitterly about his sins; but that after a time he felt great relief, and that the fear of death had been taken away from him.' It was quite evident that through the converting grace of God the lion had been turned into a lamb.

The Rev. Millard and myself visited him on Sunday evening in his cell, and administered the sacrament to him, at his own request. Next morning his soul was ushered into eternity. For half an hour before the execution there were three ministers and myself with him. Two out of three had to get permission from me to come into the cell. I never saw such a sight before; and I never want to see such another...

Little Bourke Street, at this time, was a perfect 'pandemonium'. A viler hell on earth, reeking with every description of abomination, could scarcely be found. The horrible scenes that I witnessed appalled me. Unless I had seen what I did, I could never have believed that human nature could have sunk so low — lower by far than the beast of the field...

19 December 1875 — From ten to one o'clock, I visited amongst brothels and thieves' rendezvous. I have been in the lowest parts of London, but it would be well-nigh impossible to witness more horrible scenes of moral delinquency and degradation. It was disgusting and loathsome. At half-past two, we had a prayer meeting, with the band, in the lecture hall at Wesley Church. Held a cottage prayer meeting in the house of a dying man who, a few days before, I had picked up in the street and

taken home in a cab. At a quarter to four, had an open air service, near Bilkington Square. A great crowd surrounded us. Many of the women, who were looking out of the windows and were standing at the doors, were in a state of semi-nudity, as were many of those that stood round us. Most of them were young women, from fifteen to five-and-twenty years of age.

JOHN STANLEY JAMES

A Disgrace to Our Civilisation

John Stanley James was an investigative journalist who insinuated himself 'inside' particular institutions and then published his critical accounts under his nom de plume The Vagabond. As he made clear in his column in the *Argus* on 30 September 1876, Australian Rules struck him as a barbaric degeneration of the way football should be played.

Like every athletic sport, football is followed by all—larrikins, mechanics, clerks, and (self-esteemed) young aristocrats. It seems amongst a certain class to be even more popular than cricket...and it has given me some curious ideas as to the civilisation and humanity of the coming Victorian race...

Mens sana in corpore sano I believe to be generally true, but the principle may be carried to excess, and a healthy mind certainly does not exist where cruel and brutal sports are indulged in. Football as now carried on here is not only often rough and brutal between the combatants, but seems to me to have a decided moral lowering and brutalising effect upon the spectators.

The records of the past season show that several promising young men have been crippled for life in this 'manly sport'; others have received serious temporary injuries, and laid the foundations of future ill-health, the luckiest getting off with scars which they will bear with them to their graves. Now, is the general good derived from the encouragement of physical endurance in the players and the amusement given to the spectators worth all this? I think not, and hold that the evil does not stop here, but that society is demoralised by such public exhibitions as the 'last match of the season' between the Melbourne and Carlton football clubs, which I witnessed last Saturday. I arrived early at the spacious piece of ground which has been given to our Catholic friends for religious purposes, and has been let by them for the highly religious performances of Blondin, football matches, &c....

The six or seven thousand spectators comprised representatives of nearly all classes. It was a truly democratic crowd. Ex-Cabinet ministers and their families, members of parliament, professional and trades men, free selectors and squatters, clerks, shopmen, bagmen, mechanics, larrikins, betting men, publicans, barmaids (very strongly represented), working-girls, and the half-world, all were there. From the want of reserved seats or any special accommodation for ladies the mixture all round the ground was as heterogenous as well might be. I mingled with the throng everywhere, and had a good chance of arriving at the popular verdict respecting football as at present being played.

The Carlton Club were playing on their own ground, and the feeling of the majority was in their favour, and from the commencement was so expressed rather offensively towards the Melbourne Club, which is considered, I believe, to be a little more high-toned, and consequently antagonistic to democratic Carlton. At the commencement I got a position at the rails between a seedy but highly respectable-looking old gentleman, a commercial traveller, and several hardy sons of toil...

If an intelligent foreigner had been present, watching these young men clad in party-coloured garments running after an inflated piece of leather; kicking it and wrestling for it, receiving and giving hard blows and falls, he must have thought it the amusement of madmen. The spectators, who howled and shrieked and applauded, he would have thought equally mad. It is true that as a spectacle of bodily activity and endurance the show was a fine one, but the cruelty and brutality intermixed with it, and which the crowd loudly applauded, and appeared to consider the principal attraction, was anything but a promising evidence of a high civilisation. I was told by several that it would be a pretty rough game, and they gloated in the fact.

As the play went on, and men got heavy falls, and rose limping or bleeding, the applause was immense. 'Well played, sir,' always greeted a successful throw. 'That's the way to smash 'em,' said one of my neighbours. 'Pitch him over!' and such cries were frequent, and the whole interest and applause seem centred in such work. It was no fair conflict either; a man running after another who has the ball, seizing him by the neck, and throwing him down, does not, to my mind, do a particularly manly thing. It inculcates bad blood, as the victim is sure to spot his oppressor and be down on him when occasion offers.

Early in the game it was apparent that a bad feeling existed between the players. There was a dispute as to the first goal kicked by the Melbourne Club—Was it a 'free kick' or not? The umpire's decision was loudly canvassed, and angry players congregated in the middle of the ground. 'There's going to be a scrap,' said a Carltonite delightedly, and called out to one of the players, 'Go into the ——, Jim.' Indeed, it seemed to me as if hostilities had already commenced. There was a squaring of shoulders, and the central mass heaved and surged for a minute, and then the would-be combatants were separated. Shortly after this, the umpire took up his stick, and walked off the ground, and the game was suddenly stopped. I asked this gentleman what was the matter, and he said the Carlton players used such blackguard language to him that he would not stand it; and in this, I think, he was right. One friend said, however, that he was wrong. 'The umpire always has a hard time of it,' said he; 'the only thing he can do is to wear several brass rings, if he hasn't got gold ones, and let the first man who disputes his decision have it straight.' This idea was received with great favour by the crowd, and is an instance of the good feeling generally engendered by this 'manly sport'.

After a fresh umpire was procured the game became as rough as it well could be without absolute fighting…I watched several individual players. One man would throw or push another down after he had kicked the ball, and without, as far as the play was concerned, any excuse or provocation. The aggrieved one would 'spot' his antagonist and repay him in like manner. This system of aggression was altogether, to my mind, cowardly and uncalled for, and yet was loudly applauded by the spectators.

Towards the end of the game one man fainted, several must be lame for weeks, and every man must have been bleeding or scarred. The gentleman who played in spectacles was plucky, but I would advise him to relinquish the game before he receives further injuries. The victory of the Melbourne Club proved unpopular with the larrikins, who commenced stoning the players outside the gates. One offender, however, received a good thrashing for his pains. I consider that football as played last Saturday is a disgrace to our civilisation.

RICHARD ERNEST NOWELL TWOPENY

The Best Kind of Football

British visitor Richard Twopeny's hearty enthusiasm for
Australian Rules provides an interesting contrast to James'
views. No doubt Twopeny would regard The Vagabond
as one of those 'who still have a holy horror of football'.

The popularity of football is more local than that of cricket;
but in Melbourne I think it is more intense...Of course there
are numbers of people amongst the upper and middle classes
who still have a holy horror of football as a dangerous game,
and the want of unanimity in rules prevents the two principal
colonies from meeting on equal terms.

In the older colony the Rugby Union rules are played. Victoria
has invented a set of rules for herself—a kind of compound
between the Rugby Union and Association. South Australia plays
the Victorian game. I suppose it is a heresy for an old Marlburian
to own it, but after having played all three games, Rugby, Association and Victorian—the first several hundred times, the second a
few dozen times, and the third a couple of score times—I feel
bound to say that the Victorian game is by far the most scientific,
the most amusing both to players and onlookers, and altogether
the best; and I believe I may say that on this point my opinion is
worth having.

Of course, men who are accustomed to the English games,
and have not played the Victorian, will hold it ridiculous that the
solution of the best game of football problem should be found, as
I believe it has been found, in Melbourne. But I would ask them
to remember that the Victorian game was founded by rival public-
school men, who, finding that neither party was strong enough to

form a club of its own, devised it—of course not in its present elaborate state—as a compromise between the two.

In corroboration of my opinion I would point to the facts that, while Sydney is at least as good at cricket as Melbourne, there are not a dozen football clubs in Sydney (where they play Rugby Union), as against about a hundred in Melbourne; that the attendance at the best matches in Sydney is not one-third of what it is in Melbourne; that the average number of people who go to see football matches on a Saturday afternoon in Sydney is not one-tenth of that in Melbourne; and that in Sydney people will not pay to see the game, while in Melbourne the receipts from football matches are larger than they are from cricket matches. The quality of the attendance, also, in Melbourne is something remarkable; but of some 10,000 people, perhaps, who pay their sixpences to see the Melbourne and Carlton clubs play of an afternoon, there are not a thousand who are not intensely interested in the match, and who do not watch its every turn with the same intentness which characterises the boys at Lord's during the Eton and Harrow match.

A good football match in Melbourne is one of the sights of the world. Old men and young get equally excited. The quality of the play, too, is much superior to anything the best English clubs can produce. Of course it is not easy to judge of this when the games played are different, but on such points as drop-kicking, dodging, and catching, comparison can be made with the Rugby game; and every 'footballer' (the word, if not coined, has become commonly current here) knows what I mean when I say, that there is much more 'style' about the play of at least half a dozen clubs in Victoria, than about the 'Old Etonians' or the 'Blackheath,' which are the two best clubs I have seen play in England.

Edmond Marin la Meslée

Melbourne's Mardi Gras

La Meslée emigrated to Australia in 1876. While in
Melbourne he worked as private secretary to the French
consul-general. His observations of the city and its inhabitants comprise an assortment of vignettes from 1876
to 1883. In 1878 he moved to Sydney and helped establish
the Royal Geographical Society of Australasia. On
17 December 1893, la Meslée and his wife joined a party
of thirteen to spend a day sailing in Sydney Harbour.
The yacht foundered and seven people, including the
Frenchman, drowned.

It was night when the locomotive deposited me on the platform
at Flinders Street station. Many trains came in from different
directions or set out for the southern or eastern suburbs. The
scene, although very animated, was not noisy. There was not a
single shout and the most perfect order seemed to rule this great
station despite the considerable comings and goings...

At two main city corners, and almost in the centre of the city
proper, there are two fine public buildings, the general post office
and the town hall. The last-named, particularly, does great credit
to the architect who conceived its proportions. The main hall is
used frequently for concerts at which dilettante Melburnians hear
celebrated European artists render the masterpieces of music. The
city council has installed in this hall what Victorians consider one of
the wonders of their capital, a superb organ worth 125,000 francs.
Melbourne people have a great love for music: no self-respecting
house is without its piano and even artisans' cottages have their
spinets. Rich and poor, fashionable ladies and their chambermaids,

everyone believes in the necessity of pounding, with more or less talent, or rather force, the keys of these unhappy instruments. There is not a working-girl who does not 'strum', and every barmaid would consider herself insulted if any uncouth person should permit himself to question her talent as a pianist. But in spite of their love for the art, the Australians are no more musically gifted than the English, and they will willingly pay high prices to hear it played quite badly. Whoever needs to be convinced of this has only to help in the production of some opera, especially a comic opera: the orchestra will be pitiful, the voices more than mediocre and frequent false notes will not appear to trouble the audience. As long as the scenery is well done, the dancers pretty and attractive and their costumes diaphanous, the performance will be a success...

On a hill to the east of the city stands the 1880 Exhibition Palace in the middle of a public garden of which it occupies fully a third. Its cupola dominates the city and, no matter from what direction the traveller approaches Melbourne, he cannot avoid seeing this landmark. Certainly its proportions are far from being harmonious, but on the other hand it can boast of having cost the colony almost £300,000 sterling.

But if the Victorians have no cause for satisfaction in their Exhibition Building, they have the right to glory in plenty of other institutions, among which the public library, with its attached art gallery and technological museum, should be mentioned first. After going through the gate of a fine wrought-iron fence and across a lawn, one climbs a flight of granite steps between two great bronze lions and walks first into the sculpture museum, which contains little more than reproductions of statuary of all the ages. Further on one finds another museum housing a host of Australia and New Zealand exhibits—native arms and clothing of New Zealand flax, objects from the South Sea islands, etc., etc. In a large room nearby are hung many paintings, some of them very good, and nearly all belonging to the modern school. The gallery has some French works, among them many of Gerome's charming little genre pictures: one is of an Arab interior, admirable down to the smallest detail. A huge canvas by Layraud, depicting English travellers in the hands of a band of Calabrian brigands, by itself takes up a good part of the gallery. To judge by the number of people almost always staring at it, this painting must have great merit.

They say—but I only repeat what I was told—that the dominating personage in this painting was none other than the Marquis of Lorne, and that it portrays an episode in the life of this young man before he had the supreme honour of becoming the son-in-law of Her Majesty, Queen Victoria, by marrying Princess Louise. The young lord is squiring a charming damsel whose beauty the painting suggests and whose seductive figure, well set-off in the costume of an Amazon, it shows. It would certainly have had an astonishing effect on a gang of Italian brigands in some pass of the Calabrian mountains or perhaps of the Abruzzi. The bandits let the travellers continue their journey only after they had received a heavy ransom, and the painting shows the young man just about to sign some important document.

It seems (still according to the story as I heard it) that this picture penetrated to England only some time after the Marquis of Lorne had been approved as the son-in-law of his gracious sovereign. It created a fuss, for the painter had, people said, given to his hero the features of the lucky marquis without, however, committing the indiscretion of letting the public identify those of the blonde and bewitching Miss who was sharing his unhappy fate. One felt only that she must have been beautiful. It is said that the scandal reached the ears of the Queen, and there was no lack of tittle-tattle to embellish the episode that the French artist had seen fit to represent. It would have been barbarous to destroy a fine work of art because of malicious gossip, but how was this offensive and embarrassing picture to be got rid of?

Happily a benevolent providence provided a timely solution to the problem. The city of Melbourne had begun to build an art gallery and it had commissioned buyers to hunt for celebrated canvases. The existence of Layraud's masterpiece was easily brought to their attention. They examined it and were delighted. Were they ignorant of the gossip? Who knows? In any case that is how the brigands came to adorn the Melbourne Art Gallery and to engross the attention of visitors every day. The scandal, if committed to the antipodes, does not reach so close to the throne, and the Australians will be able to admire at their leisure a French work of art for which they have paid in hard cash...

The Australians, like the English, are great horse-lovers: among them racing has been raised to the status of a national institution. The Victoria Racing Club spring meeting lasts for a week, during a good part of which the whole country celebrates. They begin on Saturday with the Derby. The following Tuesday is concentrated to the great race: Cup Day is Melbourne's Mardi Gras. The city is deserted and the whole world flocks to the racecourse. Shops, banks, government offices, establishments of every kind, shut their doors. The hotels, crammed from basement to attic with visitors from the neighbouring colonies and every part of Australia, disgorge their torrent of humanity onto the Flemington racecourse. In short, no one is left in the city but the blind, the senile, the halt and infants still too young to walk. To see the Melbourne Cup run the one-eyed beg, borrow or steal telescopes, and the lame new crutches. In fact there is no extravagance which Australians of every class and condition do not permit themselves on the great day.

At Flemington itself the spectacle is truly magnificent.

To carry the vast crowds converging thither from all points of the compass, the Victorian railways perform miracles. A specially-constructed branch-line runs right onto the field behind the grandstand and to the foot of a mound from which racegoers have a better view of the track than from anywhere else. On Cup

Day this line carries about 50,000 passengers, not to mention the thousands who come by omnibus and every other kind of vehicle that can be pressed into service for the occasion.

Alongside the superb four-horse carriage bearing some ravishing Australian girls with their correct escorts, fathers or brothers perhaps, wallows a humble buggy bulging with its load of common humanity. There go half a dozen workers, adorned with multicoloured neckties and accompanied by their sweethearts in three-shillings-a-yard silk dresses, topped off with gaudy hats on which feathers and ribbons battle for position. Gaiety shines on every face: jokes ricochet from one vehicle to another, and races start on the dusty road in anticipation of the great event which all are going to watch a little later.

People have been crowding onto the hill since early in the morning, and below on the flat surrounding the actual course a compact mass of humanity swells in number right up to the moment when the horses appear. Long before the first race, the crowd of visitors promenading on the magnificent lawn between the track and the grandstand, take their seats in the latter. There you will find gathered the fine flower of Australian aristocracy: rich squatters down from the bush with their wives and daughters for the Melbourne Cup, to win or lose perhaps two or three hundred pounds on the favourite; princes of finance, miners whom a lucky stroke of the pick has made millionaires, businessmen whose signature is worth £100,000 in no matter what the bank, and judges with a salary of £3000 a year who have abandoned their magisterial gravity for the day to mix with the Cup crowd. All Australia is there to see and be seen while some thirty superb horses, ridden by jockeys in brightly coloured silk vests and caps, compete for the much-coveted prize: the Cup and the two thousand guineas given by the city of Melbourne, loss of which may make a rich man today into a beggar tomorrow.

In the midst of this multitude of men, every one of them

engrossed with the chances of some horse or other, beautiful girls of this golden land move along almost unnoticed on the arms of their cavaliers.

Look, dear reader, at that tall young woman with the willowy figure, a bit too slender perhaps, whose complexion has the velvety look of a ripe peach and makes you want to bite it. The little you can see of her golden hair under the big picture hat dazzles you, and one glance from her great blue eyes forces you to lower yours. If you go on looking at her in that way, you will commit some outrageous indiscretion. This charming apparition is a Tasmanian. She was probably born on the picturesque banks of the River Derwent in the shade of the blue-gum and huge tree-ferns.

Let us look the other way.

The grandstand is filled from top to bottom: it is a forest of beauties decked out in laces and silks of every colour, a superb bank of living flowers, Australian roses, on this day without thorns.

There is a continuous movement up and down the aisles of the grandstands, a rustling of silks, which sometimes become a little crushed in spite of the space. Some are climbing to their seats, more are coming down to walk back and forth in front of the stands. Flocks of pretty women draw admiring glances from the young men, generally tall and slim but carrying themselves rather stiffly, as they circulate on the lawn. In the crowd can be seen a good number of the sons and the attractive daughters of Israel, generally dressed very expensively if not in very good taste.

Look at those two ladies surrounded by a veritable court of eager young men. One, evidently the mother, is wearing a marvellous satin white dress, Paris-made they say, and sent out from the salon of a world-famous couturier — I have said 'Worth'. Her daughter, who has the figure of a goddess, wears pale blue satin from the same house. Quite plain except for some beautiful pearls and a little touch of lace, which one would imagine to be very costly, the gown fits perfectly with never a crease or wrinkle. These two must be the wife and daughter of one of those squatters who count their cattle in thousands and their sheep in hundreds of thousands.

This tall, beautiful creature coming towards us whose costume, close-fitting in the latest fashion, emphasises the perfection of her figure, has a flawless complexion, and every limpid glance from her great brown eyes bestows upon its recipients, if only for a moment, a vague sensation of happiness. Her mouth is a little big perhaps; but if you see her laugh—and she has the free, pealing laugh of a child—she shows a superb set of dazzling white teeth. It is true that her hands, gloved in silk, are long, even very long; but they are exquisitely shaped and in proportion to her figure. Everything about this beautiful being, from her royal bearing to the proud way she holds her head and seems happy to be alive, suggests candour and gaiety. She has known even bluer skies and hotter suns: she was born, perhaps, in the days when gold drew to the interior of the mother colony, New South Wales, people of every class and kind. For all I know she came into the world on the goldfields at Bathurst, at Ophir or at Wattle Flat.

Beside her a pleasant young person with a less vivid complexion and a less striking figure, whose coiffure reminds one of a Creole, stands chatting with a large, carefree, laughing young man six feet tall. She is a Queenslander whose cradle was shaded by the great Moreton Bay fig-trees. Her father, a rich planter, has presented her with this trip to Melbourne to show her southern sisters that tropical beauties, though they may lack the highly-prized roses-and-cream complexion of others, yet have an elusive loveliness of their own. The young man with her seems to think so, and perhaps she is destined never again to see a great sugar plantation. Who knows? Perhaps she is fated to cross the seas with her knight-errant for he has pitched his tent, as his tall and sturdy build and fair hair suggest, in the colder climate of New Zealand...

Frantic cheers herald the appearance of the thirty magnificent horses which are going to race for the Cup and the two thousand guineas offered by the city of Melbourne. There they are, prancing impatiently and reined in by jockeys rigged out in parti-coloured satin liveries which indicate the stables of the various owners. At last the signal is given! The splendid animals, free from all restraint and urged on by their riders, shoot forward with the speed of an arrow. For a few moments they remain bunched together: not one loses his place. But as they reach the first turn the order changes suddenly.

In the grandstand, on the lawn, on the hill and on the flat every face is drawn with anxiety, and conflicting emotions succeed each other as this or that horse takes the lead. In these moments the attention of this human sea is concentrated entirely on the result of the race. Nothing else in the world exists. The judge forgets his dignity, the young man his sweetheart, the girls themselves have eyes only for the galloping mass of horseflesh thundering now along the straight in front of the grandstand.

Leading by a short head is a beautiful black beast ridden by a little jockey, almost a boy, whose vest of white satin crossed by a crimson band distinguishes him from all the others. The tense crowd raises only a feeble cheer, for the black horse, now leading the headlong group between two hedges which border the track, is by no means the favourite. But in another moment the black is outdistanced! The cheering rises to a mighty roar as the favourite takes the lead. Suddenly it is clear that none of the other horses has a chance and the crowd's whole attention focuses on the two leaders now locked in final struggle.

'Hurrah for the favourite!' roar a thousand throats as the crowd's darling appears from behind a tall rise, two necks ahead of the black horse now under the spur of its diminutive rider. But even as the cheering becomes deafening, there is another change. His flanks raked by the spurs, the black flashes past the favourite only ten yards from the judge's box—to carry off the prize of two thousand guineas and the golden Melbourne Cup itself.

Now one is struck by the despair in the faces of the losers, and there are many of these for the winner was an outsider whose name scarcely even appeared in the betting at Tattersalls or the leading Melbourne clubs. Among the gloomiest are the book-makers, the plague of racecourses in every part of the world, for the black horse had been quoted as a hundred to one in their books. It is ruin for some of them, but few racegoers feel much sorrow on that account.

First Test at the MCG

On three previous occasions an English team had visited Australia to play cricket, yet March 1877 was the first time that both teams would compete with eleven players a side. The two bowlers missing were Frederick Spofforth and Frank Allan; Allan failed to appear because of plans to visit the Warrnambool Show. Other players worth a mention include Billy Midwinter, the only player to have played for Australia against England and for England against Australia, and Ned Gregory, who has the distinc-tion of being the first man in Test cricket out for a duck.

Argus, 16 March 1877—For the reason no doubt that many disppointments have ushered in this match, the attendance of spectators at the commencement of play yesterday was more moderate than so important an event as the first contest between the cricketers of the old country and the colonies on level terms was worthy of…The people who stayed away yesterday in the belief that an eleven lacking the two bowlers of Australia could originate nothing worth the trouble of a visit to the MCC ground, missed the grandest display of batting by a colonial player which has ever been seen in these colonies...Lovely weather set in with a cool southerly breeze at midday, and the match began in the presence of about 1500 spectators. The Englishmen were well received as soon as they appeared, and cheers immediately followed for the first two batsmen, Bannerman and Nat. Thompson...

D. Gregory, the captain stepped out to the first ball from Shaw, but the quick fieldsman at long-on only permitted him one run. In the next over from the same bowler, an unwise attempt was made to steal a run, on the assumption that Jupp was asleep, and Gregory was run out.

This was the result of the first hour's play. Luncheon, which was to have lasted exactly half an hour, spun itself out to forty minutes. By the time play was resumed the attendance had grown to 3000, and before the day was over the number rose to about 4500. Only a small proportion of the spectators patronised the grandstand. The gum trees in Yarra Park bore the usual number of black clusters of free onlookers, but the elms which have grown up within the fence have deprived people of the cheap view they used to get from the hill...

Midwinter went in next, and the two big batters of the eleven got together. The spectators prepared themselves for a treat, but Midwinter played so crudely at two balls he got from Lillywhite, that his admirers felt relief when the umpire called 'over'... Midwinter now thought it time to do something worthy of a giant and recall people's attention to the events of the Christmas match; so he stepped out to Southerton, and the ball flew swiftly through the air towards the grandstand. Ulyett, stationed at the very edge of the turf, backed across the path till pulled up by the fence, then curved his back into the form of a bow, and stretched up his hands. The ball was taken and securely held...E. Gregory had a short life and a merry one. He profited not by the example of his comrade, Bannerman, who showed that the safe plan was to keep the ball down...Though the game was prolonged until the score was brought up to 166, it is not necessary to dwell further on the play.

The stumps were drawn at 5 o'clock. Both men were not out and Bannerman's total amounted to 126. To say that this excellent score was obtained by first-class cricket is inadequate praise for a performance which those who witnessed it will not forget for many a long day.

The Sentencing of Ned Kelly

Ned Kelly's confession to shooting Thomas Lonigan at Stringybark Creek left Judge Redmond Barry few alternatives for sentencing, yet the latter stages of the trial became a personal struggle between the bushranger and the judge. When the moment came for Barry to proclaim the death penalty, Kelly replied prophetically that 'a day will come at a bigger court than this when we shall see which is right and which is wrong'. We join the dramatic scene in the central criminal court immediately after the jury has re-entered the coutroom.

Argus, 30 October 1880—...The prisoner, having been asked in the usual way if he had any statement to make, said, 'Well, it is rather too late for me to speak now. I thought of speaking this morning and all day, but there was little use, and there is little use blaming anyone now. Nobody knew about my case except myself, and I wish I had insisted on being allowed to examine the witnesses myself. If I had examined them, I am confident I would have thrown a different light on the case. It is not that I fear death; I fear it as little as to drink a cup of tea. On the evidence that has been given, no juryman could have given any other verdict. That is my opinion. But as I say, if I had examined the witnesses I would have shown matters in a different light, because no man understands the case as I do myself. I do not blame anybody, neither Mr Bindon nor Mr Gaunson; but Mr Bindon knew nothing about my case. I lay blame on myself that I did not get up yesterday and examine the witnesses, but I thought that if I did so it would look like bravado and flashness.'

The court crier having called upon all to observe a strict silence whilst the judge pronounced the awful sentence of death.

His Honour said, 'Edward Kelly, the verdict pronounced by the jury is one which you must have fully expected.'

'Yes, under the circumstances.'

'No circumstances that I can conceive could have altered the result of your trial.'

'Perhaps not from what you can now conceive, but if you had heard me examine the witnesses it would have been different.'

'I will give you credit for all the skill you appear to desire to assume.'

'No, I don't wish to assume anything. There is no flashness or bravado about me. It is not that I want to save my life, because I know I would have been capable of clearing myself of the charge, and I could have saved my life in spite of all against me.'

'The facts are so numerous, and so convincing, not only as regards the original offence with which you are charged, but with respect to a long series of transactions covering a period of eighteen months, that no rational person would hesitate to arrive at any other conclusion but that the verdict of the jury is irresistible, and that it is right. I have no desire whatever to inflict upon you any personal remarks. It is not becoming that I should endeavour to aggravate the suffering with which your mind must be sincerely agitated.'

'No, I don't think that. My mind is as easy as the mind of any man in the world as I am prepared to show before God and man.'

'It is blasphemous for you to say that. You appear to revel in the idea of having put men to death.'

'More men than me have put men to death, but I am the last man in the world that would take a man's life. Two years ago, even if my own life was at stake, and I am confident if I thought a man would shoot me, I would give him a chance of keeping his life, and would part rather with my own. But if I knew that through him innocent persons' lives were at stake, I certainly would have to shoot him if he forced me to do so, but I would want to know that he was really going to take innocent life.'

'Your statement involves a cruelly wicked charge of perjury against a phalanx of witnesses.'

'I daresay, but a day will come at a bigger court than this when we shall see which is right and which is wrong. No matter how long a man lives, he is bound to come to judgment somewhere, and as well here as anywhere. It will be different the next time they have a Kelly trial, for they are not all killed. It would have been for the good of the Crown had I examined the witnesses, and I would have stopped a lot of the reward, I can assure you; and I do not know but I will do it yet, if allowed.'

'An offence of this kind is of no ordinary character. Murders had been discovered which had been committed under circumstances of great atrocity. They proceeded from motives other than that which actuated you. They have had their origin in many sources. Some have been committed from a sordid desire to take from others the property they had acquired, some from jealousy, some from a desire for revenge, but yours is a more aggravated crime, and one of larger proportions, for with a party of men you took up arms against society, organised as it is for mutual protection, and for respect of law.'

'That is the way the evidence came out here. It appeared that I deliberately took up arms of my own accord, and induced the other three men to join me for the purpose of doing nothing but shooting down the police.'

'In new communities, where the bonds of society are not so well linked together as in older countries, there is unfortunately a class which disregards the evil consequences of crime. Foolish, inconsiderate, ill-conducted, unprincipled youths unfortunately abound, and unless they are made to consider the consequences of crime they are led to imitate notorious felons, whom they regard as self-made heroes. It is right therefore that they should be asked to consider and reflect upon what the life of a felon is. A felon who has cut himself off from all decencies, all the affections, charities, and all the obligations of society is as helpless and degraded as a wild beast of the field. He has nowhere to lay his head, he has no one to prepare for him the comforts of life. He suspects his friends, he dreads his enemies, he is in constant alarm lest his pursuers should reach him, and his only hope is that he might use his life in what he considers a glorious struggle for existence. That is the life of the outlaw or felon, and it would be well for those young men who are so foolish as to consider that it is brave of a man to sacrifice the lives of his fellow creatures in carrying out his own wild ideas, to see that it is a life to be avoided by every possible means, and to reflect that the unfortunate termination of your life is a miserable death.

'New South Wales joined with Victoria in providing ample inducement to persons to assist in having you and your companions apprehended, but by some spell which I cannot understand—a spell which exists in all lawless communities more or less—which may be attributed either to a sympathy for the outlaws, or a dread of the consequences which would result from the performance of their duty—no persons were found who would be tempted by the reward. The love of country, the love of order, the love of obedience to law, have been set aside for reasons difficult to explain, and there is something extremely wrong in a country where a lawless band of men are able to live for eighteen months disturbing society. During your short life you have stolen, according to your own statements, over two hundred horses.'

'Who proves that?'

'More than one witness has testified that you made the statement on several occasions.'

'That charge has never been proved against me, and it is held in English law that a man is innocent until he is found guilty.'

'You are self-accused. The statement was made voluntarily by yourself. Then you and your companions committed attacks on two banks, and appropriated therefrom large sums of money, amounting to several thousands of pounds. Further, I cannot conceal from myself the fact that an expenditure of £50,000 has been rendered necessary in consequence of the acts with which you and your party have been connected. We have had examples of felons and their careers, such as those of Bradly and O'Connor, Clark, Gardiner, Melville, Morgan, Scott, and Smith, all of whom have come to ignominious deaths; still the effect expected from their punishment has not been produced. This is much to be deplored. When such examples as these are so often repeated society must be reorganised, or it must soon be seriously affected. Your unfortunate and miserable companions have died a death which probably you might rather envy, but you are not afforded the opportunity—'

'I don't think there is much proof that they did die that death.'

'In your case the law will be carried out by its officers. The gentlemen of the jury have done their duty. My duty will be to forward to the proper quarter the notes of your trial and to lay, as I am required to do, before the Executive, any circumstances connected with your trial that may be required. I can hold out to you no hope. I do not see that I can entertain the slightest reason for saying you can expect anything. I desire to spare you any more pain, and I absolve myself from anything said willingly in any of my utterances that may have unnecessarily increased the agitation of your mind. I have now to pronounce your sentence.'

His Honour then sentenced the prisoner to death in the usual form, ending with the usual words, 'May the Lord have mercy on you soul.'

'I will go a little further than that, and say I will see you there where I go.'*

JOHN COWLEY COLES
Ned Kelly Condemned

Coles' ministry at Melbourne Gaol saw him rubbing shoulders with a huge diversity of felons. Although Ned Kelly was a Catholic, the Protestant Coles could not resist a visit to this most famous of inmates.

The warder went to the condemned cell and I received a message that Kelly desired to see me. In the cell he could hear everything that I had been saying in reading the Bible or while I was preaching.

The man by no means looked a ruffian. He had rather a pleasant expression of countenance. He was one of the most powerfully built and finest men that I ever saw. He treated me with great respect, listened to all I had to say, and knelt down by my side when I prayed. I refused to hear anything from him about his bushranging exploits, but I kept him to this—that we might die any moment. I might not live another half-hour; but if he did not

* Barry died on 23 November 1880, twelve short days after Kelly's life ended at the end of a rope.

die before he was sure to be executed on a certain day, and that he was a sinner standing in need of a Saviour. I find that the following entry in my journal about this, my first visit to Kelly: 'He evidently wanted to make me think that he did not care for his position, and that he would see it out like a man.'...

After preaching, at Kelly's request, I went into the condemned cell. On entering I said to him, 'Do not think, Kelly, for one moment that it is out of any foolish curiosity to see you that I have sought these interviews with you; nothing of the sort. Indeed, I wish I could be spared the pain of seeing an intelligent young man like you in such an awful position. My sole object in speaking to you this morning is to impress on you the fact that you have a soul to be saved, or for ever lost; that Christ died for the chief of sinners, and if you will but be sorry for your sin and confess it to God and ask for mercy for Christ's sake, He will have mercy on you.'

He answered me, 'I have heard all that you said this morning,' referring to the address, the text being 'Prepare to meet your God.' 'I believe it all. Although I have been bushranging I have always believed that when I die I have a God to meet.' He added, 'When I was in the bank at Jerilderie, taking the money, the thought came into my mind, if I am shot down this moment how can I meet God?'

I knelt down in the cell and prayed with him, he kneeling by my side. As he rose from his knees he crossed himself and thanked me.

This was my last interview with Kelly. Shortly after this he was executed. I did not go to see it. I could have done the man no good by doing so, and was saved the pain of seeing a fellow creature ushered into the presence of God.

SHERMAN FOOTE DENTON

Gun-happy!

Sherman Denton was employed as artist to the US Fish Commission at the time he wrote *Incidents of a Collector's Rambles*. The book records his travels in Australasia between 1881–83 with brother Shelley and father William, who died in New Guinea in 1883 while collecting birds of paradise. William was a psychic, sideshow spruiker and lecturer on various topics and, in an age before wildlife protection, the brothers supplemented the family income by collecting exotic fauna. Here we meet Sherman and Shelley as they blaze their way through the Victorian countryside, principally around Panton Hill, about thirty kilometres north-east of the city. At the same time Denton's father leads Melbourne's citizens on a pillaging expedition of the fossil beds at Beaumaris (here called Cheltenham), following a public lecture on geology.

I was awakened at daylight by the most uproarious laughter proceeding from across the way. Poking my head out of the window, I saw on the limb of a gum tree three laughing jackasses indulging in a morning song. In great haste I seized my gun, and soon reduced the trio to a duet. The bird was not dead when I picked him up, and he bit my fingers desperately. The laughing jackass is about the size of a crow and coloured white, grey and blue. He belongs to the kingfisher family, and lives largely on snakes and lizards, which he squeezes to death between his mandibles. A person who has never tried the experiment, can form very little idea of the interest and excitement attending the first expedition with a gun into the forests of a new country.

Every bird one sees is game, and a careful observer see hundreds of things to delight his mind.

I shall never forget my first morning in an Australian 'bush'. At home most of the sounds one hears in the woods are as familiar as human voices; but out here, under the gums, all is new, and I often found myself speculating on what the creature could be that made some of the noises. There were whistling, shouting, squeaking, crying, laughing, twittering, cooing, and sounds impossible to name or describe. I soon began to distinguish the cries of certain birds, and, before I left Panton Hill, most of the songsters in that vicinity were old friends. They were in fine plumage, and some of the skins we made here are the brightest in our cabinet...

We went off with Barelli* one bright moonlight night after opossums. He, Barelli, had a little dog, which could find the animals faster than we could shoot them. As soon as the dog barked, we started for the spot, and always found him sitting under a tree, looking up into it. Getting the tree between ourselves and the moon, we could soon see the opossum, and bring him down. We had shot seven or eight opossums, three native cats, spotted pouched mammals—so named, I should imagine, from their dissimilarity, rather than their resemblance, to that domestic animal—and were on our way home when we came to a very high tree with a large animal crouching near the top. I put a handful of buckshot into each barrel and let him have it. The gun kicked me so badly that I judged it must have done considerable execution at the other end; but the beast evidently had no intention of coming down, so Barelli put a bullet through him, and a shower of blood followed by the creature itself came to the ground. It proved to be an Australian bear, a pouched animal, weighing about fifty pounds.

One day when returning from shooting, we came across

* A Frenchman who had given a number of public talks about the fauna around Panton Hill, prompting Denton and his brother to investigate.

another bear in a tree, but, having used all our ammunition, I armed myself with a stout club, and started for the top of the high tree. Crawling out on a branch near the bear, I struck him with my club, but, instead of knocking him off, only succeeded in angering him, and, before I could deal him another blow, he was upon me. My first thought was to let go my hold, but I soon changed my mind when I thought of the distance to drop. I took a firm hold of a limb with my left hand, and began pounding him with my fist in the most approved pugilistic manner, and, with a final crack on the nose, sent him to the ground, where Shelley soon dispatched him…

We started off one morning, well loaded down with ammunition, food, and blankets, for a couple of days' stay on the Upper Yarra River…After wandering about the river until we were well tired out, we applied at a neighbouring farmhouse for a night's lodging. A Fury, personified, with a lower lip like the trap-door of a tarantula's nest, informed us that it was the Lord's Day—a fact that had not occurred to us before; further adding that she would admit no one to her house who would desecrate the sabbath.

I fear our estimation of religious zeal was not heightened as we turned away to trudge back through the woods to Panton Hill. Rain prevented us from camping in the forest. No houses were in sight except on the other side of the river, and we could find no way to cross. We lost our way several times, and became so tired that further progress seemed impossible. It was Monday morning before we arrived at our comfortable little room in the hotel. As Shelley crawled into bed, he grunted out— 'By George! wake me up next week.'

The next morning, leaving our luggage to come on in a cart, we started for a trip in the Plenty Ranges…We were just in the middle of 'Tramp, Tramp', when a long, clear whistle, with a crack like a pistol-shot at the end, stopped us short. Sitting down on the roadside we listened, and soon the whistle began again; then followed the most exquisite mimicry of many of the songsters of the wood, varied by sounds resembling the clear tones of a distant bell, the rattle of a rickety wagon, rasping and gratings that made the cold chills run down one's back, whispers, moans, cries and laughter. I clearly distinguished the coarse high laugh of the giant kingfisher, the cooing of the dove, the call of the black and white shrike, the song of the rusty-backed thrush, the scream of the hawk and the hoarse screeching of the cockatoo. Sometimes the song, with a volume like a large organ, was loud and sweet, and it seemed as if the musician must be within a stone's throw; then, again, it died away to the faintest whisper.

There was a mellow richness in parts that reminded me of the liquid notes of the clarinet. We sat spellbound till the song ceased. I have heard most of our American songsters, and some of them are very fine, with voices rich and mellow; but the mocking bird himself cannot compare with this prince of songsters, the Australian lyrebird.

This one was just below us in a gully thick with tree-ferns and scrub, and we did not get sight of him. As we walked on, the trees grew larger, the lower growths more dense, and but the time we reached Pheasant Creek, our destination, we were in a forest of the finest trees I have ever seen—some of them towering to a height of three or four hundred feet, and twenty feet in diameter at the base. They are not so disappointing as the 'California big trees', which start from the ground enormous, and before they reach fifty feet have dwindled to one-third their former size; but these carry their bulk well up, and their circumference is not much less at one hundred feet than it is at the ground...

21 August—When we woke this morning, we could hear, coming from the scrub near the creek, the liquid notes of a lyrebird, and after swallowing a hasty breakfast we started in pursuit. I concealed myself in the scrub, while Shelley went down stream and returned, keeping up a low whistle as he came towards me, to

prevent my shooting in his direction, as he drove the bird past. I had not waited long when I saw a bird running on a fallen tree, and with a snap shot I secured the prize. It was a female in very good plumage, and I was very much delighted.

Then we went farther down stream, seeing and hearing several more, but they were so shy and so quick, that we shot only one. They are about the size of a common fowl, slate-coloured, with soft, fluffy feathers, and seem to depend for escape on their legs rather than their wings. They have stout claws for scratching, and their eyes are placed on the sides of their heads, in such manner that they can see in all directions. I saw one male bird only, and his tail gave him a very peacock-like appearance, as he flashed past me in the thick scrub…We found the lyrebirds very hard to skin, as their heads are so large in proportion to their necks, that the skin has to be cut to get it over.

22 August—We tried lyrebird for breakfast this morning, but found it very tough, and not especially well flavoured. Not a stone's throw from our cabin, we shot three of the beautiful king-parrots; and as I went to the spring for water I saw a kangaroo feeding on the tender grass. Unfortunately I did not have my gun, so he got away as fast as his great hind-legs would carry him, jumping over the bushes as he went.

Wombats, large mammals, the size of half-grown pigs, are very common here, but so far we have seen nothing but their holes, which are large enough for a man to crawl into. While out we saw several trees stripped of their bark from top to bottom, and a miner informed us that it was done by the black cockatoo, but we did not see any of the birds.

As we were coming home, we shot a large bear, which was all we could carry; and in turning over a piece of bark for beetles we found a very fierce-looking lizard, which bit at everything within its reach. This reptile, about a foot and a half long, is covered with large, hard, scales, and has a good set of sharp teeth and a bright blue tongue. A miner to whom we showed the animal called him a 'sleeping Dick'. He certainly was not very sleepy when we caught him, for he looked perfectly ready to amputate a finger...

24 August—This morning, early, we saw one of the strangest sights imaginable: as we were walking along the hillside, we saw, stretched upon the soil, what looked for all the world like an animated bicycle tyre. It was about four feet long and one inch in diameter, and, on inspection, proved to be a gigantic earthworm. His length depended much on the state of his mind, for the moment we alarmed him, he shortened up into a stumpy sausage, bristling with minute spines. I regretted that we had no way of preserving such a curiosity, as he certainly would have made a sensation in America. We have since learned that they are quite common, and have been found six feet in length. It is a wonder some enterprising Yankee does not start a factory among the Plenty Ranges, and ship these worms to America as first-class bologna sausages.

25 August—This morning, walking several miles toward the other side of the range, we reached the head of a gully, where the lyrebirds seemed to be holding a jubilee. The morning was fair and warm, but everything was covered with dew. Shelley walked cautiously through the scrub, while I went ahead on the outside and entered some distance below, where I sat very quietly watching for the birds. Our first trial was unsuccessful, although there were several birds between us. The next time I saw a fine male, but the gun missed fire in both barrels, on account of the very poor quality of the caps, which were not waterproof. I was disgusted; as nothing so exasperates a hunter as to have his gun misfire. At the next trial we did not see a bird, but one commenced singing right across the creek from me, and I began the difficult task of crawling upon him. The leaves and ferns were still wet, and I must have made very little noise, as he kept on

singing without an interruption. I had to smile several times at his
odd noises, and once came very near exploding with laughter at
his version of a concert between laughing jackasses.

Part of the way I was obliged to crawl on my hands and knees,
trembling so with excitement, I doubted my being able to shoot
when I had the chance. I approached till within few yards of him;
but, as I rose from the ground, the music suddenly ceased, and
with a whistle and a crack he was off like a meteor. I sent a dose of
shot after him, as he flashed for an instant among the ferns, but on
reaching the spot the tip of one of his long tail-feathers gave
evidence of my failure. It began to look as if we were not going to
have a male bird, with all our hard work, but we tried once more;
and this time a female flew across the creek and ran along the
opposite bank. A charge of shot put a stop to her career; and,
just as I was about to pick up the fluttering bird, a fine male came
out of the bushes to investigate matters, and as I had left my gun
behind, of course I did not get him. The very fates seemed to be
against us, for every time I had seen a male bird 'fair and square',
there was some hitch about the rest of the programme, and when
I did get a good shot, it was always a female…I began to think I
was sold again when, just as I was getting up to go, I saw a bird
run out of the scrub and make for the fern on my left. Taking
deliberate aim, I fired. The smoke came back into my face, so
that I could not see the effect of my shot. I ran down the bank,
jumped the brook, and there on his back lay a fine male lyrebird,
in the best of plumage. His tail was more than a yard long, and
beautifully banded with dark brown, rusty red and white. I felt
happy enough as I started up the bank, carrying my prize, his
beautiful tail half spread and nearly touching the ground. Shelly
had shot a female lyrebird, and fired at a large wombat, which
was asleep in its hole, with its head half out. The creature had
life enough left to crawl back, where it was impossible to get him.

We had a long trudge through the woods back to our little

cabin, reaching here, tired and hungry, after dark. Tomorrow we leave for Panton Hill, and for Melbourne on Monday...

Melbourne is a very social city, and while there we met many agreeable people, and had many a good time. My engagements were so numerous, in fact, that it became necessary to keep a list of them for daily consultation. Frequently I did not get to bed till it was growing light, and I sometimes found myself speculating on what day it was when I awoke. At last, one morning, after having been out until the small hours—and they were not so very small either—I came to the conclusion that the sooner I returned to a natural and rational manner of living the better.

Perhaps, for the sake of my appearance, it was well I came to this decision, for I had begun to grow thin from loss of sleep, and the sun had seen me so seldom, that I looked as pale as a stalk of celery. I have 'roughed' it by the week, lived on all kinds of food, camped in the snow, waded icy streams on the mountains, and been without dry clothing for days together, but I never felt so thoroughly worn out as after those few weeks of dissipation. In order to live such a season one would need the constitution of a mustang, and the digestion of an ostrich.

Father had interested the people so much in geology, that one fine day over two hundred went down with him to Cheltenham to look at a fossil whale, which he had discovered. They chartered a train, and went prepared to spend the day. There was very little of the whale left when they started for home.

FRED CATO

FRED CATO

Gumsucker Love

During 1882–83 young Fred Cato sent a series of missives
to his absent fiancée Fanny, in which he provides a
delightful account of Melbourne's sights, sounds and
goings-on. Fred and Fanny finally married in December
1884, a union that would last more than fifty years.

6 March 1882 — When I got home tired on Friday night last, I
was quite cheered at having a letter handed to me with your
writing on the envelope. After reading through it, I seemed
ready for anything. Well, dear Fanny, I hardly know what I
would not give to have you beside me now, and listen once
again to your voice. It seems so far far in the distant future,
before we shall have the mutual pleasure of clasping one
another in our arms, and telling of joys and troubles that we
have had.

My nationality you will know by this time. I am, in colonial
phraseology, a 'Gumsucker', i.e. a native of Victoria. But as my
parents hail from England and Scotland, and as these people are
found on every part of the earth's surface and I was not born
in either England or Scotland, I may justly style myself a
cosmopolitan — especially as I am divided between Victoria and
New Zealand. My second name is Jack or rather John. By the
bye, have you a second name?…

Every morning now, I have a walk of about two miles to work,
and the same walk back in the evening. I am working at
Brunswick Street. They want me to take the management of the
shop but I hardly care about being tied to any particular one. We
close at that shop at 7 p.m. I do not go home to dinner but walk

from Fitzroy to Smith Street, Collingwood, where there is a large coffee palace, at which I get my midday meal. Sometimes I get my tea as well there, while at other times I wait till I walk home. There is a coffee tavern in Brunswick Street as well, but once to go there was enough for me. The waitress approaches with an unheavenly expression on her face, and, when asked what she has got to eat, exclaims, 'Chapps, steak, sausages.' Even if you go there fifty times, the same sad tale is told. For tea, she gives what I describe as hot water through which a Chinaman must have run before it was boiled, and that was the closest approach to tea that ever came near it...

4 December—...So you have all been scared by the comet. I saw it Saturday night, but it did not look very terrifying. Your imagination has carried you too far, when it caused you to believe that a like consternation concerning the comet falling into the sun exists in Melbourne. This is the first I have heard of it, except some idle twaddle at the time when getting up early in the morning to view the wondrous sight was the fashion. People in Melbourne I think are too much engrossed in business affairs, etc, to be much troubled with comets colliding with suns or joining with them to give fiercer heat.

But I shall tell you what the Melbourne public are concerned with just now, and that is about the worst railway accident that has ever occurred on the Victorian lines. It occurred on a Saturday night. Between thirty and forty people are wounded, but not many dead yet, as far as I know. You must understand that on a number of our lines there are trains running every few minutes, and sometimes a number of express ones besides, so that it requires very good generalship to keep all things right. From what I at present know of the accident, I believe it due to one train starting four minutes before its turn. I have not seen any papers yet, although 'Herald extraordinaries' were being sold yesterday. I met three urchins trying to sell the papers as I went up to Sunday school. One of them yelled out, 'H. Exy. Case of suicide. A man cut his throat with a bar of soap and turned himself into a reel of cotton'; another followed with, 'H. Exy. Ship-wreck in a gutter', and so on...

2 January 1883 — ...Instead of going to our own church tonight, I went to the Salvation Army meeting*. It is held in the Temperance Hall, Queensberry Street. I do not think that I ever saw such a low assembly before — the riff-raff of society, present and future. Thieves and I believe, murderers physiognomically, I would condemn the greater number. The meeting is conducted very rowdily. Several officers have charge and their gesticulations are at times very absurd. Whistling, talking, laughing, coming in and going out are occurring during the whole of the service. Revival hymns are sung, and between them short addresses are delivered by men and by women. While I was there, two of the former, and three of the latter spoke. The speakers as a rule are very illiterate. For instance, one woman tonight repeated several times with great emphasis that she belonged to 'a *Harmy* of God, and not a *Harmy* of the Devil'. To the uninitiated, it looks very much like profanity, and yet I would not be the one to condemn them. They have done good, and God grant that they may do more. There are certain classes in all large cities, at whom it is very hard to get with the gospel. The Salvation Army therefore adopt street singing marching, etc, etc, in order to get them inside. I don't think they would ever have any effect upon an educated mind. Poor fellows, they do not get very much at their collections. I suppose the plate had been a third of its distance around when it came to me — there were three or four threepences and one half-penny...

5 November — ...'Please to remember the 5th of November', etc. This day always brings to mind my boyhood pranks, when I

---

* The Salvation Army was established in Melbourne in 1882.

indulged in crackers, etc, in honour of the immortal Spaniard Guy. The air is now redolent with the fumes of Chinese fireworks that Master Len has been letting off. Tomorrow will be run the great event of the year at the Flemington grounds. The whole of the Australian colonies, with bated breath, will await the result. Joy will be brought to some; sorrow, degradation and suicide to others. Gambling in connection with the racing carnival is the plague of Victoria, especially of Melbourne.

GEORGE AUGUSTUS SALA

Marvellous Melbourne

It was English journalist George Sala who coined the term Marvellous Melbourne, succinctly summing up the city as it was in the 1880s. As special correspondent for the *Daily Telegraph*, Sala lodged stories with the paper from round the globe. Here he reports from a city made fabulously wealthy by gold, and a vast metropolis sprung from nothing in a single lifetime.

It was on 17 March, in the present year of Grace, 1885, that I made my first entrance, shortly before high noon, into Marvellous Melbourne...Melbourne at the noonday of which I speak was *en fête*. This is essentially holiday-making country. The Queen's Birthday, the Prince of Wales's Birthday, St George's Day, St David's Day, St Patrick's Day all find crowds of merry celebrants; every trade and craft has its periodical outing, and not the least exuberant of their festivals is, I am told, the Undertakers' Picnic.

The French critic of our manners was good enough to observe with a sneer that, when an Englishman had nothing to do he was wont to say, 'Let us go out and kill something'. With much greater reason might it be hinted that whenever he had a chance of escaping from the irksome thraldom of labour the Briton in Australia says, 'Let us go out and enjoy ourselves'...

It is desirable, for many reasons, that I should explain why I have called Melbourne a marvellous city. The metropolis and seat of government of the colony of Victoria has at present, within a ten-mile radius, including the city and suburbs, a population of more than 282,000 souls...Omnibuses, hansoms, and hackney wagonettes swarm in the streets, and very soon an extensive system of horse-tramway cars will be thrown open. The Anglican and Roman communions have splendid cathedrals, and there is a multitude of handsome and commodious places of worship for other denominations. The town hall is gigantic and imposing; the general post office vast, comely and admirably arranged. There is a splendid university...There are half a dozen theatres, more or less. There is a very grand permanent exhibition building and a fine aquarium...There are asylums, markets, hospitals, coffee palaces, public and private schools, clubs, parks, gardens, racecourses; and recreation grounds in profusion in and about the city; and I need scarcely say that there are any number of big banks and insurance offices, which in their architecture are more than palatial. The whole city, in short, teems with wealth even as it does with humanity. Well, you may say, what is there wonderful in all this? Melbourne is the prosperous capital of a prosperous British colony. What is there to marvel at in its possession of all, or nearly all, the features of the most advanced civilisation? But there is thus much that is marvellous in Melbourne. The city is not fifty years old...

I have never revisited Melbourne without finding plenty of blazing sunshine say for about four days out of seven, and without being grateful for the gentle umbrageousness afforded by the arcades which lead from Bourke Street.

Let me see. The first of the Bourke Street arcades is the Royal, nearly opposite the Post Office, which was erected a few years since by the Hon. H. Spensley, at a cost of some £20,000. Further east, nearly opposite the Theatre Royal, a handsome and commodious structure, you will find the second Melburnian arcade, the Victoria, which was built and opened by Mr Joseph Aarons in 1876. The cost, including that of a building called the Academy of Music, was about £40,000. Then, still further on, close to the vast Eastern Market, is the Eastern Arcade, erected by a well-known coach-proprietor named Crawford. The admission to all these pretty avenues is free, and they are all open and brilliantly lighted until ten at night. In this last respect the Melbourne arcades present a pleasant contrast to our Burlington, the gates of which are pitilessly bolted and locked at 8 p.m. — precisely the hour when people, especially foreigners, who have just dined, would most gratefully appreciate the advantages of a covered promenade. But they order these things differently and better in France — and at Melbourne. Indeed, but for the fact that prohibitions on smoking are conspicuously placarded about in the Royal, the Victoria, and the Eastern arcades, you might, without any very violent stretch of the imagination, fancy on a fine night that Bourke Street was one of the Paris boulevards instead of being a highway hewn not fifty years ago out of the trackless Bush, and that you were a *flâneur* from the Café du Helder, who had just strolled into the nearest passage to saunter from shop to shop, the contents of which you may have seen five hundred times before, and to rub shoulders with a throng whose faces from long acquaintance should be perfectly familiar to you. But does a Paris boulevard *flâneur* ever grow tired of sauntering?

...In the daytime the arcades at Melbourne are affluent in well-dressed womankind, and the shops are full of feminine finery and knickknacks. Anglo-Saxon womankind at home, in the States, and in Australia abhor the odour of tobacco; while in the last-named country indulgence in the weed takes at least two very objectionable forms. In the first instance, cigars at the Antipodes, as I have elsewhere hinted are, as a rule, atrociously bad. In the next place the short pipe, charged with the strongest tobacco and reeking with essential oil, is the favourite calumet both of the beardless, sallow, weedy 'cornstalks'*, with their hats at the backs of their heads, and of our full-bearded, broad-shouldered, brawny brother—and master—the Australian Working Man...

I think that it was the night after my arrival in the metropolis of Victoria that a great fire broke out in a warehouse in William Street, next door to Menzies' Hotel. Both buildings are of stone, and there were some inches of clear space between the wall of the burning warehouse, which was full of combustible merchandise, and the wall of the hotel; still the propinquity of the incandescent to the unfired edifice was far too close to be pleasant. There was, naturally, a prodigious scare among the guests at Menzies'...Fortunately, the brigade were early on the scene of action. The local substitute for Captain Eyre Massey Shaw, C.B., did his work admirably; the police mustered in force, and did good service; the crowd, although dense, was, on the whole, well behaved. Soon after midnight the firemen had obtained a mastery over the flames, by three o'clock in the morning the conflagration had burned itself out; and the estimable Widow Menzies and her guests were able to return to rest, and to murmur, if they felt so disposed, 'For this relief, much thanks'. But throughout that eventful night I had been conscious of a sound, reiterated at brief intervals, solemn, measured, strident, and, as I thought, minatory. It was the sound of a human voice, grimly sonorous, but to my ear, at first, not articulate. The flames roared, the water from the hose flashed and hissed and bubbled and gurgled from the main;

* A term generally applied to New South Welshmen. It refers to the willowy, slim build and height of the 'new' nineteenth-century Australians.

the crowd shouted, the firemen clattered hither and thither; the crash of broken glass and falling timbers was incessant; but still the lugubrious chant of that human voice, now near, now distant, relaxed not in its monotonous cadence…Had some member of the Salvation Army felt a call to cry, 'Woe to Melbourne!'? At length, when surcease came to the roaring of the flames, when the crowd had dispersed, and the last dog had barked itself mute, the lugubrious chanter had things all to himself, and I could make out what he said. His cry was of polonies. Yes; polonies. That variety of sausage tribe is, I hear, amazingly popular at the Antipodes. So are saveloys.

FRANCIS WILLIAM LAUDERDALE ADAMS

Where They Go Ahead

Francis Adams was a radical social commentator, poet and novelist. He arrived in Melbourne in 1884, where he found it difficult to scrape together a living. These observations on the city were published in 1886. In 1890 and, as he explained it, 'Mind-sick of Australia', Adams departed permanently for Europe. His legacy in the Australian union movement and in early sociological studies, however, long endured.

The first thing, I think, that strikes a man who knows the three great modern cities of the world—London, Paris, New York—and is walking observingly about Melbourne is that Melbourne is made up of curious elements. There is something of

London in her, something of Paris, something of New York, and something of her own. Here is an attraction to start with. Melbourne has, what might be called, the *metropolitan tone*. The look on the faces of her inhabitants is the *metropolitan look*. These people live quickly: such as life presents itself to them, they know it: as far as they can see, they have no prejudices. 'I was born in Melbourne,' said the wife of a small bootmaker to me once, 'I was born in Melbourne, and I went to Tasmania for a bit, and I soon came back again. *I like to be in a place where they go ahead.*' The wife of a small bootmaker, you see, has the *metropolitan tone*, the *metropolitan look* about her; she sees that there is a greater pleasure in life than sitting under your vine and your fig-tree; she likes to be in a place where they go ahead. And she is a type of her city. Melbourne likes to 'go ahead'. Look at her public buildings, her new law courts not finished yet, her town hall, her hospital, her library, her houses of parliament, and above all her banks! Nay, and she has become desirous of a fleet and has established a 'naval torpedo corps' with seven electricians. All this is well, very well. Melbourne, I say, lives quickly: such as life presents itself to her, she knows it: as far as she can see, she has no prejudices.

As far as she can see.—The limitation is important. The real question is, *how* far she can see? How far does her civilisation answer the requirements of a really fine civilisation? What scope in it is there (as Mr Arnold would say) for the satisfaction of the claims of conduct, of intellect and knowledge, of beauty and manners? Now in order the better to answer this question, let us think for a moment what are the chief elements that have operated and are still operating in this Melbourne and her civilisation...

On one of the first afternoons I spent in Melbourne, I remember strolling into a well-known bookmart, the bookmart 'at the sign of the rainbow'. I was interested both in the books and the people who were looking at or buying them. Here I found, almost at the London prices (for we get our twopence and threepence in

the shilling on books now in London), all, or almost all, of the
average London books of the day. The popular scientific, theo-
logical, and even literary books were to hand, somewhat cast into
the shade, it is true, by a profusion of cheap English novels and
journals, but still they were to hand. And who were the people
that were buying them? The people of the dominant class, the
middle-class. I began to inquire at what rate the popular, scientific,
and even literary books were selling. Fairly, was the answer. 'And
how do Gordon's poems sell?'

'Oh, they sell well,' was the answer. 'He's the only poet we've
turned out.'

This pleased me, it made me think that the 'go-ahead' element
in Victorian and Melbourne life had gone ahead in this direction
also. If, in a similar bookmart in Falmouth (say), I had asked how
the poems of Charles Kingsley were selling, it is a question
whether much more than the name would have been recognised.
And yet the middle-class here is as, and perhaps more, badly—
more appallingly badly—off for a higher education than the
English provincial middle-class is. Whence comes it, then, that a
poet like Gordon with the cheer and charge of our chivalry in
him, with his sad 'trust and only trust,' and his

　　weary longings and yearnings
　　for the mystical better things:

whence comes it that he is a popular poet here? Let him answer us
English for himself and Melbourne:

　　You are slow, very slow, in discerning
　　that book-lore and wisdom are twain:

Yes, indeed, to Melbourne, such as life presents itself to her, she
knows it, and, what is more, she knows that she knows it, and her
self-knowledge gives her a contempt for the pedantry of the old
world. Walk about in her streets, look at her private buildings,
these banks of hers, for instance, and you will see this. They *mean*
something, they *express* something...They express a certain sense

of movement, of progress, of conscious power. They say: 'Some thirty years ago the first gold nuggets made their entry into William Street. Well, many more nuggets have followed, and wealth of other sorts has followed the nuggets, and we express that wealth—we express movement, progress, conscious power. Is that now what your English banks express?' And we can only say that it is not, that our English banks express something quite different; something, if deeper, slower; if stronger, more clumsy.

But the matter does not end here. When we took the instance of the books and the people 'at the sign of the rainbow', we took also the abode itself of the rainbow; when we took the best of the private buildings, we took also the others. Many of them are hideous enough, we know; this is what Americans, English and Australians have in common, this inevitable brand of their civilisation, of their determination, their pitiless strength. The same horrible 'pot hat', 'frockcoat', and the rest, are to be found in London, in Calcutta, in New York, in Melbourne.

Let us sum up. 'The Anglo Saxon race, the Norman blood': a colony made of this: a city into whose hands wealth and its power is suddenly phenomenally cast: a general sense of movement, of progress, of conscious power. This, I say, is Melbourne—Melbourne with its fine public buildings and tendency towards banality, with its hideous houses and tendency towards anarchy. And Melbourne is, after all, the Melburnians. Alas, then, how will this city and its civilisation stand the test of a really fine city and fine civilisation? How far will they answer the requirements of such a civilisation? What scope is there in them for the satisfaction of the claims of conduct, of intellect and knowledge, of beauty, and manners?

Of the first I have only to say that, so far as I can see, its claims are satisfied, satisfied as well as in a large city, and in a city of the above-mentioned composition, they can be. But of the second, of the claims of intellect and knowledge, what enormous room for improvement there is! What a splendid field for culture lies in this middle-class that makes a popular poet of Adam Lindsay Gordon! It tempts one to prophesy that, given a higher education for this middle-class, and fifty—forty—thirty years to work it through a generation, and it will leave the English middle-class as far behind in intellect and knowledge as at the present moment, it is left behind by the middle-class, or rather the one great educated upper-class, of France.

There is still the other claim, that of beauty and manners. And it is here that your Australian, your Melbourne civilisation is, I think, most wanting, most weak; it is here that one feels the terrible need of 'a past, a story, a poet to speak to you'. With the library are a sculpture gallery and a picture gallery. What an arrangement in them both! In the sculpture gallery 'are to be seen', we are told, 'admirably executed casts of ancient and modern sculpture, from the best European sources, copies of the Elgin marbles from the British Museum, and other productions from the European continent.' Yes, and Summers stands side by side with Michaelangelo! And poor busts of Moore and Goethe come between Antinous and Louvre Apollo the Lizard slayer! But this, it may be said, is after all only an affair of an individual, the arranger. Not altogether so. If an audience thinks that a thing is done badly, they express their opinion, and the failure has to vanish. And how large a portion of the audience of Melbourne city, pray, is of the opinion that quite half of its architecture is a failure, is hideous, is worth only, as architecture, of abhorrence? How many are shocked by the atrocity of the medical college building at the university? How many feel that Bourke Street, taken as a whole, is simply an insult to good taste?

...Things move more quickly now than they used to do: ideas, the modern ideas, are permeating the masses swiftly and thoroughly and universally. We cannot tell, we can only speculate as to what another fifty—forty—thirty years will actually bring forth.

Free trade, federalism, higher education—they all go together.

The necessities of life are cheap here, wonderfully cheap; a man can get a dinner here for sixpence that he could not get in England for twice or thrice the amount. 'There are not,' says the *Australasian Schoolmaster*, the organ of the state schools, 'there are not many under-fed children in the Australian (as there are in the English) schools.' But the luxuries of life…are dear here, very dear owing to what I must be permitted to call, an exorbitant tariff, and, consequently, the money that would be spent in fostering a higher ideal of life, in preparing the way for a national higher education, is spent on these luxuries, and the claims of intellect and knowledge, and of beauty and manners, have to suffer for it…

Free trade, federalism, higher education—they all, I say, go together; but if one is more important than the other, then it is the last. Improvement, real improvement, must always be from within outwards, not from without inwards. All abiding good comes, as it has been well said, by evolution not by revolution…

We know, or think we know (which is, after all, almost the same thing), that these three questions—free trade, federalism, higher education—are the three great, the three vital questions for Australia, for Melbourne. We know that, sooner or later, they will have to be properly considered and decided upon, and that, if Melbourne is to keep the place which she now holds as the leading city, intellectually and commercially, of Australia, they will have to be decided upon in that way which conforms with 'the intelligible law of things,' with the *Tendency of the Age*, with the *Time-Spirit*. For this is the one invaluable and, in the end, irresistible ally of progress—of progress onward and upward.

HUME NISBET

The Chinese Quarter

Hume Nisbet resided in Australia from 1865 until 1872. He also visited in 1886 and 1895. An accomplished artist and writer, Nisbet seems to have been drawn to the seamy side of life. Here, in a piece written for *Cassell's Picturesque Australasia*, he takes us to the opium dens of Little Bourke Street.

Little Bourke Street is a world apart from the city of Melbourne, and the race which occupies its crowded courts seems to have no connection with the other people who by day or night promenade along the pavements of Bourke Street proper. Few Victorians who look with just pride upon the vast, clean-kept streets and lofty buildings of their monster city know or dream of the life so far removed from all their ideals of home comfort which is seething quietly a few feet from where they are walking and laughing in happy ignorance. Let me begin by lifting a single corner of the veil which nicely covers up all, and show a scene or two from the Chinese quarter. With two detectives as our guides, for no sane man would think if venturing into these quarters alone, particularly at night, we did the round, and as might be expected under the circumstances, saw everything *coleur de rose*.

Our visit had evidently been expected. Men talk of the advances of civilisation, of telephones, and the like, but the rapidity with which news can circulate through thieves' quarters surpasses all the inventions of modern science. We began our walk at 9 p.m., having made out arrangements with the courteous head of the police about five hours before; but we had not advanced ten yards into the street before a woman hailed one of the guides with the cheerful words, 'They all know you are coming down tonight with two gentlemen, so you won't see much fun.' Possibly we had been seen and watched coming from the detective station, and so the password had travelled to and through the whole district...

It seems a strange combination, but all the Chinese gamble, and all smoke opium, yet they are industrious and cleanly, rising early and working late, and on Saturdays their week's savings go to the Lottery Bank or the Fan-Tan. Some people deny the cleanliness, but writing from personal experiences of the Melbourne Chinese, I boldly affirm that cleanly they are.

Some of these Chinese shops are delicious in colour and picturesqueness—lanterns swinging about, throwing down soft light on the assembled figures; jars and grotesque china monsters standing on the shelves; bills, boxes, and packages; vermilion labelled with quaint Chinese characters; rice books set before the markers, who were dotting off tickets with their vermilion or black paint pots and pointed poonah-brushes. Groups of forbidding-looking Europeans, or rather a conglomeration of nationalities, half-castes and white men, were lounging about, casting scowling, yet timid, hangdog glances on the intruders, muttering sounds like maledictions, yet not plain enough to be resented. Above the counter-top stood an altarpiece with its hideous god, or rather complex symbol of Nature, and before it the daily offering, a cup of tea, which no European is allowed to touch. All was cleanly and sweet-smelling, except when the filthy European mongrels chewed tobacco and spat about the floor...

Into alleys where no one could dream of finding a passage we stumbled, every little hole and corner laden with its own burden of depravity and crime. Here, in a dark corner, with fearful-looking, tumbledown sheds on three sides of the yard, and the damps and chills of foulness underground, one of my guides had lain a whole night watching for some daring burglars, and had been rewarded by catching them. Lighting a match, he pointed out to me strange dens and hiding-places. In one an old sack and some straw flung in a corner on the bare floor told us that the birds had not yet forsaken their vile nest. In another alley the policeman showed us where he had recovered a large 'plant' of jewellery. In capturing the Chinese receiver he had nearly been killed by a blow on the head with a cleaver. As we were standing listening a figure slid softly past, yet not too softly to evade the sharp ears of the detective, who called out the name, and received in reply, 'Good night.'

Shifting a loose paling aside, our guide crushed through; we followed, and lo, another land lay revealed. It was no longer Little Bourke Street, but a vast territory of horrible dens of infamy. What we saw was vile enough, but yet innocence itself to what we could not see, as our visit had been notified, and the inmates were mostly out, or if in, hiding and pretending to be out. Most of these dens had Chinese characters upon the lintels; and as we went on we passed shambling, indistinct figures, who kept to the shadow side of the wall, and tried to move past unseen, yet all had to announce some errand to the vigilant policeman. The graceful outline of a well-dressed girl brushed past me in passing, and she tendered her excuse for coming against me in a soft tone and educated accent. 'Going home, Nance?' inquired the detective. 'Yes, sir,' sweetly returned the young girl, and became lost in the obscurity. 'That girl is a perfect slave to the opium-habit,' I was informed by my guides.

Presently we came to another wooden building, on its last legs, or, rather, piles. It slanted down sideways amidst the mud, and rags filled up the holes of windows, while the thin morning breeze flapped some loose boards with a dismal sound. A loud knock against the door, to which no reply was given; then a rough shove, and the door yielded, and we entered an apartment pitch-dark.

'Take care of your feet,' muttered our guides, 'and walk softly.'

We groped our way along until a turn revealed to us a low light burning in a far-off room, like a candle in a fog, while the pungent odour of opium smoke filled our nostrils with its rather pleasant perfume. On we went, and presently entered upon the scene where the habit was being indulged. Here we saw a hideous, yellow-visaged, shrunken-eyed Chinaman and a young woman about twenty, neatly dressed and comely, while between them stood a tiny oil-lamp, the light of which had shown us the way in, and near the lamp a little saucer with a dark, treacly substance at the bottom. She held the long opium pipe to her lips, and waited; he slowly extracted a small quantity of the glutinous liquor from the saucer on the point of a needle, and, rolling it round like a pea, held it over the lamp flame. He rolled it round and round till it frizzled, swelled, and then became reduced in size, so as to fit into the tiny aperture of the pipe which the woman held glued to her lips. As he pushed it in, and held the filled pipe over the flame, the girl inhaled one long, sucking breath, which she swallowed, and then it was all over—to begin again after we left, pipe after pipe—one long suck to each elaborately prepared pipe.

We went into other dens. In some we saw Englishmen indulging in the pernicious habit; in others young females, with sweet, pure-looking faces and gentle manners, who would have deceived me as to their vocation if seen elsewhere. Yet others there were in which Chinese alone congregated, to prepare and smoke their evil pipes: and these dens were invariably clean. In one I tried four pipes, but evidently I had not done the business right, for I felt none of the delightful sensations which de Quincey so vividly describes. I only rose with a dry, nasty taste in my mouth, feeling nothing more than I felt before; and the taste was only in a measure removed by a visit to the cookshop, and a plate of long soup, with the native sauce added to it, followed by a saucer of cut chicken...

In one English house which we entered—filled to the door

with harsh-voiced women and coarse-looking men—I seemed to recognise for the first time the noisy vice of London slums. In all the other places we had seen refinement and gentleness—the gentleness of demons—an air of courtesy and education which appalled me more than the worst language of Billingsgate. We are accustomed to associate vice with curses and blasphemy; but it seemed more hideous and revolting when accompanied by gentle tones and educated language. Victoria swarms with state schools and free education, and yet villainy is not stamped out, but rather intensified, by the power which books have given.

There were no brutal ruffians in the dens I saw, with the exception of this one house. I heard no vulgar jests or blood-curdling oaths. Those of English race spoke gently, as the Chinese did, and in set phrases, the men looking like world-worn gentlemen, while the women spoke like blasé ladies, with modest attire and girlish figures. Only here and there in the lanes might be seen a recognisable blackguard, smoking coarse tobacco, or a bloated, unmistakable nightbird; and these were merely the prowlers of the dark outside. Inside, refinement and villainy blent too readily not to be suggestive of the poetic ideal of the damned.

But in this one dark-covered house were assembled larrikins and females with coarse features and corresponding figures. Here were arms tattooed, scowling faces, unkempt locks. We were prepared at a glance for anything, from the garrotter down to the kinchin-layer*, and left with the feeling that all the surroundings were in accordance with the proper fitness of natural laws outraged. This was ordinary vice, and about it we thought no more. Does not the poet say:

'Vice is a monster of so frightful mien,
    As, to be hated, needs but to be seen'?

* A thief who steals from children.

And this was a case in point. But the Chinese lepers of morality gave us more concern. We could not but wish Little Bourke Street demolished and the plague-spot wiped out altogether, warehouses built in the dilapidated quarter, crime crushed and the vermin driven out...

It was growing very near daylight, and we were utterly tired out, and disgusted to the heart's core with our eight hours' experiences. In the last house that we visited, we saw on one bed of the opium den three young colonials lying making up their own pills, languidly sucking at the pipe-stems one after another. Here we also saw a Chinaman and a lovely girl of about sixteen years, while her companion, also about the same age, with a bundle of purchases at her side, was sitting down. Behind the door on a chair, in half shadow, sat a most ladylike woman of about twenty-five. As our eyes grew accustomed to the dim light, we saw a blear-eyed old hag with a face wrinkled and marked like a parchment record of iniquity, and, most pathetic sight of all, a young man tenderly nursing a baby.

'Ha! Tom, lad, is the youngster any better?' inquired one of the detectives.

'Not much, sir,' quietly replied the young man. 'Yet since Nelly came out he has been easier with his cough.'

'So you are there, Nell?' asked the detective, looking at the woman behind the door.

'Yes, sir.'

'Nice girl, isn't she, gentlemen,' he continued, waving his hand carelessly, with the air of the proprietor of a wild beast show, 'and the smartest pickpocket in Melbourne, ay, or the world either, for that part, as I think we can nearly beat Creation in the way of the under professions.'

'Yes, I think I have seen more of real blackguardism tonight than in my previous life's experience, and I have seen a few places pretty bad.'

The woman sat with her hands folded on her knees, and gently smiled, while the three young colonials made a motion as if to rise.

'Don't stir, gentlemen, we are going in a moment.'

The three young men sat back languidly on the bed, and prepared another opium puff.

'Where is the pleasure in this?' I asked one of the pleasantest-faced, as he lay back looking passively at me with half-closed eyelids.

'Well, you see, when a working man like myself'—he certainly did not appear like a hard worker—'comes home of a night too tired to eat or sleep, we come here and take a pipe or two, and feel as if we could go fresh to work once again without needing either to sleep or to eat. You have read de Quincey, haven't you?'

'Yes,' I replied, feeling a sudden interest in this opium victim.

'Well, he tells you all about it.'

'But are you all working men?'

'Certainly,' replied the other two young fellows, who had not spoken before.

'None of your lies!' harshly broke in one of the detectives, with a sudden scowl; and at his voice the young man seemed to shrivel up. 'I'll tell you what they are. That fellow you have been speaking to is not two days out of gaol for a case of burglary and violence. The other two were in the same haul, only we hadn't the evidence enough to convict them. Better luck next time. This young man is a sort of all-round man, although I know his tricks best in shoplifting. He is the friend of Nelly over there, and the baby he is nursing is hers, before she took up with him.'

'And the others?'

'Old Mother Murphy, with crimes enough to sink a frigate, past all use except opium-sucking now; and these two on the bed— well, they are called ladies by day, and keep a villa in one of the fashionable outskirts of Melbourne; only they cannot exist without their pipe, and come here under cover of night to enjoy it quietly.'

The people described never stirred, nor showed the least emotion, but acted as if we were not there or he had not spoken.

With another last glance round, I passed out, filled with hopeless pity for women so besotted. Yet there was one ray of light through all the gloom of that murky fog—the tenderness of the love of that young housebreaker for the pickpocket Nelly, which constrained him to nurse her child, the sickly souvenir of an earlier passion.

JOHN FREEMAN

Winkling Out a Living

John Freeman was an acute observer of life in late nineteenth-century Melbourne. Here he follows the fortunes of some of the lowest on the social ladder, the destitute men who gathered periwinkles for a living. The molluscs were easily overexploited and soon became rare close to Melbourne, much to the discomfort of those whose livelihood depended upon them.

The few men who go about Melbourne selling winkles belong to the loafer class, and are mostly old men. As a rule, they patronise the sixpenny lodging-house, when they save the wherewithal to pay for the bed; when they haven't they usually 'doss it' where they can, which is usually in an old boiler or empty malt tank in winter, and *sub Jove* in summer.

At one time these men could fill their baskets at Williamstown or St Kilda, but for the last few years they have been rather scarce in those localities, owing to the number of excursionists who, when there, make 'winkle-hunting' part of the day's amusement. Consequently, those who want them for sale have to look elsewhere for them.

It is but a hard and precarious living the 'winklers' get at the best. With basket on arm, they trudge along the road in all weathers to the few remaining spots where the tiny molluscs are yet to be found. Sometimes they are so fortunate as to be able to fill their baskets at Brighton, but frequently they have to go as far as Morehalloe[*], and sometimes further than that. Leaving town early in the morning, they may be able to get to Brighton, fill their baskets, and return to Melbourne in time to sell them that same night. If, however, they have to go beyond the latter-named place, all they can do is get there in one day and return the next.

It would be a weary walk for these elderly gentlemen if they could not get an occasional lift on the road. But, fortunately for them, there are plenty of carts or empty drays going the same way as themselves, the drivers of which will always give them a ride, if civilly asked for permission to 'jump up'.

The winkles are found loose among the gravel or sand upon the beach in greater or lesser quantities, more frequently the lesser. They also hide themselves in the friendly shadow of the loose boulders lying about, which have to be removed before the searcher can reach his prey, often not an easy task for men whose muscles have become softened, and whose strength has been sapped by a perpetual soaking in 'colonial'.

Having filled his basket, which, by the way, is no light load, our winkle man gets on the 'back track', as he calls it. Having arrived in town, he goes to the place he stays at, and begins to prepare his stock for the market. The first process the winkles undergo is washing—a very necessary operation, as the sand clings to them with great tenacity, and can only be removed by repeated

[*] Mordialloc.

rinsings under the tap. Having washed them to his satisfaction, the next thing our friend has to do is to boil them, and a few minutes suffices for that, if he can get anything to boil them in. The culinary arrangements of these six-penny lodging-houses are not always of the most perfect description. Neither does the manager or chucker-out consider it part of his duty to provide boilers for cooking winkles in, as the only recognised cooking in these establishments is the preparation of whatever small articles of food the lodgers may bring in, and for that a saucepan and gridiron are at their service. Should the saucepan be engaged at the time the winkle man wants to cook his winkles, he borrows a billy, and does as many as it will hold, and repeats the operation until all are cooked.

Having prepared his stock for sale, all that remains for him to do now is to sell it, and before he can do that he has to travel up one street and down another for many weary miles in search of customers. The great bulk of his patrons are to be found in hotels, among the half-drunken people lounging about the bars, whose appetites being somewhat palled by drink, are tickled by these tasty little things, and restored to their normal condition. Many people, especially new arrivals, like them with their bread and butter at tea-time. Others are fond of them, but cannot command sufficient patience to extract them from their shells; and some 'can't a-bear' them on account of their strong resemblance to snails.

If our friend can get back to town with a peck of winkles he considers himself very fortunate. Mostly, however, he has to content himself with about half that quantity, which being sold a threepence the half-pint leaves him something like four shillings for his trouble, and as it sometimes takes him two days to gather and sell them, it cannot be said his business is a lucrative one.

The possession of money is not always an unmixed blessing. Strange as it may sound, people sometimes have more money than is good for them, that is, when they make an injudicious use of it. It is much better for our friend that his income is limited to about two shillings a day, as out of that he must pay for a bed, and at least one meal, Sunday included, and that will not leave him sufficient for a very extended 'drunk', whereas, if he had more he would never be sober. He is tolerably contented, however, and accepts his position with great philosophy, saying, 'If I cannot get drunk every day, I will as often as I can.' In carrying out that resolve, he hangs about his favourite tap till all his money is gone, and then he and his basket disappear till the following evening, when there are other rinsings and another boiling, soon after which the streets are again resonant with 'Periwinkle…'

In summer when the weather was hot, our friend used to go to the banks of the Yarra, between the falls and Princes bridges, and having washed his shirt in the stream, would spread it out on the banks for the sun to dry it. While the drying was going on, he usually lay down to have a nap, till one day, on awaking, he found his shirt had disappeared. He never knew if it had been blown into the river, or whether it had been stolen by some loafer who had thought it a favourable opportunity of getting a change of linen. He inclined to the former belief, because, as he observed, the shirt was in such a dilapidated state that any loafer must be hard up indeed who would think it worth the trouble of walking off with. Ever after that, he said, he always took the precaution of going to sleep with one eye open till the garment was sufficiently desiccated to be resumed.

When washing day came round he used to go to the Public Library and take a piece of soap out of the lavatory in the full belief that he had a perfect right to do so, and when we informed him he had committed a larceny for which he was liable to imprisonment, he was not only greatly surprised, but highly indignant as well.

'Wasn't it bought with the public money?' he asked, 'and put there for the public use, and haven't I, as one of the public, as much right to it as anyone else?'

'Of course you have, but you must go there to use it.'

'They wouldn't let me wash my shirt there, would they?'

'Not if they knew it.'

'Well then, what benefit is the soap to me if I can't take it to where I can do my washing?'

'My good fellow, you must understand the trustees do not find soap for washing shirts, either there or anywhere else. It is placed in the lavatory for the use of those visitors who want to wash their hands before they handle the books, and you may go there and use it as often as you like and as much as you like.'

'But if I have the right to use the soap at all, what difference can it make whether I use it inside the building or outside?'

'None whatever, as far as the soap is concerned, but the law says you must not take it away.'

'The law be hanged. Right's right, and wrong's no man's right.'

Hume Nisbet

Tripping through Paddy's

Here Nisbet has emerged from opium dens to trudge the beat at the Eastern Market, affectionately known as 'Paddy's'. As this piece makes clear, even at the height of marvellous Melbourne there was much poverty and despair in the city.

Paddy's Market is one of the institutions of Melbourne. It is all covered in now, and lighted with electric lamps, which have a beautiful, fairy-like effect. With the vegetable and fruit stalls, it presents a busy, lively scene on a Saturday night, full of character and colour, something for a painter to revel in.

Fifteen years ago it was not all covered in, and had no electric lights. Tramps, outcasts, and homeless vagabonds used to congregate here and pass the night out of the dew, for there were corrugated-iron roofs over some parts of it.

I had to pass here nightly, after the theatre was over, to reach my lodgings in Little Collins Street, and witnessed some piteous sights—men, women, children, honest and dishonest, virtuous and vicious, all lay huddled together for warmth, mostly starving.

Why? Perhaps they had come out to the country without considerations, and in ignorance of what it was. Emigration at the time had something to do with it. Unscrupulous home agents, for the sake of their fees, had launched out hordes of subjects unfit for the land. The labourers and tradesmen were all right, also the domestic servants; they got places easily and made money, and found comforts such as they could not afford in England. It was the professionals who suffered: writers, lawyers, governesses (ladies and gentlemen), who lay here huddled together, starving, helpless, and hopeless.

Some of those who loved virtue and honesty better than life, went down to the river Yarra and found a solution of their difficulties there; but the bulk of them had not the courage to die, or the brains to think it fully out, so, instead of turning their backs on town and old traditions, they loafed about the streets by day, and lay under the shelter of Paddy's market by night.

I used to disturb them sometimes as I picked my way amongst them in the dark; sometimes I trod by accident on dainty limbs, to hear a groan or a moan in answer to my apology...

I had taken shelter from a shower of rain under a verandah in Spring Street; there was only one young woman standing waiting, like myself, on the shower passing—a Jewess, as I could see by her dark, Semitic features, and not too beautiful; yet, perhaps, the misery that was upon her had robbed her of some of her usual attractions...Backwards and forwards she walked restlessly, while

I stood still under the lamp shadow and watched the light play over her face as she crossed it, having nothing else to do. She was making up her mind for something, I could see, and I was speculating in a vague way upon what it could be, when all at once she stopped and faced me, saying, 'Do you think this rain will last long?'

'I don't think so,' I replied, and then a long pause, while we both stood together looking at the drops pouring over the gutter of the verandah.

At last she spoke again. 'Would you mind doing me a favour, sir?'

'No! That is, if I can. What is it?'

'I want some medicine from the chemist over there, but he will not give it to me; perhaps he might give it to you if you tried.'

'Perhaps. What kind of medicine do you want?'

'A shilling's worth of laudanum. Will you try?'

'Certainly,' I said, taking the money from her and starting off; then a thought struck me, and I turned back and faced her. 'What do you want it for, Miss?'

'Toothache. I have it frightfully tonight.'

'No you haven't,' I said quietly. 'It is heartache which ails you, and you want to kill yourself—is that not true?'

'Yes, you are quite right, I want to kill myself. Now, I suppose, you will be for giving me in charge.'

'No. I would rather help you to die if you are quite sure that you are done with life. But are you sure? Tell me about it before I go for the poison.'

Then she told me how she had offended her kindred, the Jews, by becoming a Christian, and how they had cursed her and discarded her. She was a tailoress, but most of the trade was in the hands of the Jews, and they would not employ her, while the Christians had no room for her.

'I have just 3*l.* left now, the sum required to bury me and settle what I owe for lodgings; and I don't want to die in debt, or have a pauper's funeral.'

'But have you tried every shop in Melbourne?'

'Yes, all of them, without a hope of success.'

'Then I'll get you the laudanum; only I want a favour from you also before I get it.'

'What do you want?'

'I want you to live until tomorrow night and try all round once more. If you don't get a job tomorrow, then meet me here at six o'clock, and I'll do my best to get it for you; but if you do get a job, don't come. Now you know, I'll be here from six to half past, so that if I don't meet you I shall know that you have been lucky. Is it a promise?'

'Yes, I promise to try once more, and do nothing rash until tomorrow night.'

I returned her shilling, and we shook hands and went separate ways; the rain was over by this time. Next night I waited at the place from six till half past without seeing her; she had passed out of my life.

Six months afterwards I was waiting at the post office to ask about letters, when a pretty, laughing-faced young woman came up the steps, with a young man beside her. As soon as she saw me she darted forward and shook me warmly by the hand. I recognised the Jewess whom I had met under the Spring Street verandah.

'I got a job next day, so that I did not need to come back to you. Wonderful! wasn't it; and better, I also got a husband. I say, dear,' she cried to her companion, who came up to us, and who I also saw belonged to her own race, 'this is the young fellow who made me go the round once more.' To me: 'This is my husband; I got a place, after all, in a Christian shop, the first I tried, and he was the foreman there. We have been married two months.'

'And are you still a Christian?' I asked, curiously.

'No! he cured me of that,' she answered, with a merry laugh.

Edmund Finn

Birrarang Long Gone

Here Edmund Finn, as Garryowen, laments the transformation of the once beautiful Birrarang into the Yarra
of colonial times. In the 1830s and early 1840s this river
was home to fish of all sorts, and dolphins—here
referred to as porpoises—ventured as far as Richmond.

The Birrarang (water coursing through mist and umbrageousness), as Aboriginally designated, but accidentally named the
Yarra Yarra by Mr Charles Wedge under circumstances elsewhere
narrated was, when first seen by white men, a stream shrouded in
romance, and wrapped in a grand grotesque wildness, to which its
waters and its banks within the Melbourne circuit have long been
strangers.

From the spot whereon Melbourne was afterwards built to
the Saltwater River confluence, the Yarra Yarra flowed through
low, marshy flats, densely garbed with tea-tree, reeds, sedge and
scrub. Large trees, like lines of foliaged sentinels, guarded both
sides, and their branches protruded so far riverwise as to more
than half shadow the stream. The waters were bright and
sparkling; and, wooed by the fragrant acacias, shaking their
golden blossom-curls, how different in aspect and aroma from
the Yarra of today—a fetid, festering sewer, befouled amidst the
horrors of wool-washing, fellmongering, bone-crushing and other
unmentionable abominations! Some of the contiguous timber
attained to a considerable height in the region of the present
Queen's Wharf, and the Yarra basin constituted a natural reservoir
which, viewed from the adjacent eminences, offered a spectacle
for which eyes would now seek in vain.

The eastern and western, the Emerald and Batman's hills formed an immense cordon of she-oak, gum- and wattle-tree forests, which it would hardly be imagined would ever succumb to the fire and axe of civilisation. As for herbage, it luxuriated everywhere, and two persons still living, who walked through un-streeted Melbourne in 1836, have informed me that in the places now known as Collins, Bourke, Elizabeth and Swanston streets, they waded through grass as green as a leek, and nearly breast high. The blacks, the emus, the bellbirds, parrots, and magpies had the northern quarter all to themselves, for the kangaroos mostly affected the southern side of the river, satisfied with the immense scampering area afforded them throughout that then practically illimitable region. The Yarra also swarmed with a sort of black fish, bream, flounder and herring, which afterwards became a source of much sport to European anglers. The porpoises used not only to venture out of the bay into the Saltwater River, but were sometimes rash enough to indulge in an aquatic stroll as far as Richmond. The Yarra falls were primarily a rocky ledge barring the river, but in the centre was a fissure sufficiently wide to permit small laden boats to ascend at high water, and such had been known to do so occasionally. The salt water flowed up the river sometimes as far as Studley Park and into Gardiner's Creek. Shoals of sharks would now and then, like a hostile squadron, take a reconnoitring look in at Sandridge and Williamstown, and seals have been caught at the place now known as Fisherman's Bend. For years after the white occupation an excursion up the river was most enjoyable; along by the new Botanic Gardens and round towards Studley Park and the Yarra Bend, which, with two or three nooks in the Merri Creek, were the favourite haunts for the Aborigines—'the forest primeval', tenanted with trees of every age and condition, which had weathered many thousands of storms…

On arriving in Port Phillip, I was an expert swimmer for many years, and, one hot summer day, jumped into the Yarra, in the vicinity of the now Punt Road ferry. The river was deep, and down I went, but was astonished to find that my ascent to the surface was impeded by a kind of suction drawing me downward, and it required all the muscular power in my body to get up again, when I effected a safe landing, and never after ventured into Yarra running water. Several instances have occurred where some of the best white swimmers in the colony suddenly and unaccountably lost their lives in this river. As for the blacks, they are amphibious by habit and necessity, and no one ever heard of one of them meeting such a fate...

I have before mentioned the circumstance of a native black being rarely if ever known to be drowned in the Yarra, in consequence of the perfection acquired in what was to the Aboriginal race not merely an accomplishment but a necessity, *viz*, the art of swimming. The children (male and female) were inured to the creeks and rivers almost as soon as they could toddle. They were pitched in like balls, watched for a short time, and the youngsters soon learned to 'paddle their own canoe'. They would perform wondrous feats in swimming and diving, and the mode of water travelling was unlike the European system, as the swimmer instead of lying flat on the water, went on his side with hand struck out from the shoulder as a steering apparatus, and the other hand and feet acting as powerful propellers. Alluding to my previous reference to many mishaps occurring on the Yarra, Mr Russell writes: 'The drownings which have occurred in the Yarra are, as you know, numerous. The first I remember was that of a blackfellow. Mr C. H. Le Souef and I were sculling our little boat across, when we saw what we took to be a black dog in the water, but on pulling it up we found a blackfellow attached to the shock of hair. It was in Dr Cussen's time, and it was found that intoxication had been the cause. Subsequently a Mr Gall, of Messrs Campbell and Woolley's establishment, came to his death by the same undercurrent of which you speak in the *Herald*. He was said to have been a good swimmer. The only son of John Batman, playing on the brink of the 'Falls' was also accidentally drowned. He was very young. It is melancholy to think of his dead body being carried down by the tide and sweeping round the very hill that bore his father's name.'

Whilst the Yarra chapter was quietly flowing through the *Herald*, the writer has been honoured with half-a-dozen communications, three of which raise some questions, and one of them notably supplies a few facts so interesting (though this in no way impugning the general accuracy of my narrative) that I am induced to append this postscript, as a means of making special reference to them.

One correspondent, whilst expressing admiration of the sketch in general, confesses himself sceptical as to the veracity of the assertion that porpoises not only travelled up the river, but even ventured to show their noses at Richmond. He was in the settlement in 1836, and he never beheld or heard of such an excursion. In reply, I may say that the fist intimation I had about the Yarra porpoising was from the late Mr W. F. Rucker, who died in 1882. He assured me that he saw porpoises more than once popping about in the Yarra basin at the wharf, and when I ventured to express doubt, he declared positively there could be none. Two other old colonists confirmed this statement, and there is still alive at Kew a gentleman (whom I am authorised, if necessary, to name) who with his brother (recently dead) carried on a lucrative wood-cutting business some miles up the river, and not only once or twice but a score of times, were porpoises, not in shoals, but in twos or threes, passed and repassed between Melbourne and the present bridge at Richmond, the connecting link between a Church and a Chapel Street. The 'falls' in its primitive state, presented no obstacle to their advance, for, as already stated, there was in the centre of the ledge of rocks a rift sufficient in width for a small laden boat to pass through; and whatever a vehicle of this class could accomplish in water, it is not assuming too much that a porpoise could do the same.

A Predatory Captain Blood

For decades the *Argus*, founded by William Kerr, in 1846, was Melbourne's leading daily newspaper. Its initial popularity lay in its ruthless attacks on perceived deficiencies of the administration and defence of town and trading interests. In the 1860s the paper became captured by the conservatives of the colony and was slowly overtaken by the *Age*. Here the *Argus* reports on one of the most singular and scandalous thefts in the history of the city. The missing mace prompted many explanations as to its whereabouts; one of the most intriguing was that it was used in a mock-parliamentary sitting in Madam Brussell's brothel, off Little Lonsdale Street. More than 110 years later this 'emblem of constitutional liberty' is still at large.

Argus, 10 October 1891 — A confidential report made at the offices of the Criminal Investigation Branch yesterday evening gives the bare details of the most extraordinary robbery ever heard of in the colonies, probably indeed without parallel in the constitutional history of the world. More than once some predatory Captain Blood has made attempts upon the Crown jewels, but never until yesterday has an instance been known in which any sacrilegious hand dared to disturb the inviolate sanctity of the emblem of constitutional liberty — the mace. It has remained for Victoria to add that proud distinction to her laurels, for yesterday morning, in broad daylight, as it would seem, the mace was seized by some daring thief, its case broken open with scant regard for the privileges of the House, and the golden bauble itself spirited clean away.

How it happened and when it happened no one can tell with any certainty. All that is known is that when the House adjourned after an unusually long sitting after midnight on Thursday—or to be more correct—Friday morning, the mace was carefully taken away, and locked up in its case in the Speaker's anteroom. Theoretically its custody is delegated to the assistant clerk of the Legislative Assembly, Mr Geo. Upward; but for practical purposes it is looked after by the caretaker, who acts at night as the custodian of the whole building. In the old days, before the new façade had been added, the caretaker and the mace were almost bed-fellows, but the improvements of modern times have relegated the caretaker to a more convenient set of apartments in the basement of the new building, while the mace still retains its old home in the Speaker's anteroom. But when the room was entered yesterday morning it was found that the case had been broken open and that the mace was gone. And that is all the evidence upon which the three detectives engaged in the task here have to work.

The mace was made entirely of Victorian gold, and was valued roughly at about £250. It would, of course, prove a most valuable booty, but it is difficult to understand how so cumbrous an article could have been carried away—in daylight presumably—without awakening attention. Still, those familiar with Parliament House will well comprehend the ease with which a perfect stranger may walk about the building, and gain access to its most private rooms undisturbed.

*

Argus, 12 October 1891—…In spite of all the efforts of the detectives not the slightest clue has been found to the mysterious disappearance of the Speaker's mace from Parliament House early on Friday morning. The when and how of the robbery have been fairly well established, but the whereabouts of the booty is so far a secret…Has the mace been stolen for its inherent value, or is it being held for reward? In the latter case, a little adroit management of the 'no questions asked' order may perhaps restore it to its accustomed place on the table of the Legislative Assembly when the House resumes next Tuesday…

The box on which the mace rests at night is of somewhat peculiar construction. It stands on end at the side of a cupboard to which it is firmly screwed, and it opens exactly as a portmanteau would do if placed in a similar position. In fact, supposing a stranger to have entered the room on the search for whatever property came first to hand, this box is the last thing which he would be likely to examine…

It will be evident from these facts that the robbery was committed by someone having a very intimate—a very peculiarly intimate—knowledge not only of the plan of the building, but of the weak points of the defence, of the sleeping places of the attendants, in fact of the whole system in vogue at Parliament House…Is it not rather to be presumed that the mace was taken by someone who appreciated its political value, and who meant to turn that knowledge to the best possible advantage?

RUDYARD KIPLING

Secondhand American

Like most famous visitors to Australia's shores, Rudyard Kipling was pounced upon by the press almost before he had stepped ashore. His evident confusion about the nature of the place he was in is thus forgivable. This interview by a zealous *Age* journalist was published on 13 November 1891.

To say a word first of Mr Kipling's personal appearance, his physique and manner are those of a rapid thinker and worker. He is of medium height, with a solid, nuggetty build; a sharp, lively face, with the bronzed complexion of India; bright, quick eyes looking through light gold spectacles, and short hair, nearly thinned down to baldness on the top of the head. He has a lightning power of forming and phrasing his impressions, which are expressed with a lighting of the face like sparks under a blow on a hot iron.

While he has been in Australasia his sense of humour has been excited by the 'steep' yarns the 'boys' have been telling him, mistaking him for an Englishman instead of a colonial, for as an Anglo-Indian he belongs to a race as un-English as the Australians themselves; and he has now and then smiled inwardly at the 'precipitous' tales of alligators, mosquitoes, fish and snakes that have been poured into him by the deluded yarn spinners...

Since reaching Melbourne Mr Kipling has been seized with a sense of the Americanism of the place. 'This country is American,' he says, 'but remember it is secondhand American, there is an American tone on the top of things, but it is not real. Dare say, by and bye, you will get a tone of your own. Still, I like these American memories playing round your streets. The trams — those bells are like music; those saloons and underground dives are as Yank as they can be. The Americanism of this town with its square blocks and straight streets, strikes me much. I can't say anything about the people, for I have not met any of them, but I gather this much that they are very much pleased with their own town. They don't seem to follow the Americans in their habits so much as the city itself. I asked a man today where the depot was, but he didn't know I meant the railway station... These trams are as good as the trams of 'Frisco which was the home of the cable car and started it first. The clang of that bell sounds to my ear like "Hello, Central!" used to sound in the ear of the Yankee at the court of King Arthur.'...

The internal affairs of this country have not escaped Mr Kipling's notice, and he particularly notes the place which the labour question takes in Australian politics. He thinks we have too much politics for a young country with its character still to make, and that the claims of labour occupy too prominent a place in proportion to other branches of politics, just as politics as a whole receive more than enough attention in proportion to real and solid development of the country...'Is it not rather early in your history,' he asks, 'with a mere handful of population, to have half that population crowded into the cities while the lands lie an idle wilderness, and men are striking against overwork while governments are paying big wages on relief works for the unemployed?...

'It seems to me to be taking a ridiculously elevated estimate of one's own importance to think that it is your mission in life to go around and insult countries when you are only a man among men, and especially a man who can't get even his boots on'—for Mr Kipling was now struggling with a new pair of boots, being due for an evening at the Austral Salon. 'I got these boots in Fourteenth Street,' he explained. He meant Swanston Street, which seemed to him the Fourteenth Street of Melbourne, while Collins Street recalled something of that other New York thoroughfare, the Fifth Avenue. Time was up and a very pleasant interview came to an end.

FERNANDO VILLAAMIL

Salute to the Victorian Navy

The Spanish corvette *Nautilus* slipped through the Heads in 1893 on a round-the-world tour celebrating the fourth

centenary of Columbus' discovery of the Americas. At
the time Victoria had a splendid navy and Captain
Fernando Villaamil reviewed the fleet, met her commander, and enjoyed all the hospitality a recession-struck
Victoria could muster. The city, he felt, compared
favourably with New York, London, and even Paris.

Melbourne and its extremely beautiful surrounding areas,
Toorak, Collingwood, Fitzroy, Carlton, North and South
Melbourne, Prahran and St Kilda, covers a considerable area of
land which can only be crossed with ease thanks to the existence
of transportation by cable tram; that said, and as a testimony of
my admiration for the industrial society that created this system
(which, I might add, is not particularly lucrative), I shall attempt
to give an idea of the impression that Melbourne as a city had on
my spirit, and of the inhabitants whose acquaintance I had the
good fortune to make, and whom I shall recall for many years to
come.

To my mind, Melbourne is the queen city of the South; Africa,
South America and Oceania cannot boast a city as beautiful as this
one, and I say beautiful only because I cannot find another adjective
that better describes the way I see it. London, for example, is greater
than Paris in size, population and perhaps in artistic wealth, something which all travellers can admire; but nevertheless, Paris is more
pleasing than London, and if asked why this is, perhaps a simple
answer would be: Paris is beautiful, and London sad, very sad.

So Melbourne is a modest Paris, or rather a New York, lacking
the size of either of these capitals, understandable if age and stage
of development are taken into account. Forty years is very little
time to create a fully-fashioned Paris at the antipodes of Europe,
even if one considers the money and activity that abound in this
part of Australia.

In general, the city's appearance has something of London, more of New York, and a considerable amount of Paris. The majority of the buildings are of an English style, providing comfortable dwellings for a single family of only one or two storeys; while those buildings which have been constructed for specific ends, such as hotels and offices, are colossal in height and size.

Melbourne's inhabitants have a completely Yankee spirit, apparent in their way of doing things and in their bringing projects to fruition, for nothing is impossible for the English or the Victorian colonials when they believe something should be done. What can be done today is never left for tomorrow; and it is only if one thinks and lives in this spirit that a piece of virgin Australia can be transformed in so little time into the colony which, today, fills its settlers with pride and astounds first-time visitors.

Melbourne has American customs and looks like an English city. But anyone who is familiar with the people to be found in the streets of New York and London will not find any resemblance at all to those seen in the streets of Melbourne. If it were not for the fact that one hears perfect English spoken, anyone would think that they had been transported to Barcelona, Naples or Marseilles. For every Anglo-Saxon man or woman there are fifty or more whose physical appearance recalls southern Europe.

The profusion of public houses peculiar to all English cities has been replaced here by large tea-rooms, which are somewhat like cafés or restaurants. These establishments are frequented by respectable people who enter and leave with the freedom characteristic of the Americans.

Victoria, unlike any other Australian colony, has its own fleet, consisting of a battleship, two cruisers and four torpedo boats, a force which, when in reserve, or rather, during peace time, is commanded by an English naval captain, who is stationed on a kind of moored vessel, at that time the frigate *Nelson*.

On visiting this young and agreeable Captain White, as was

my duty, he was kind enough not to waste the first opportunity that presented itself to introduce the officers of the *Nautilus* to the most select Melbourne society. Thus, during the first afternoon that we spent at the port we went to the small navy yard in Williamstown, where a game of lawn tennis was under way. The players were young ladies accompanied by their lady chaperones, for the male sex, as we have been able to observe during the course of our excursions, works by day and rests in the evenings, taking little part in the recreational activities which are regularly enjoyed by the fairer sex.

One of the chaperones we met that afternoon, the wealthy and very pleasant Mrs Lande, invited us for two days hence to visit her sumptuous Toorak house, or rather palace, to take tea and learn to play tennis under the tutelage of those lovely young ladies, who were surprised at the Spaniards' poor display of skill in the most fashionable and most *de rigueur* of all the games enjoyed by English high society.

I believe that despite the good intentions of both teachers and disciples all those who submitted themselves to this training were forced to admit to ineptitude in skilful racquet technique; in contrast, they were awarded outstanding marks for other games and diversions, especially for dancing.

Melbourne balls, as in all places, are the most propitious occasions for the foreigner to strike up and deepen friendships with those people whom he finds most agreeable; and when we were invited either in an official or private capacity it was necessary to turn to English dictionaries and vocabularies in order to avoid unfortunate incidents.

Balls with splendid suppers, garden parties, bazaars, concerts, *tableaux* and other pleasant invitations of this kind were received daily, for there is no doubt that of all the cities in the world Melbourne's high society enjoys itself more than any other and delights in continual festivities. While admiring this luxury, I had occasion to discover that because of the crisis the banks were experiencing at that time the occasions for merrymaking had declined; I was assured by several individuals that under normal circumstances there were not enough hours in the day to attend to the multitude of invitations to spend afternoons and evenings engaged in the most delightful of pastimes.

NAT GOULD

Painful to See

Nat Gould sailed to Australia in 1884 and worked as a journalist and sportswriter on various papers in Queensland and New South Wales. His observations of Melbourne as it was in 1894 were first published in his most famous book *Town and Bush* in 1896.

During the many times I have been in Melbourne I have explored most of its suburbs, and seen a good deal of its people. There is a vast difference between the people of the various cities of Australia. Melbourne people are go-ahead, and have plenty of push. They move about smartly, and, like Londoners, never seem to have a moment to spare. I do not think the people who rush most get through more solid work than others who go about their work in a slower way. As far as I can judge, I should say there is more solidity about Sydney than Melbourne.

The Melbourne ladies dress well, and there are few slovenly men. There may be more style about Melbourne than Sydney, but I doubt if the people as a rule, are more prosperous. Melbourne has suffered much from over-speculation and land booms…The last time I had a look round Melbourne suburbs was in 1894, and then it was positively painful to see the vast number of houses to let. It was not only moderate-sized houses that were tenantless, but gentleman's residences were closed, or merely left in charge of a caretaker. In some instances there was no one in charge, and the once beautiful grounds, that were gay with flowers and echoed with the merry laughter of children, were neglected and solitary. It must have cost many a heartache leaving these lovely spots, full of old associations and connected with the happiness of families.

Let us hope that before long a change will come over the scene again, and the transformation be of a brighter character. I was told by a gentleman, well informed, that at this time there were over twenty thousand houses to let in and around Melbourne. Many of these houses will go to ruin. Vagabonds go round to the empty tenements and strip them of everything portable. They break into houses and remove the fixtures, and even the piping is not safe from them, as they tear it up to sell it for old lead. Coppers are coolly carted away; and I have seen houses literally stripped of everything by these thieves.

In more prosperous times Melbourne did not suffer more than other cities of similar size from these thieves; but the scarcity of employment drove men, who would otherwise have been honest, to desperation.

Joshua Slocum
Imaginary Habits of Fish

Captain Joshua Slocum was the first person to sail single-handed around the world. He was fifty-one when he set out from Boston in 1895 in the *Spray*, a vessel measuring thirty-six feet, which he had built himself. The round

journey would take him three years and two months to
complete. Slocum disappeared in 1909 while on a solo
expedition to explore the Amazon and Orinoco rivers.

January 1897—...The *Spray* paid no port charges in Australia
or anywhere else on the voyage, except at Pernambuco, till
she poked her nose into the custom house at Melbourne, where
she was charged tonnage dues; in this instance, sixpence a ton
on the gross. The collector extracted six shillings and sixpence,
taking off nothing for the fraction under thirteen tons, her exact
gross being 12.70 tons.

I squared the matter by charging people sixpence each for
coming on board, and when this business got dull I caught a
shark and charged them sixpence each to look at that. The shark
was twelve feet six inches in length, and carried a progeny of
twenty-six, not one of them less than two feet in length. A slit of
a knife let them out in a canoe full of water, which, changed
constantly, kept them alive one whole day. In less than an hour
from the time I heard of the ugly brute it was on deck and on
exhibition, with rather more than the amount of the *Spray*'s
tonnage dues already collected. Then I hired a good Irishman,
Tom Howard by name—who knew all about sharks, both on
the land and in the sea, and could talk about them—to answer
questions and lecture. When I found that I could not keep abreast
of the questions I turned the responsibility over to him.

Returning from the bank, where I had been to deposit money
early in the day, I found Howard in the midst of a very excited
crowd, telling imaginary habits of the fish. It was a good show;
the people wished to see it, and it was my wish that they should;
but owing to his over-stimulated enthusiasm, I was obliged to let
Howard resign. The income from the show and the proceeds of
the tallow I had gathered in the Strait of Magellan, the last of

which I had disposed of to a German soap-boiler at Samoa, put me in ample funds.

24 January—found the *Spray* again in tow of the tug *Racer*, leaving Hobson's Bay after a pleasant time in Melbourne and St Kilda, which had been protracted by a succession of south-west winds that seemed never-ending.

In the summer months, that is, December, January, February, and sometimes March, east winds are prevalent through Bass Strait and round Cape Leeuwin; but owing to a vast amount of ice drifting up from the Antarctic, this was all changed now and emphasised with much bad weather, so much that I considered it impracticable to pursue the course further. Therefore, instead of thrashing round cold and stormy Cape Leeuwin, I decided to spend a pleasanter and more profitable time in Tasmania, waiting for the season for favourable winds through Torres Strait, by way of the Great Barrier Reef, the route I finally decided on. To sail this course would be taking advantage of anticyclones, which never fail, and besides it would give me the chance to put foot on the shores of Tasmania, round which I had sailed years before.

I should mention that while I was at Melbourne there occurred one of those extraordinary storms sometimes called 'rain of blood', the first of the kind in many years about Australia. The 'blood' came from a fine brick-dust matter afloat in the air from the deserts. A rainstorm setting in brought down this dust simply as mud; it fell in such quantities that a bucketful was collected from the sloop's awnings, which were spread at the time. When the wind blew hard and I was obliged to furl awnings, her sails, unprotected on the booms, got mud-stained from clue to earing.

The phenomena of duststorms, well understood by scientists, are not uncommon on the coast of Africa. Reaching some distance out to sea, they frequently cover the track of ships, as in the case of the one through which the *Spray* passed in the earlier part of her voyage. Sailors no longer regard them with superstitious fear, but our credulous brothers on the land cry out 'Rain of blood!' at the first splash of the awful mud.

Charles Fredericksen
There Was a Lot of Life

Charles Fredericksen was born near Maryborough in 1872. After the gold rush his family moved to Melbourne, where they settled in Fitzroy. Charlie led a varied life, including stints as a vaudevillean and acrobat. In 1908 became a spruiker outside Hoyts' theatre, in which role he attained minor celebrity status. Here are excerpts from his memoirs written in the 1950s.

I left school at twelve years of age, my first job was beating the drum in the band outside the old Lyceum opposite the Melbourne Hospital. I made too much [noise] so I got the sack. I next got a position in Grand Opera at the Old Bijou Theatre, there were eight boys about the same age. We did acrobatic song and dance, a Chinese turn in the palace scene of the opera *Bobabid*...After I got a job at George & George in Collins Street, as a cash boy and later a junior salesman. I left there to go boot finishing and worked at the EBC Exhibition Boot Company, run by Rollen and Burdett, then I went barbering, putting the soap on men's faces and making a lather. I soon got full up on Saturday— the drunks came in and their breath would nearly knock you over...I wanted to get away with a show, eventually I got a job to go away with a Japanese troupe. There were wire walkers, acrobatics, sword walkers and contortionists, a very clever crowd they were. We first showed at the Colac Show…we travelled to Melbourne by road, showing at the towns to only fair business, and we all had to work hard. Driving the pegs in for the big tops and digging the rings, putting up the seats, doing a parade with the band wagon and all in costumes, have your tea, then play in front of the show to get the crowd, then give the show. Pull down after and pack the wagons ready for the next town. Believe me, we had a full-time job, but we enjoyed it all.

We eventually arrived in Melbourne and played most of the suburbs. The drought was on, it was nothing to see twenty to a hundred men camping under the bridges along the route. How they lived is hard to say. All you had to do, was to go to Treasury and they would give us a free pass to any town in Victoria. They were glad to get the unemployed out of the city, but when they got in the country there was nothing there.

I wanted to settle a bit, so I got a billet at a tannery and fell-mongery at South Richmond, near Church Street right on the Yarra. I would do odd jobs at night, entertaining and singing to illustrated pictures—nearly all the town halls in the suburbs had pops once a week. Later I got married so that stopped my roaming.

When I was working on the tannery, me mate on the pits with me was Billy Smeaton. We had an experience, while we were working. Two small boys ran up to us, very excited and shouted, 'Mister, there's been a murder. We have just pulled a box out of the Yarra, and there is a body in it.'

Billy and myself rushed down. There was a boot box with a wire around it and a big stone attached to it. Where the handle of the box fits, that board was missing and you could see the body of a woman in it. I told the boys to go to the police station in Church Street not far away. The police arrived and removed the trunk and the body to the morgue, and that was the famous Boot Box Tragedy.

★

What I know about Melbourne...

In Stephen Street, now Exhibition, there was a lot of life. Pigeons were all the rage there on Saturday nights. The road would be almost blocked with bird fanciers, young and old, buying and selling their birds. There were some beautiful birds about...they went in for fancy breeds mostly, saddle-back and tumblers. They never troubled much about homers, and when they flew their tumblers it was a fascinating sight to watch. There was a bird shop in the market building. I remember the stall-holder trying to sell a talking cockatoo to a chap who stuttered very much. He said to Alf, 'How how-h mu-much do do y-you wa-want fo-for it, and ca-can h-he to-talk?'

And Alf said, 'If he can't talk better than you I would screw his neck.'

Just past the Majesty Theatre was the Japanese Village, a very entertaining show, built of timber and iron roof...When they left, the building was pulled down, and on the vacant land along came a Yankee doctor. He had a golden chariot that was drawn through the streets by horses and a band playing. For his publicity he sold his Prairie flower remedy. He was a quack who gently grafted his way to fortune. He would pull teeth 'painlessly' with the aid of a brass band. The band would play its loudest and out came the tooth. The doctor remarked that none of his patients had ever been heard to yell.

Then there was Jim Crilly, a great showman in his day, and a master of fake shows. Jim showed in Bourke Street, and a horse with its head where a tail ought to be—the horse was backed into the stall. Jim also showed the canoe-footed pony. It was a pony found in the hills of Gippsland, and its hooves grew that long the animal could hardly walk. He showed it in the Exhibition, he gave it the chaff in a red fire-bucket, with the word 'fire' painted on it and he told the public it was inside eating fire. Jim also showed the Dancing Ducks. They had to dance whether they liked it or not—they were put on hot bricks.

He also showed in Bourke Street, 'Jim Crilly's Living Skeleton'. The unfortunate man was in the last stages of consumption. The doctors gave him two weeks to live. Jim didn't mind. He showed him in a shop in Swanston Street, opposite the town hall for two weeks. The show was draped in funeral black, the skeleton stood in a coffin. And while the show was going on, a boy took pity on him and offered the skeleton a bun. Jim put the boy out, telling him he was trying to ruin his show. Jim next showed him at Prahran, but he passed out there, so that was the end of the skeleton.

Then there was the Apollo Hall, in the Eastern Arcade. It went through to Little Collins Street. There were all classes of shops and a wine saloon downstairs. Upstairs [at] the Bourke Street end was the Apollo Hall. They ran the minstrels and fights. Big heavyweights would fight for a fiver, and a lot would fight for a shower—sometimes they only got 4/- or 5/-. At the other end was Donegan's Dance Hall and there were some larrikins at the dances but they were orderly.

Where the Salvation Army is was once the Nugget Theatre. They put on minstrel shows and dramas, and on Sunday nights Joe Lyons the free thinker would lecture and put on high-class singers. Tom Thumb and his midgets appeared here. Tom and his wife would drive to the theatre in a tiny carriage made to look like a half-walnut shell. Sometimes the hall was used for afternoon seances by 'spiritists'.

There was a mechanical show just above Russell Street and it was a masterpiece, and W. H. Bruce the tailor, who would make you a suit of clothes for 27/6. He'd take your order today and it would be ready tomorrow night. There was Ike Bitten, who had an oyster shop, just below the Eastern Arcade. Ike was that big he had to sit in front of his shop in two chairs, and he wore a big gold dog chain across his pantry…There was the Bull & Mouth Hotel [where] the rats would come up to the trough, have a sip or two, get shot, and the barmen would knock them over.

There were restaurants all over the place. You could go to Thorpey's next to the Melbourne Hotel in Bourke Street and get a three-course meal for fourpence. There were Pretty's and Sheppard's: lower down they were sixpence. There were tea and toast shops—a pot of tea, a small jug of milk and two large slices of toast and two small rolls of butter all for threepence—and all served clean. There were sausages-and-potato-mash shops. They cooked sausages and potatoes in a big silver grill at the Windsor and charged fivepence a plate.

Opposite Myers stores, when they pulled down the Bull & Mouth, the cellar left a big pit. Along came a showman, he had a lady snake-charmer, and she had a large reptile around her neck. It looked a bit sick, so the showman got a mouse out of a box and offered it to the lady to give to the reptile. She said, 'Not me, I couldn't handle a mouse.'

There were a lot of characters in Melbourne. Jack Donovan, he was a chap who would do anything. One day, a bookmaker said to him, 'Jack, I will give you a fiver if you punch Jim Mase on the nose.' Jim was running the Old England at the time. He said, 'Give me the fiver.' He handed the money to Jack.

Mase was leaning on the bar, Donovan went to Mase and gave him a lovely punch on the nose, then ran out of the hotel. When he ran a few yards he slipped and fell. Mase grabbed him and a crowd congregated and Donovan said, 'Jim, you wouldn't hit a man down', and Mase, like a good sport, let him go.

Donovan later had a bulldog and he thought he could beat the world. He was walking down Collins Street when a sheepdog rushed out of a chemist shop and the dogs started to fight. The sheepdog killed Jacki, so he picked it up by the tail and threw it through the window and said, 'You've killed my dog, you can bury it.'

There was a two-up school in the lane opposite the Eastern Market, run by Sammy. They ran the school very decent—if you went there you would get a fair go. There was the nit-keepers posted away from the school, also the door-keepers and the police had a hard job to catch them. When they did get in all they found was a ring with two men boxing in it and a crowd sitting watching them. The place was run very strict and there was no dirty work and it went on for years.

E. W. Cole was an elderly bearded gentleman who loved books. He started with a stall up at the Eastern Market. In 1883 he moved into the old Spanish Restaurant building opposite Buckley's and created his famous book arcade with its great rainbow sign. Here he had not just thousands and thousands of books, but monkeys, birds, ornaments, sheet music and his own orchestra of cornet, violin, piano and organ. There were funny mirrors that made you look fat or thin and an advertising sign turned by little mechanical sailor men. (After Cole's closed in 1929 the little men went up to the Science Museum. The funny mirrors were put in the Giggle Palace at Luna Park.)

Before the sewerage, the gutters in Little Bourke Street always had fast running water, so the city Rat push, who were a pretty tough crowd, would hold their races there. They had matches for boats and they would start the race from Russell Street and race to the winning post near Swanston Street. The betting was keen; they would bet from one penny to ten shillings on a match. They had the Short Soup Trial, the Beef Steak Handicap. There was no photo-finish and sometimes there would be a box on over who won a race, There were Irish Mick, a big willing chap, and Mick Sixty and Snowy Boys and a lot of others, and they could all fight a round or two. Rough diamonds, but not bad sort of chaps.

HWUY-UNG

A Chinaman's Opinion

This letter by a Chinese visiting in 1900, is one from a collection translated into English by J. A. Makepeace titled *A Chinaman's Opinion of Us*. It remains a marvel of cross-cultural misunderstanding.

The people in the streets of this city seem to be always in a hurry; they appear to be flying in all directions, like hungry ghosts seeking peace and rest. When first I noticed this, and the look of anxiety on their eager faces, I asked my cousin if any public calamity had befallen. For answer, he smiled and said: 'No, Hwuy-ung; what is wrong with them is not enough to hang upon the teeth; each one fears he may be after the appointed hour to begin work; to deliver a message or to dispatch a letter; to conclude some business—in most cases, matters of a few *taels*—or one or more of the Five Hindrances.'

I replied, 'They should receive in the heart the Master's words: "When internal examination discovers nothing wrong, what is there to be anxious about, what is there to fear?"'

'That is so,' replied my cousin. 'They treat life so seriously that there is little hope of their being joyful.'

I then recalled to mind the words of our great sage, Lao-tze: 'The people make light of death because they seek to live in wealth...'

On Polite Worship day no one is permitted to work. The ten factories must be closed. All who claim to have virtue are that day seen in the temples. Those who do not go there are known to be bad. This is a very serviceable distinction; for knowing this, one may choose company with discretion. It is a sad day; as tasteless as cold rice. Ten thousand things are dead, and ten thousand people are as if struck by a paralysis.

As many of these laborious people must do something, they go by back door into the *shamsu*-shops. These trade better on the Worship day than on others. Each trade has regular holidays, when the workmen go with their families by the steam-horse to the sea or the hills. Lazy people, who do not take count of these days, have to fast if they have not before brought food supply.

Australia Asserts Herself

Melbourne arguably enjoyed its greatest success on 10 May 1901, when it hosted the opening of Australia's Federal Parliament. The city was to remain the new nation's seat of power until Parliament moved to Canberra in 1927.

Argus, 10 May 1901 — ...By the hand of royalty, in the presence of the greatest concourse of people that Australia has seen in one building, and with splendid pomp and ceremonial, the legislative machinery of the Commonwealth was yesterday set in motion. The day was full of smiles and tears, the smiles predominating. Rising gloomily, the dispersing clouds allowed the bright sun to peep through, and when the great ceremony was in progress in the Exhibition building the atmosphere was radiant, and illuminated the vast spaces of the building and the great sea of faces with a bright Australian glow.

Again there was the same great teeming crowd in the streets

which the welcoming day saw—but probably increased by thousands who have come to the metropolis since. Every suburb poured in its thousands, and happy were those on the nearer railway station who, after seeing several trains go by, at last found a carriage in which there remained an inch of standing-room. Stands and balconies on the line of route were as thickly peopled as before, though there were about 12,000 persons in the Exhibition building, and once more the Royal Duke and his gracious consort passed in regal state through streets lined everywhere with enthusiastic and loyal people.

A sight never to be forgotten was the assemblage which, in perfect order but with exalted feeling, awaited the arrival of the Duke and Duchess in the great avenues which branch out from the vast dome of the Exhibition building.

Twelve thousand people seated in a vast amphitheatre—free people, hopeful people, courageous people—entrusted with the working out of their own destiny, and rejoicing in their liberty, must be impressive by reason of numbers alone.

There have been many more exciting moments in the long struggle for federation than this one, when the splendid consummation was reached. Order was well observed, and there was no noise of loud talking, but everywhere the irrepressible murmur of expectancy and the never-ceasing footfalls of those who, coming late, found themselves on the outskirts of the throng, and ever moved restlessly from place to place. All through the ceremony this murmur was heard from those too far off to hear, and, not content, as they might have been, with reflecting on the fact that they had lived to be present at such a momentous scene. There are many thousands of people in Australia who will envy them the mere fact of making one of the units of such a memorable occasion...

When the Duke stepped forward to deliver his speech to the two Houses a 'Hush!' ran around the assembly, and everyone listened intently, but the sound of the ever moving feet on the boarded floors went on. His Royal Highness spoke deliberately, in a clear, strong voice, and the speech he read was distinctly heard by thousands of those present. It was a dignified, a graceful, a kindly, and a congratulatory speech, and it expressed a confident belief that the new powers granted to Australia will only strengthen the affection of the people for the throne and empire. At the final words, 'I now declare the Parliament of the Commonwealth of Australia open,' the Duchess touched an electric button, which gave the signal outside for the hoisting of the Union Jack on all the state schools of the colony, and for the sending of a message to England declaring the object of the journey of the Royal envoys accomplished. Trumpets rang out the signal, and outside was heard the booming of cannons in a Royal salute.

After a brief pause, the Duke of Cornwall and York stepped forward once more, and read a special cable message of congratulations from His Majesty the King. And now Australia asserted herself, she had been suppressing her feelings to show that she knew how to behave with old world decorum in the presence of Royalty, but this message, direct from the King himself, was too much — they simply had to cheer. And cheer they did. It was done without order or without concert. It was taken up time after time by sections of the audience; it ran round the aisles, and surged through the galleries; a hearty, spontaneous, irrepressible Australian cheer.

ALFRED BUCHANAN

Melbourne Moods

Alfred Buchanan, English novelist and dramatic and literary critic, published this remarkable reflection on the city in 1907. He seems to have visited around 1903. What shines through so strongly to me is his remarkable ability to capture the sweet-and-sour essence of the place, which persisted as the city continued to develop in its second century of existence.

To leave Sydney and go to Melbourne is to enter a new world. Instead of resemblances there are contrasts. In place of Australianisms there are Anglicanisms, Americanisms, and foreign 'isms' of various kinds. Climate may have something to do with the difference, and topographical conditions may have something more. The reception that Sydney gives you is that of a woman in a luxurious room, with soft lights falling on rich curtain hangings, with glitter of glass and silver ornament, with lavish display of elegance and outward charm. The woman rises seductively, looks at you languorously and invites you, not so much by word as by gesture, to make yourself at home. It is delightful; but yet there is something wanting. The reflection comes that you are not being specially favoured; that this is the manner of the hostess to all and sundry; that there may be something unhealthy in this mellifluous atmosphere...

The reception you get from Melbourne is of quite another character. The woman this time is cold and calm, and superbly indifferent. If she seems to smile it is probably the reflection of your own hopefulness. She offers you nothing; she barely acknowledges you; she does not want you; it is certain that she is not anxious to know you. All her panoply of architectural ornament is arrayed against you. And yet the thought supervenes that this cold woman may be better worth knowing in the end than the other one; that her harder outlines may conceal a more genuine worth; that her good opinion may be better worth striving for than that of the other—the one with the redder lips, and the flaunting, unchanging smile.

But the wide streets and the flat unoccupied spaces of Melbourne are an outward semblance calculated to strike the newcomer with a shuddering sense of chill and desolation. More especially if they are encountered for the first time on a winter's afternoon. For the winter that merely dallies and trifles in Sydney, and makes but a pretence of bringing with it cold weather, is genuine in the Southern city.

There is no bleaker thoroughfare on earth than Collins Street or Bourke Street on a blustering July day. From Spring Street to the railway station there is a clear, unbroken passage for the Arctic wind. The occasional tramcar and the infrequent pedestrian are cheerless objects around which the sou'wester disports itself, seeking always, in return for some ancient grievance, a grim and unnecessary revenge. If the day happens to be a Saturday, or a public holiday, the outlook is rendered ten times more dismal by the deathly appearance of the streets, from which all but an unreal semblance of life and movement has departed. A wilderness of grim-looking window shutters, and a Sahara of pavement—that is all. The wind drives the dust in front of it, then follows on shriekingly. When it has finished playing with the dust it brings in the rain. And Melbourne, with its wide, shelterless streets swept from end to end by a rainstorm—Melbourne with its blank spaces and its vanished crowds—is the one place on earth where the new arrival would choose not to be...

Presently the sun will shine again. Presently the holiday will be over; and the people who have been abroad in the suburbs, or cultivating their garden patches, or hiding themselves in their own houses, will once more be visible, and the pavement will once more echo to the sound of feet. By a seeming miracle the streets have become almost full. Melbourne has become an intelligible place to live in. The shops, now that the window shutters are down, are seen to be beautifully fitted up. The buildings are for the most part new, and they are never grimy. One remembers that in the heart of Sydney there are pervading evidences of smoke and grime. One must give Melbourne its due. It has something to boast about. It has been magnificently laid out. Its measurements are on a generous scale. It is fine and large and bracing. One forgets the chill sensation left by those deserted streets and those grim-looking window shutters. The Block has become a centre of bustle and animation. Again the thought presents itself that this place may have a heart of its own, that it may have a personality, even a warmth, concealed behind those set features and those formal lines.

Further acquaintance with Melbourne increases the respect felt for it. One gets to like it for the same reason that the Londoner gets to like London. It is not a question of beauty, or simplicity, or gentleness of form and feature. One gets to like it because of its greatness, and because of its strength; perhaps also, in the case of the older residents, because of the thought of the splendid life and animation that were part of it fifteen or twenty years ago, and that may be part of it again. The Melbourne man, after a certain lapse of time, acquires a personal feeling for his self-contained, self-respecting city. He learns to recognise its various moods—for even Melbourne has moods—and enter into them all. He would not care for it if it were flashy and volatile like other places. He can admire it for its reserve and its silences. He knows that, go where he will, he will not find a cleaner, wider, more spacious city to dwell in. And he is fully aware that for him Melbourne reveals much of what she keeps hidden from the stranger; that she will show to him as to one of her lovers a warmth and friendliness that are the more satisfying because not universally shared.

Commercially, Melbourne is not what it used to be. It has lost the sparkle, the animation of other days. Yet, whatever else it has lost, it has retained the consciousness of former prosperity. It is as proud as ever; in fact more proud than in the days when people were pouring into it by thousands, and when fortunes were being made every five minutes in its principal streets. Diminished prosperity has caused it to hold its head higher. And at stated times, like some proud but impecunious beauty, it insists on recalling itself to the mind of the world. On Cup Days and *fête* days it scores a triumph: it arrays itself in the festival garment of the early nineties, and queens it to the admiration of the stranger within its gates. On these occasions Melbourne is incomparable. It has no need to be envious, because it is the admired of all admirers. When the cheering is over, and the crowds have departed, and the lights have been put out, Melbourne retires moodily into itself, goes about its daily business with an abstracted air, and consoles itself intermittently by talking of the long deferred prosperity which it insists must come…

Meantime, the business of keeping up appearances goes on. Melbourne has become accustomed, through sheer force of insistence on its individual merits, to regard itself as everything a modern city ought to be, and as most things that other cities are not. It prides itself on a great deal—on its music, its art, its culture, its architecture, its good looks, and its intelligence. In the matter of dress it aspires to set the fashion for Australia. Men and women join in the amiable rivalry. The girl of the Victorian capital is more severe in demeanour, more classic in pose, and more punctilious in attire that her Sydney sister. She takes herself more seriously. She has few *negligé* airs and graces; she does not cultivate the irresponsible freedom of the gown of Nora Creina; she arrays herself for the Block with a firm resolve to compel critical admiration. And in this she generally succeeds. The men of Melbourne live in starched shirts and expensive broadcloth. They cling tenaciously to that fading relic of an earlier civilisation—the bell-topper hat. Social life in the city would be impossible without one. The University keeps up its quota of students, whether the parents can afford to pay or not. The theatres can attract audiences even for a performance of Wagner, or a revival of Shakespeare. The city fathers set an example of dignity to the rest of Australia. The politicians rarely call each other bad names, and never indulge in free fights on the floor of Parliament.

Behind all this outward seeming there is, it need hardly be said, a great amount of make-believe. Melbourne is only the temporary capital to the Commonwealth, but it is the permanent centre of—to use an ecclesiastically sounding word—attitudinarianism. Its mental life is more the expression of a desire to be thought superior to others than the outcome of any set of inborn predilections. Its intellectuality has the motto, *videri quam esse*. There is not one of its learned pundits or *littérateurs* or its native-born poets who has won much outside reputation. Its scrupulous regard for dress is the screen for much actual poverty. Its vaunted cosmopolitanism has no real existence. Its social circle is, only too often, the playground of snobs. Its professed public virtue deceives no one. In Sydney the spectacle of vice undraped is more insistent and more familiar. But in Melbourne there is as much for the Women's Christian Temperance Union to grieve over, though there may be less that meets the casual eye.

When the last word has been said on the subject—when it has been admitted that Melbourne pretends a great deal and poses a great deal, and hides a great deal—it is yet a fact that the city retains among its people much of sterling worth, and many of the elements of greatness. From the army of those who are not what they claim to be, or not what they would have you think them to be, may be picked out a leaven of those who are entitled to respect, and perhaps to something more. Alert, quick-witted, well-read, well-mannered, tolerant and scrupulously fair—that is the type which may be encountered if the search is keen enough. Hereafter, this type may set the standard. At present, all that can be said of it is that it is there.

The fact must always stand to the credit of Melbourne that it is capable of generous enthusiasms. When it lets itself go, it does so without reserve. Carlyle has remarked that a man who can laugh unrestrainedly, even if he only laughs once, is not wholly bad. A city that can cheer unitedly and unreservedly, whether for a singer or orator, an actor or a returned contingent, has at least some prospect of emerging from the wilderness of shams in which it happens to be located. Melbourne rises to greatness the moment it forgets itself.

ACKNOWLEDGMENTS

Michael Heyward and Melanie Ostell of Text Publishing played such key roles in the production of this anthology that in truth it is the result of a true partnership. Michael first suggested publishing such a book and gave me the courage to persist with the task. Melanie worked tirelessly throughout the production process, tracing sources, editing and organising materials. She also unearthed some gems that I would never have found.

Lisa MacKinney contributed in the early stages of research and I'm particularly grateful to Angus Curry for locating John Mason's unpublished journal in the Museum of the Confederacy, Virginia, USA. George Thomas proofread the manuscript, bringing order and accuracy to the enterprise and Alexandra Szalay made suggestions to the introduction which greatly improved it.

Any such work relies heavily on the enthusiasm and goodwill of the custodians of records. Des Cowley and the many State Library of Victoria staff that helped with this project are owed special thanks. Without their unfailing support this book would not have seen the light of day.

Notes on Sources

General

Shirley W. Wiencke's *When the Wattles Bloom Again: The Life and Times of William Barak, Last Chief of the Yarra Yarra* provides an excellent overview of the fate of the Melbourne Aborigines following settlement. I thank her for sending me a copy of her book. Robyn Annear's *Bearbrass: Imagining Early Melbourne*, published by Vintage, is a highly entertaining and well-researched work that breathes life into the infant settlement. James Grant and Geoffrey Serle's *The Melbourne Scene 1803–1956*, first published by Hale & Iremonger in 1957, is a comprehensive history of the city and a useful work for those interested in further reading. With Michael Cannon as editor in chief, the eight volumes that comprise *The Historical Records of Victoria* also contain a treasure-trove of material, published by the Public Records Office, Melbourne, 1991–98.

Francis William Lauderdale Adams (1862–93)

The piece 'Melbourne and her Civilisation' was published in Adams' famous collection *Australian Essays*, William Inglis & Co, Melbourne, 1886.

Anonymous

'Melbourne As It Is, and As It Ought to Be' is a thirteen-page pamphlet printed by J. Harrison, Geelong, 1850–51. It is part of Volume 23 of the Victorian Pamphlet Collection held at the State Library of Victoria.

Anonymous

This piece that foreshadowed Eureka first appeared in an anonymous London publication called *Social Manners and Life in Australia: Being the Notes of Eight Years' Experience* in 1861. It is also in C. M. H. Clark's *Select Documents in Australian History*, Angus & Robertson, Melbourne, 1955.

Clara Aspinall

Three Years in Melbourne, L. Booth, London, 1862. The years spanned are 1858–61.

William Barak (d. 1903)

Barak's brief history of Melbourne is held in the La Trobe Australian Manuscripts Collection, State Library of Victoria, MS 1956. A biography of Barak was privately published in 2000 by Shirley W. Wiencke under the title *When the Wattles Bloom Again*.

John Batman (1801–39)

John Batman's diary is held by the La Trobe Australian Manuscripts Collection, State Library of Victoria. Batman's letter to John Montague appears in *Historical Records of Victoria*, Volume 1.

LUDOVIC DE BEAUVOIR (1846–1929)
A Voyage Round the World, John Murray, London, 1870.

RICHARD BOURKE (1777–1855)
A transcript was made of this letter from Volume 6 of Sir Richard Bourke's papers, held in the Mitchell Library, State Library of New South Wales, A 1733.

ALFRED BUCHANAN
The Real Australia, T. F. Unwin, London, 1907.

CURTIS CANDLER (1827–1911)
'Notes on Melbourne Life' together with Candler's manuscript copy of the diaries of Captain Frederick Charles Standish (c. 1848–77), original bound manuscript, MS 9502, La Trobe Australian Manuscripts Collection, State Library of Victoria.

FRED CATO (1858–1935)
Growing Together: Letters between Frederick John Cato and Frances Bethune, edited by Una B. Porter, Queensberry Hill Press, Carlton, 1981.

CÉLESTE DE CHABRILLAN (1824–1909)
Un Deuil au bout due monde was first published in 1877. The English-language edition, translated and with an introduction and notes by Patricia Clancy and Jeanne Allen, is *The French Consul's Wife: Memoirs of Céleste de Chabrillan in Gold-rush Australia*, Miegunyah Press, Carlton, 1998. The extract is reproduced here with kind permission.

JOHN CHRISTIE (1845–1927)
Transcripts were taken from Christie's case papers held by the La Trobe Australian Manuscripts Collection, State Library of Victoria. Not yet cata-logued. A largely paraphrased account of Christie's experiences as an officer of the law was published in *The Reminscences of Detective-Inspector Christie*, related by J. B. Castieau, George Robertson & Co, Melbourne, 1911.

JOHN COWLEY COLES (B. 1822)
The Life and Christian Experience of John Cowley Coles was published by M. L. Hutchinson, Melbourne, 1893. The title page reveals that it is 'the history of twenty-seven years of evangelistic work in the colony of Victoria' and that it was 'written at the request of many friends'.

DAVID COLLER
This letter was suggested for use by the library at the Royal Botanic Gardens. The letter is housed at the Public Records Office W70/5147, unit 576, VPRS 3991/P, marked inward registered correspondence VA 475.

DAVID COLLINS (1756–1810)
David Collins held the offices of deputy judge-advocate and secretary at Port Jackson, and later that of lieutenant-governor of Tasmania. The extract used here is from a facsimile edition of Collins' *A voyage to establish a settlement in Bass's Straits, to which is added a description of Port Phillip and an account of the landing at the Derwent in 1804*, edited by John Curry, Colony Press, Melbourne, 1986.

KINAHAN CORNWALLIS (1839–1917)
The two-volume work *A Panorama of The New World* was published by T. C. Newby, London, in 1859. Cornwallis' Australian experiences are dealt with in the first book.

EDWARD CURR (1820–1889)
Recollections of Squatting in Victoria: Then Called the Port Phillip District (From 1841 to 1851), Rich River Printers, Echuca, 1883.

PATRICK EDWARD CUSSEN (1792–1849)
Cussen's letters to William Lonsdale and Charles Joseph La Trobe both appear in *The Historical Records of Victoria*, Volume 3.

SHERMAN FOOTE DENTON
Incidents of a Collector's Rambles in Australia, New Zealand, and New Guinea, Lee & Shephard, Boston, 1889.

ALEXANDRE DUMAS (1825–95)
Le Journal de Madame Giovanni was first published by Cadot, Paris, 1856. Marguerite E. Wilbur translated the work and the extract was taken from *The Journal of Madame Giovanni*, Liveright Publishing, New York, 1945.

LUCY ANNA EDGAR
Among the Black Boys: Being the history of an attempt at civilising some young Aborigines of Australia, Emily Faithfull, London, 1865.

EDWARD EYRE (1815–1901)
Autobiographical Narrative of Residence and Exploration in Australia 1832–1839 is from an original manuscript held in the Mitchell Library, State Library of New South Wales, A1806. The extract here is taken from an edition edited by Jill Waterhouse, published by Caliban Books, London, 1984.

ANTOINE FAUCHERY (1827?–61)
Lettres d'un Mineur en Australie was first published in 1857. This 1965 translation by Professor A. R. Chisholm appears in *Letters from a Miner in Australia*, Georgian House, Middle Park, 1965.

JOHN PASCOE FAWKNER (1792–1869)
One of Melbourne's first settlers, Fawkner was a prolific diarist and letter-writer. Many of his journals and papers can be found in the La Trobe Australian Manuscripts Collection at the State Library of Victoria. The diary extracts selected here, which deal with his first year at 'Phillipi', were edited by C. P. Billot in *Melbourne's Missing Chronicle, Being the Journal of Preparations for Departure to and Proceedings at Port Phillip by John Pascoe Fawkner*, Quartet Books, Melbourne 1982.

EDMUND FINN (1819–98)
The extracts used here have been taken from a facsimile edition of *The Chronicles of Early Melbourne 1835 to 1852: Historical, Anecdotal and Personal*, compiled by Neil Swift, published by Heritage Publications, Melbourne, 1976. *The Chronicles* was first published by Fergusson & Mitchell, Melbourne, 1888.

JAMES FLEMMING
Flemming travelled with Grimes aboard the *Buffalo* in 1802 on a voyage to investigate Bass Strait. The extract used here is from John Shillinglaw's *Historical Records of Port Phillip: The First Annals of the Colony of Victoria*, first published 1879. A facsimile edition, edited and introduced with notes by C. E. Sayers, was published by William Heinemann, Melbourne, 1972.

MATTHEW FLINDERS (1744–1814)
A Voyage to Terra Australis was first published in two volumes in 1814. This extract was taken from *Terra Australis: Matthew Flinders' Great Adventures in the Circumnavigation of Australia*, Text Publishing, Melbourne, 2000.

JANE FRANKLIN (1791–1875)
This piece from the Franklin papers, held in the National Library of Australia, was published in *Life Lines: Australian Women's Letters and Diaries 1788–1840*, edited by Patricia Clarke and Dale Spender, Allen & Unwin, St Leonards, 1992.

CHARLES FREDERICKSEN (1872–1966?)
Transcripts were made, with kind permission, from personal papers held in the Charles Fredericksen Collection, Performing Arts Museum, Victorian Arts Centre.

JOHN FREEMAN
Lights and Shadows of Melbourne Life, Sampson Low, Marston Searle & Rivington, London, 1888.

NAT GOULD (1857–1919)
Town and Bush, George Routledge & Sons, London, 1896. A facsimile edition was published by Penguin Books in 1974.

JOHN GURNER (B. 1854)
Life's Panorama, Being Recollections and Reminiscences of Things Seen, Things Heard, Things Read, Lothian Publishing, Melbourne, 1930. Gurner's recollections span the 1860s through to the 1890s.

GEORGE HAMILTON (1812?–1883)
Experiences of a Colonist Forty Years Ago: A Journey from Port Phillip to South Australia in 1839 and a Voyage from Port Phillip to Adelaide in 1846 was authored by 'An Old Hand' and published by J. Williams, Adelaide, 1880. It was republished by the Libraries Board of South Australia in 1974.

ROBERT HODDLE (1794–1881)
A transcript taken from extracts in copied form of Robert Hoddle's diary, MS 000092, Box 35/7, held by the Royal Historical Society of Victoria, Melbourne.

CARL TRAUGOTT HOEHNE (1805–72)
Extracts from the letters of Carl Hoehne in translation have been reproduced with permission. They are found in *From Hamburg to Hobsons Bay: German Emigration to Port Phillip (Australia Felix) 1848–51* by Thomas A. Darragh and Robert N. Wuchatsch, Wendish Historical Society, Melbourne, 1999.

R. H. HORNE (1802–84)
This extract appeared in Horne's *Australian Autobiography*. It was reprinted in *Australia Brought to Book: Responses to Australia by Visiting Writers 1836–1939*, compiled and edited by Kaye Harman, Boobook Publications, Balgowlah, 1985.

JOHN HENRY HOWITT (1831–43)
This letter, MS 10241, Box 1055/3, is housed at the La Trobe Australian Manuscripts Collection, State Library of Victoria.

RICHARD HOWITT (1799–1870)
Impressions of Australia Felix During Four Years' Residence in That Colony: Notes of a Voyage Round the World: Australian Poems, &c., Longman, Brown, Green & Longman, London, 1845.

WILLIAM HOWITT (1792–1879)
Land, Labour, Gold or; Two years in Victoria: with visits to Sydney and Van Diemen's Land, Longman, Brown, Green & Longman, London, 1855.

HOWQUA
The interview with Howqua reproduced here is from a collection of reports in facsimile titled *The Chinese in Victoria: Official Reports and Documents*, edited by Ian F. McLaren, Red Rooster Press, Ascot Vale, 1985.

WILLIAM HILTON HOVELL (1786–1875) AND HAMILTON HUME (1797–1873)
Journey of Discovery to Port Phillip, New South Wales by Messrs W. H. Hovell and Hamilton Hume in 1824 and 1825, compiled and edited by William Bland (1789–1868), A. Hill, Sydney, 1831. A facsimile of the first edition by the Libraries Board of South Australia appeared in 1965.

HYUW-UNG
A Chinaman's Opinion of Us, translated by J. A. Makepeace, was published in London in 1927. It also appears in Grant and Serle's *The Melbourne Scene 1803–1956*.

JOHN STANLEY JAMES (1843–96)
James' *Argus* columns were published in a collection, *The Vagabond Papers*, introduced and edited by Michael Cannon, Hyland House, Melbourne, 1983.

CHARLES KEAN (1811–80)
This letter was drawn from *The Oxford Book of Australian Letters*, edited by Brenda Niall and John Thompson, Oxford University Press, Melbourne, 1998. The original is held at the Alexander Turnbull Library, National Library of New Zealand, qMS 1086.

WILLIAM KELLY (1813?–72)
Kelly's two-volume work *Life in Victoria or Victoria in 1853, and Victoria in 1858*, Chapman & Hall, London, 1859, was dismissed as silly and inaccurate when first published. Perhaps his depictions of the rich and powerful, and his empathy with the Chinese earned him the scorn of many of his contemporaries.

JOHN HUNTER KERR (1821–74)
Glimpses of Life in Victoria penned by 'A Resident' was first published in Kerr's native country by Edmunsen & Douglas, Edinburgh, 1872. It was reissued in 1996 with an introduction by Marguerite Hancock by Miegunyah Press, Carlton.

PHILLIP PARKER KING (1791–1856)
King's diary of his visit to Melbourne in March 1837 appears in *The Historical Records of Victoria*, Volume 1.

EDMOND MARIN LA MESLÉE (1852–93)
La Meslée's account of Australia in the early 1880s was published as *l'Australie Nouvelle*, E. Plon, Paris, 1883. This extract is from *The New Australia: Edmond Marin La Meslée 1883*, translated, introduced and edited by Russel Ward, Heinemann Educational, London, 1973.

GEORGE LANGHORNE
George Langhorne's 1836 remembrances of Victorian Aborigines were taken

from *Historical Records of Victoria*, Volume 2A. The extracted statement comes from miscellaneous papers collected by Harry F. Gurner.

CHARLES JOSEPH LA TROBE (1801–75)
A copy of La Trobe's letter to George Gipps is at the La Trobe Australian Manuscripts Collection, State Library of Victoria, Gipps–La Trobe correspondence (boxes 71–73); the original is housed at the Dixon Library, State Library of New South Wales. La Trobe's dispatch to Lord Earl Grey in October 1851 was drawn from C. M. H. Clark's *Select Documents in Australian History*, Angus & Robertson, Melbourne, 1955.

WILLIAM LONSDALE (1800?–64)
This extract can be found in *The Historical Records of Victoria*, Volume 1.

GEORGE GORDON MCCRAE (1833–1927)
'Some Recollections of Melbourne in the "Forties"', *Victorian Historical Magazine*, No. 7, November 1912. The full piece was read before members of the Historical Society in November 1911 and April 1912.

GEORGIANA HUNTLY MCCRAE (1804–90)
Georgiana's Journal: Melbourne 1841–1865, 2nd edition, Angus & Robertson, Sydney, 1966.

JOHN THOMPSON MASON (B. 1844)
Mason's journal which begins on 3 January 1865 is from Volume 4 of the manuscript collection, Eleanor S. Brockenbrough Library, The Museum of the Confederacy, Richmond, Virginia, USA. Reproduced with permission.

MELBOURNE COURT REGISTER
The cases drawn from the Melbourne Court Register appear in the *Historical Records of Victoria*, Volume 3.

JOHN MURRAY
The Logbooks of the Lady Nelson: *With the Journal of Her First Commander Lieutenant James Grant R.N.*, Ida Lee, Grafton & Co, London, 1915.

HUME NISBET (1849–1923)
The first Nisbet piece used here appeared in *Cassell's Picturesque Australasia*, edited by E. E. Morris, Cassell & Co., London, 1887. The second is from Nisbet's own two-volume work, *A Colonial Tramp: Travels and Adventures in Australia and New Guinea*, Ward & Downey London, 1891.

JOSEPH ORTON (1795–1842)
This extract is part of a report that the Reverend Orton wrote to the Wesleyan Missionary Society in London in May 1839. It appears in *The Historical Records of Victoria*, Volume 2A.

GEORGE AUGUSTUS SALA (B. 1828)

Sala's reportage for the English *Daily Telegraph* during his 1885 visit is collected in *The Land of the Golden Fleece, George Augustus Sala in Australia and New Zealand in 1885*, edited by Robert Dingley, Mulini Press, Canberra, 1995.

JOSHUA SLOCUM (1844–C. 1910)

Sailing Alone around the World was first published in 1900. The piece extracted here was taken from a new edition, edited and introduced by Thomas Philbrick, published by Penguin Putnam, New York, 1999.

JAMES SMITH (1820–1910)

'Diary of James Smith 1863', microfilm MS 9191/71, La Trobe Australian Manuscripts Collection, State Library of Victoria. The original diary is held by the Mitchell Library, State Library of New South Wales.

WILLIAM STRUTT (1825–1915)

Strutt wrote of his time in the country and his Australian Journal 1850–1862 is where his account of Black Thursday first appears. It is also in *Documents on Art and Taste in Australia: The Colonial Period 1770–1914*, edited by Bernard Smith, Oxford University Press, Melbourne, 1975.

ANTHONY TROLLOPE (1815–82)

Australia and New Zealand, Chapman & Hall, London, 1873.

RICHARD ERNEST NOWELL TWOPENY (1857–1915)

Town Life in Australia, Elliot Stock, London, 1883, and reprinted by Sydney University Press, Sydney, 1973.

JAMES HINGSTON TUCKEY (1776–1816)

An account of a voyage to establish a Colony at Port Philip [sic] *in Bass's Strait, on the south coast of New South Wales, in his Majesty's Ship* Calcutta, *in the years 1802-3-4*, first published by Longman, Hurst, Rees & Orme, London, 1805, and in facsimile by Colony Press, Melbourne, 1987.

FERNANDO VILLAAMIL (1845–98)

Villaamil's voyage was published as *Viaje de circunnavegación de la corbeta* Nautilus, Sucesores de Ribadeneyra, Madrid, 1895. It was reprinted by Editorial Naval, Madrid, 1989. The extract used here was translated from the Spanish by Imogen Williams and hailed from a commemorative publication entitled *A Visit to Australian Ports by the Spanish Corbeta* Nautilus, *1892–1893: An extract printed with permission in Australia*, [n.p], 1988.

WILLIAM WATERFIELD (1795–1868)

Diary extracts appear in *The Historical Records of Victoria*, Volume 3.

JONATHAN BINNS WERE (1805–85)
A Voyage from Plymouth to Melbourne in 1839: The Shipboard and Early Melbourne Diary of Jonathan Binns Were, C.M.G. After this document was found in the late 1950s it was published exclusively for J. B. Were & Son clients in 1964. We are pleased to acknowledge the assistance of the Melbourne offices of J. B. Were & Son in reproducing this extract.

HORACE WILLIAM WHEELWRIGHT (1815–65)
Bush Wanderings of a Naturalist, by 'An Old Bushman', was first published by Routledge, Warne & Routledge, London, 1861.

NOTES ON ILLUSTRATIONS

Wilbraham Frederick Evelyn Liardet (1799–1878), *Corroboree on Emerald Hill in 1840*, c. 1870s. Watercolour and pencil. Courtesy of the La Trobe Picture Collection, State Library of Victoria, H28250/3.

Henry de Gruchy and Stephen Leigh, *Isometrical Plan of Melbourne and Suburbs*, 1866. Coloured lithograph. Courtesy of the La Trobe Picture Collection, State Library of Victoria, H291.

John Adamson, *Melbourne, Port Phillip*, c. 1841. Coloured lithograph. There are a couple of different treatments of this image by Adamson, though all are based on an 1839 work titled *Melbourne from the South Side of the Yarra Yarra 1839*, drawn by Adamson and engraved by J. Carmichael. Courtesy of the La Trobe Picture Collection, State Library of Victoria, H6262/2.

Robert Hoddle, *Melbourne, Port Phillip, 1840, from Surveyor-General's Yard*, c. 1830s. Watercolour and pencil. Courtesy of the La Trobe Picture Collection, State Library of Victoria, H258.

Elisha Noyce (lithographer) and William Knight (artist), *Collins Street, Town of Melbourne, Port Philip* [sic], *New South Wales*, 1840. Chalk lithograph. The National Library of Australia holds a watercolour in the Rex Nan Kivell Collection, which may be after the lithograph by Noyce. Courtesy of the La Trobe Picture Collection, State Library of Victoria, H18111.

Unknown artist, *Richmond Ferry, Looking South across Yarra River to Punt Road, South Yarra*, c. 1856. Photograph. Courtesy of the Royal Historical Society of Victoria, S-181.

Charles Rudd, *Collins Street, Looking East from Elizabeth Street*, c. 1890s. Photograph. Courtesy of the La Trobe Picture Collection, State Library of Victoria, H39357/11.